# THE BIG BOOK OF VEGAN COOKING

# THE BIG BOOK OF
# VEGAN
## COOKING | 175 Recipes for a Healthy Vegan Lifestyle

## Dianne Wenz

Photography by Kate Sears

ROCKRIDGE
PRESS

Series Design: Katy Brown
Interior and Cover Designer: Patricia Fabricant
Art Producer: Sara Feinstein
Editor: Rebecca Markley
Production Editor: Sigi Nacson
Author photo by Dennis Mason
Photography © 2020 Kate Sears. Food styling by Lori Powell.
Author photo courtesy of Dennis Mason.
Cover photo: Spinach Artichoke Galette, page 138

ISBN: Print 978-1-64876-501-8 | eBook 978-1-64739-589-6
R0

For the animals

Portabella Chimichurri
Tacos, page 112

# CONTENTS

# INTRODUCTION

I went vegetarian in 1992 for ethical reasons, and then went vegan in 2001 after reading about the dairy and egg industries. A lot has changed since then. *The Economist* declared 2019 to be "The Year of the Vegan," something I never thought could be possible back in the early aughts, when people thought vegans were extraterrestrial life-forms that hailed the planet Vega.

Young vegans don't know how lucky they have it. Back in the old days, we'd have to walk uphill in the snow barefoot to buy powdered soy milk and boxed veggie burger mixes from obscure health food stores. The kind of store where all the signs were handwritten in magic marker on the back of cereal boxes and there was one bare, flickering light bulb hanging from the ceiling. Now you have your choice of nondairy milk in most coffee shops and almost every fast-food joint serves vegan burgers.

I lived with my mom when I stopped eating meat, and meals became a subject of great dispute. I remember one particular dinner that consisted of beef flavored Rice-A-Roni and microwaved frozen cubed carrots and peas, with "Well, I don't know what you eat anymore!" yelled at me from the kitchen as I stormed off and slammed my bedroom door.

I grew up eating packaged foods that could be taken out of the freezer and quickly heated up in a microwave or poured out of a box and mixed together in a pot. Since vegan convenience foods were scarce in the early '90s, I had to teach myself how to cook. I got a subscription to *Vegetarian Times* and started doing my own grocery shopping. I started simply, with meals like black bean tacos and chickpea salad sandwiches. After getting comfortable with plant-based ingredients, I soon began whipping up concoctions such as tofu vegetable curry and lentil veggie burgers.

Through veganism, I've found a love of cooking. With vegan meats and nondairy cheese available in just about every grocery store now, you can still find me in the kitchen, making meals from scratch. It's a creative outlet for me, and the truth is that I just feel better when I eat homemade food. There's no "I shouldn't have eaten that" feeling while my meal sits like a rock in my stomach. I sleep better at night, and I have more energy during the day now than I did when I was younger.

In this book, I'm sharing with you some easy basics for those who are new to vegan cooking, as well as some of my favorite creative meals for seasoned vegans. I hope that you, too, will find a love of home-cooked, meat-free meals.

# CHAPTER ONE

# BEGINNINGS

As with all things in life, we need to start at the beginning, so this chapter is an introduction to veganism. For those of you who are new to this way of eating, consider it a crash-course in vegan cooking. Here I'll help you make over your kitchen in order to create an animal-free-friendly space, and I'll also help you stock your pantry with the ingredients you need to put together delicious, cruelty-free meals. I will share my top tips for being vegan in a nonvegan world, too. Veganism is a lifestyle rather than a diet, but since this is a cookbook, I'll be focusing on the food.

# WHY VEGAN

There can sometimes be a little confusion as to what "vegan" food is. I like to think of it this way: Vegans don't eat anything that came from a critter that had a mom. Meat, eggs, milk, cheese, and honey are no longer on the menu. There's also a hard pass on animal-derived ingredients, such as gelatin and carmine. Don't worry—I promise there will still be plenty of mouth-watering foods from the plant kingdom to eat!

## FOR YOURSELF

There are countless studies that show the health benefits of ditching animal-based products. It could be because vegan food doesn't contain any of the nasty stuff that's found in meat, like saturated fat and cholesterol. Or it might be because plant-based foods are loaded with the good things our bodies need to thrive, such as fiber, vitamins, minerals, and phytonutrients. It's most likely a combo of both.

There's no cure-all that can prevent disease and keep us 100% healthy, but a plant-based diet can certainly help. Because fruits, veggies, whole grains, and legumes are loaded with so many nutrients, they've been shown to protect against ailments such as heart disease, certain cancers, type 2 diabetes, liver disease, and kidney disease. Plant-based foods can also boost energy and improve mood, making vegans generally nicer to be around. (It hasn't been scientifically proven that vegans are nicer people. This is just a theory I'm working on.)

Dumping dairy can also greatly improve health in many ways. It's believed that about 65 percent of the world's population lacks the enzymes needed to digest lactose, the sugar found in cow's milk. Lactose intolerance can lead to digestive problems, and who wants to walk around with gas and bloating all the time? Certainly not me! Dairy products can also lead to acne and hormonal issues. And because consuming dairy can lead to excess mucus production in the body (*yuck!*), it can exacerbate allergies and lead to sinus infections, too.

## FOR THE ANIMALS

It's difficult to deny the fact that animals are being raised and killed solely for the purpose of putting food on our plates. If you spend any amount of time with a pig or a cow, you'll find they're really no different from your dog or cat. They are capable of experiencing love and pain, and they get upset when they're separated from their families.

Many people, some vegans included, have a "don't tell me, I don't want to know" attitude when it comes to animal welfare, but it's important to know what goes on in factory farms. The more we know, the more we can institute changes in the industry.

Contrary to popular belief, cows don't walk around begging to be milked. They need to have recently given birth in order to produce milk, so dairy cows are artificially impregnated. In fact, most animals raised for meat are the result of artificial insemination, and they are frequently taken away from their mothers when they're just wee babies. They're often kept in overcrowded, filthy pens where diseases run rampant. Most animals are overfed to fatten them up quickly before they're sent to the slaughterhouse.

Chickens are probably the most mistreated animals in factory farms. Male chicks aren't considered useful, so they're killed at birth. Hens aren't wandering around the barnyard popping out eggs every few days. They're kept in little pens in conditions that could rival those depicted in the scariest horror movies. Once hens are no longer "useful," they're sent to the slaughterhouse, where they suffer the same fate as other animals in the factory-farming system.

## FOR THE EARTH

Let's face it—Mother Earth isn't as healthy as she used to be. Animal agriculture is behind quite a lot of her ailments, as a large amount of the planet's resources are being used to house and feed animals.

Nearly half of all water in the United States goes to raising animals. The amount of water needed to produce a pound of beef is astronomically high compared with that used for vegetable production. It can take up to 2,400 gallons of water to produce 1 pound of beef, whereas vegetables need around 25 gallons per pound.

And speaking of water, the waste from factory farms has to go somewhere, and it quite often ends up in rivers and waterways. Farm animals in the United States produce approximately 1.5 billion tons of manure a year, which means there's a *lot* of poop in our water. That water can sometimes pollute vegetable crops, which in turn leads to nationwide produce recalls.

Animals raised for food need a place to live, and the growing desire for meat means more land is needed to house them and grow their food. As a result, forests around the globe are being cleared to make more room. The Amazon rainforest in Brazil is being torn down at an alarming rate: the World Wildlife Fund estimates that 27 percent of the rainforest will be gone by 2030 if the current rate of deforestation continues.

Much like some humans I know, cows can get a little gassy (okay, a *lot* gassy), and the methane they produce is considered a greenhouse gas. A UN study showed that animal agriculture is responsible for 18 percent of greenhouse emissions, which is more than the exhaust from all forms of transportation combined.

# VEGAN NUTRITION

Skeptics worry that a vegan diet lacks proper nutrition, but I can assure you that this can be an extremely healthy way to eat. (Seriously, getting protein is *not* a problem.) If you eat a wide variety of plant-based foods, chances are you're getting most of the vitamins and minerals your body needs from plants, with the exception of a couple of nutrients that vegans need to be mindful of.

## PROTEIN

Contrary to popular belief, protein is abundant in the plant world. It can be found in beans, nuts, grains, and even vegetables. In addition, we humans need a lot less protein than most people realize. Most of us need to eat 0.8 grams of protein per kilogram (2.2 pounds) of body weight per day. So, a 150-pound person would need about 55 grams of protein a day.

## CALCIUM

Most people think that cow's milk is necessary to keep our bones in tip-top shape, but calcium from plant-based sources can actually be more easily absorbed in the body. It's recommended that younger adults get 1,000 mg per day, whereas those over age 50 should have an intake of 1,500 mg. Calcium can be found in abundance in leafy green vegetables, dried fruits, almonds, tahini, and beans.

## IRON

The body doesn't absorb iron from plant-based sources as easily as it absorbs iron from animals, but that doesn't mean vegans are stumbling around, weak from anemia. Iron can be found in grains, beans, nuts, seeds, dried fruits, and leafy greens. Vitamin C helps boost its absorption, whereas compounds in tea can actually block it. It's suggested that women of childbearing age get 32.4 mg of iron a day, whereas other adults should get 14.4 mg.

## OMEGA-3 FATTY ACIDS

On a vegan diet, it can be a little tough to consume sufficient quantities of EPA and DHA, types of omega-3 fatty acids, but it's not impossible. Omega-3s can be found in chia seeds and chia oil, flaxseed and flax oil, leafy green veggies, seaweed, soybeans, walnuts, and wheat germ, and supplements are widely available. It's recommended that adults get 250 mg a day.

## VITAMIN B$_{12}$

Vitamin B$_{12}$ is actually the by-product of bacteria, and it's pretty impossible to find in plant-based foods, so it's crucial that vegans supplement with it. In his book, *How Not to Die*, Michael Greger, MD, recommends a daily dose of 250 mcg per day for adults under age 65, with the recommended amounts increasing to 1,000 mcg for those who are 65 and older.

## Not So Vegan

Nonvegan ingredients can sneak their way into seemingly "safe" foods, so it's important to check ingredient labels when buying packaged foods. I like to take a look at the label's allergy info first, because it will clearly state if the food contains egg or dairy products. I'm okay with products that have been made on equipment shared with these ingredients, because cross-contamination is minimal, but if you have an allergy, be careful, because it could cause a problem.

Some dairy-based ingredients to look out for are whey, lactose, and casein, which somehow find their way into lots of otherwise vegan foods. Albumin (or albumen) is a protein that comes from eggs, and it's sometimes used in cookies and candies. Gelatin, an ingredient found in candies, marshmallows, and jellies, is derived from a source so disgusting, I'm not sure you want to hear about it. (It's made by boiling animal skin, tendons, ligaments, and bones. See, I told you you didn't want to know.)

Some other animal-derived ingredients to keep your eye out for include beeswax, confectioners' glaze, cochineal or carmine, isinglass, castoreum, and lard. Oleic acid, L-cysteine, and lactic acid can be derived from either animals or plants, so if you see these ingredients on a label, check with the manufacturer to make sure the product is vegan.

# KITCHEN MAKEOVER

While changing your diet, you're also going to want to give your kitchen a makeover. Don't run out to HomeGoods and hand over your paycheck just yet, though. I recommend doing a big cleanout of nonvegan items and then gradually adding things as you need them.

Most vegan kitchens contain the same types of gadgets and gizmos found in nonvegan ones. I do recommend a few pieces of equipment that might be new to you, though. The same goes for pantry ingredients. Foods like quinoa and seitan might sound foreign now, but I promise you'll be a pro at cooking with them in no time.

## EQUIPMENT

### Food Processor

A food processor is sort of like the Swiss Army knife of the kitchen, and I use mine more than any other gadget. It chops, slices, shreds, blends, and even kneads dough, so I can use it for everything from cutting vegetables to making sauces.

### Blender

Blenders are great for . . . uh, well . . . blending. I use mine to make smoothies, dressings, and dips. A high-speed blender is nice for making creamy nut-based cheeses and sauces, but it's not a necessity for the vegan kitchen. Immersion blenders can be handy for soups and sauces, but if you don't have one, you can use your upright blender.

## Quality Set of Knives

When I was growing up, my family chopped everything, vegetables included, with steak knives. It wasn't until I was in my 30s that I got my first good, sharp knife, and it was an immediate game changer. The right knife for you is one that feels comfortable in your hand and that you enjoy using. I recommend having a paring knife and a serrated bread knife as well.

## Nut-Milk Bag

If you want to be one of those DIY vegans who makes their own almond milk and fancy dairy-free cheeses, it's a good idea to have a nut-milk bag: a drawstring bag made out of a fine-mesh fabric that's used to strain the solids from blended liquids. Cheesecloth can also be used, but with its wider mesh, I find that it doesn't strain as finely as nut-milk bags do.

## Fine-Mesh Sieve

Grains should be rinsed before cooking, and it's best to do so in a fine-mesh sieve. This handy tool is also great for sifting flour and sugar, draining pasta, and straining lumps out of sauces. Look for one that has hooks or a metal loop on its frame, opposite from the handle, so it can be placed over a pot or a bowl without falling in.

## Glass Canning Jars

I like to make dressings and sauces in big batches and store them in the fridge or freezer so they're ready to go when I'm hungry, so glass jars are a must. I also sometimes use them to prep meals such as salads and smoothies in advance. They can be handy when making your own jams and preserves, too.

## Mandoline Slicer

A mandoline can slice veggies super thin, and although it's by no means a necessity in any kitchen, it does come in handy from time to time. I use my mandoline for making homemade Veggie Chips (page 36) and Zucchini Manicotti (page 133).

# INGREDIENTS

## Whole Grains

Repeat after me: Carbs are not my enemy. Carbohydrates are the body's fuel, and consuming whole grains is one of the best ways to fill your tank. Wheat, oats, brown rice, corn, and quinoa are the most popular grains, but you might want to also try farro, amaranth, and millet. If you follow a gluten-free diet, you should avoid grains from the wheat family, such as farro, spelt, Kamut, and bulgur, as well as barley and rye.

## Beans and Legumes

Beans and legumes are known for their protein content, and they're really versatile, too. They can be thrown into salads and soups, wrapped up in a tortilla to make burritos or tacos, and blended with spices to make dips. Some of my favorite varieties include chickpeas, black beans, lentils, peas, and peanuts.

### Dairy Substitutes

It's a great time to be vegan, because nondairy versions of animal-derived foods such as cheese, sour cream, and butter are now easy to find in just about any store. When I went vegan, my "milk" choices were limited to soy and rice, but now the choices include coconut, almond, macadamia, flax, oat, walnut, and even pea.

### Nutritional Yeast

I know the word "yeast" doesn't sound very appetizing, but I guarantee you'll be sprinkling this stuff all over your food by the time you finish chapter 2. Nutritional yeast is known as "nooch" in vegan circles, and it can be added to dishes to give them a cheesy, nutty flavor.

### Herbs and Spices

Quite frequently, when people rave about a meal, they're actually talking about the herbs and spices that flavored it. A full spice rack is a necessity for every kitchen, vegan or not. In addition to salt and pepper, I frequently find myself reaching for garlic powder, onion powder, red pepper flakes, basil, and thyme.

### Alternative Proteins

Animals are no longer needed to make protein-rich meals (honestly, they were never actually needed), because

## Fresh vs. Frozen vs. Canned

When buying veggies, fresh is best, but I know it's not always practical. Sometimes access to fresh can be difficult, and eating fresh produce every day can require frequent trips to the grocery store, which might be close to impossible for busy vegans. And then there's the danger of produce going bad before you have a chance to eat it (I'm looking at you, mushy cucumbers!).

Frozen vegetables are a good sub for fresh. They're frozen as soon as they're picked, so they may actually be fresher than "fresh" vegetables, which can take days to be shipped to you from across the country. When cooking with frozen veggies, there's no need to defrost them first—they can usually be added straight to your recipe from the freezer (and the recipe will indicate if thawing ever is necessary).

Canned vegetables are another option, although they might not be as nutritious or tasty as fresh and frozen. Veggies can lose nutrients in the canning process, and salt is frequently added for flavor. I grew up eating mostly canned vegetables, and I now find them to be too limp and tasteless. I make an exception for tomatoes, artichoke hearts, and hearts of palm, which are handy to have in the pantry and are easy to add to meals.

meat-free meat is all the rage these days. You can find vegan versions of everything from burgers and steak to bacon and sausage. But don't forget the classics: tofu, tempeh, and seitan.

### Soy Sauce

I use soy sauce a lot in my cooking, in dressings as well as in stir-fries. If you're sensitive to gluten, use tamari, which is a wheat-free soy sauce. It typically has a darker color and richer flavor, and it's less salty than traditional soy sauce. Coconut aminos and Bragg Liquid Aminos are good subs, too.

# TIPS FOR VEGAN EATING

## GO SLOWLY

If you're new to veganism, you might be tempted to jump in headfirst. While that approach works for some, most people end up feeling overwhelmed and giving up before they've really gotten going. I don't want you to give up, so here's my advice: Most people do best when they ease themselves into this new lifestyle, trying new foods and replacing nonvegan items gradually.

## DON'T BREAK THE BANK

It's a myth that veganism is expensive. If you're buying gourmet cashew cheeses and powdered superfoods on a weekly basis, it certainly can be pricey. But beans and rice are pretty inexpensive. Stick with the budget-friendly basics and treat yourself to the more expensive stuff every once in a while.

## DON'T LISTEN TO OUTSIDE NOISE

There are many vegan naysayers out there, and they tend to have loud voices. When they start to talk, strap on your noise-canceling headphones, because you don't need that kind of negativity in your life. You do you, and continue down the vegan path. Hit up the internet to look for vegan groups to join (both online and IRL) for outside support.

## READ LABELS

Make sure you read the labels, checking for animal-based ingredients, on all packaged foods you buy, even if it's something you've purchased before. Manufacturers love to change their formulas without warning, and even I've accidentally bought chocolate containing milk and pasta made with eggs. Fortunately, vegan food is hot right now, and a lot of companies are clearly labeling their products as "vegan" or "plant-based."

## PLAN AHEAD

It's getting easier to find vegan food in the wild, but there are still vegetable deserts out there. If you're going out to eat, it's good to check the area to see what's available. It can be helpful to take snacks (or even meals) with you, too. Stopping for takeout on the way home from a long day at the office can be tempting, so meal prepping in advance can also be beneficial.

## EAT YOUR VEGGIES

With so many vegan convenience foods at the ready, it can be really easy to go through the day without eating any vegetables. Sure, those foods are yummy and easy to make, but they're not the healthiest options available. Make sure you're getting at least 1 to 3 cups of veggies a day.

## HAVE FUN!

I think a lot of the world has stereotyped vegans as super-serious activists who eat nothing but twigs and berries, which makes us sound pretty boring. Most of the vegans I know are happy people. Whatever your reason for adopting a vegan diet, have fun with your food and enjoy yourself!

# ABOUT THE RECIPES

Let's get into the kitchen! I've developed these recipes to capture a variety of flavors. I've also been sure to use a range of ingredients so you can familiarize yourself with vegan options. Vegan food is more than just salad! (Not that there's anything wrong with salad.)

I've included the following labels to help you navigate to the recipes that meet your needs:

**Nut-Free:** These recipes are made without nuts, for those with allergies or sensitivities.

**Gluten-Free:** If you have issues with gluten, these recipes are for you!

**Soy-Free:** Soy not your thing? Look for this label.

**Kid-Friendly:** The whole family will love these recipes.

**30-Minute Meal:** From prep to table, these dishes are ready in 30 minutes or less.

**One-Pan/One-Pot:** These recipes can be made in a single vessel with a limited amount of equipment.

Broccoli and Sun-Dried Tomato Quiche, page 26

# CHAPTER TWO

# RISE AND SHINE

## BREAKFAST AND BRUNCH

# PEANUT BUTTER CUP SMOOTHIE

**SERVES 2 | PREP TIME:** 5 MINUTES

A peanut butter cup for breakfast? Sign me up! This smoothie seems decadent, but the hidden spinach makes it sneakily healthy. I promise no one will notice that there are greens in the mix. If you'd like an extra boost of nutrition, you can add a scoop of vegan protein powder.

**2 cups Almond Milk (page 214) or store-bought nondairy milk**

**2 cups tightly packed spinach**

**2 frozen bananas, peeled and sliced**

**¼ cup unsweetened cocoa powder**

**¼ cup creamy natural peanut butter**

**1 teaspoon pure maple syrup**

In a blender, combine the almond milk, spinach, bananas, cocoa powder, peanut butter, and maple syrup. Blend on high speed until smooth and creamy. Pour into 2 glasses and serve.

**Substitution Tip:** If you're allergic to peanuts, try almond butter or cashew butter instead. Sunflower seed butter is a great alternative to nut butter.

PER SERVING: CALORIES: 467; FAT: 24G; SATURATED FAT: 3G; CHOLESTEROL: 0G; PROTEIN: 19G; FIBER: 12G; SODIUM: 154MG

# CHOCOLATE-FOR-BREAKFAST OVERNIGHT OATS

SOY-FREE, KID-FRIENDLY, ONE-PAN/ONE-POT

**SERVES 2 | PREP TIME:** 5 MINUTES, PLUS CHILLING TIME

We all have our vices, and mine is chocolate. I'm a much nicer person once I've had my daily fix, so eating some chocolate first thing in the morning makes my day run a little smoother. To make breakfast extra decadent, you can top your oats with chocolate chips, cacao nibs, chopped nuts, and/or fresh berries.

**1½ cups Almond Milk (page 214) or store-bought nondairy milk**

**1 cup quick-cooking rolled oats**

**3 tablespoons unsweetened cocoa powder**

**2 tablespoons chia seeds**

**2 tablespoons pure maple syrup**

**1 teaspoon pure vanilla extract**

In a jar or container with a lid, combine the almond milk, oats, cocoa powder, chia seeds, maple syrup, and vanilla. Stir well to combine. Cover with the lid and refrigerate for at least 5 hours or overnight. If the oat mixture has separated, give it a stir before serving.

**Substitution Tip:** If you don't like chocolate—*Gasp! How do you even function?*—you can omit the cocoa powder and double up on the vanilla extract. Try a little almond extract and a pinch of cinnamon, too, if you like.

PER SERVING: CALORIES: 456; FAT: 12G; SATURATED FAT: 2G; CHOLESTEROL: 0G; PROTEIN: 18G; FIBER: 14G; SODIUM: 101MG

# PEANUT BUTTER AND JELLY CHIA PUDDING

GLUTEN-FREE, SOY-FREE, KID-FRIENDLY

**SERVES 4 | PREP TIME:** 10 MINUTES, PLUS CHILLING TIME **| COOK TIME:** 5 MINUTES

I don't want to start a fight here, but what we here in the United States call "jelly" is actually jam. Jelly is made with fruit juice. It's clear and kinda wobbly, hence the phrase "shook like a bowl full of jelly." Jam is made with whole crushed fruit. So technically this is "peanut butter and *jam* chia pudding," but that doesn't sound as catchy. This quick strawberry jam is thickened with chia seeds; feel free to use it on sandwiches and muffins, too.

FOR THE JAM

**2 cups fresh strawberries, chopped and lightly mashed**

**2 tablespoons pure maple syrup**

**2 tablespoons chia seeds**

**2 teaspoons fresh lemon juice**

FOR THE CHIA PUDDING

**2 cups Almond Milk (page 214) or store-bought nondairy milk**

**½ cup creamy natural peanut butter**

**¼ cup chia seeds**

**2 tablespoons pure maple syrup**

**1 teaspoon pure vanilla extract**

1. **Make the jam:** In a small pot, cook the strawberries over medium heat until they begin to break down, about 5 minutes.

2. Remove the pot from the heat and stir in the maple syrup, chia seeds, and lemon juice. Let the jam cool for 5 minutes (it will thicken as it cools), then transfer it to an airtight container with a lid, cover, and refrigerate for at least 5 hours or overnight.

3. **Make the chia pudding:** In a medium bowl, combine the almond milk, peanut butter, chia seeds, maple syrup, and vanilla. Cover and refrigerate for at least 5 hours or overnight.

4. To serve, spoon alternating layers of chia pudding and jam into bowls or parfait dishes.

**Substitution Tip:** Any type of fresh berry can be used in place of the strawberries. Defrosted frozen berries can be used if fresh aren't available. Any type of nut butter, or even sunflower seed butter, can be used in place of the peanut butter.

PER SERVING: CALORIES: 443; FAT: 26G; SATURATED FAT: 2G; CHOLESTEROL: 0G; PROTEIN: 15G; FIBER: 13G; SODIUM: 71MG

# SWEET POTATO BREAKFAST BOWL

GLUTEN-FREE, SOY-FREE, KID-FRIENDLY

**SERVES 2 | PREP TIME:** 10 MINUTES | **COOK TIME:** 1 HOUR

Sweet potatoes elevate breakfast, taking your bowl out of the cereal-and-oatmeal rut. We often enjoy these orange-hued spuds for lunch and dinner, so why not breakfast? This warm bowl, made with cinnamon, maple syrup, and almond butter, will cure what ails you on a chilly autumn morning, but it can also be enjoyed cold, straight from the fridge, on hot summer days.

2 medium sweet potatoes (about 1 pound total)

½ cup Almond Milk (page 214) or store-bought nondairy milk

2 tablespoons pure maple syrup

2 tablespoons smooth natural almond butter

2 teaspoons pure vanilla extract

1 teaspoon ground cinnamon

½ teaspoon salt

1 cup fresh blueberries

1 banana, sliced

¼ cup chopped almonds

1. Preheat the oven to 400°F. Line a baking sheet with parchment paper.

2. Using the tines of a fork, poke a few holes in each sweet potato, then place them on the prepared baking sheet. Bake for 45 minutes to 1 hour, or until the potatoes are soft and can easily be pierced with a knife.

3. Remove the pan from the oven and let the sweet potatoes cool slightly. Using a spoon, scoop the flesh into a food processor or blender; discard the skins. Add the almond milk, maple syrup, almond butter, vanilla, cinnamon, and salt and puree until smooth.

4. Divide the mixture evenly between 2 bowls. Top with the blueberries, banana slices, and almonds to serve.

> **Time-Saving Tip:** You can roast the sweet potatoes ahead of time. When you're ready for breakfast, simply make the puree and then heat it in a small pot over medium heat for about 5 minutes. If you're really short on time, you can substitute a 15-ounce can of sweet potato puree for the roasted sweet potatoes.

**PER SERVING:** CALORIES: 483; FAT: 17G; SATURATED FAT: 1G; CHOLESTEROL: 0G; PROTEIN: 11G; FIBER: 12G; SODIUM: 689MG

# BAKED APPLE CINNAMON OATMEAL SQUARES

SOY-FREE, KID-FRIENDLY, ONE-PAN/ONE-POT

**MAKES 9 SQUARES | PREP TIME:** 10 MINUTES | **COOK TIME:** 40 MINUTES

I'm not a big fan of stovetop-cooked oatmeal. It's kind of like the oatmeal has an identity crisis: It's not really creamy, but not quite chewy—what exactly is it? When oatmeal is baked, however, it really finds itself. These squares cook up nice and firm, with a hearty, chewy texture. They're a terrific grab-and-go option for busy mornings.

2½ cups quick-cooking rolled oats

3 tablespoons flax meal (ground flaxseed)

2 teaspoons baking soda

1 teaspoon ground cinnamon

½ teaspoon ground ginger

½ teaspoon salt

1¼ cups Almond Milk (page 214) or store-bought nondairy milk

2 medium bananas, mashed

½ cup pure maple syrup

1 teaspoon pure vanilla extract

1 medium apple, peeled, cored, and chopped

½ cup chopped pecans

1. Preheat the oven to 350°F. Line an 8-inch square baking pan with parchment paper.

2. In a large bowl, combine the oats, flax meal, baking soda, cinnamon, ginger, and salt. Stir well.

3. Add the almond milk, bananas, maple syrup, and vanilla and stir until just combined. Fold in the apple and pecans.

4. Pour the mixture into the prepared baking pan. Bake for 35 to 40 minutes, until a toothpick inserted into the center comes out clean.

5. Let cool in the pan, then cut into 9 squares to serve.

**Substitution Tip:** The apple and pecans can be swapped for other fruit and nuts. Try 1 cup blueberries and ½ cup chopped almonds, or 1 cup chopped hulled strawberries and ½ cup chopped macadamia nuts.

**PER SERVING (1 SQUARE):** CALORIES: 323; FAT: 9G; SATURATED FAT: 1G; CHOLESTEROL: 0G; PROTEIN: 10G; FIBER: 7G; SODIUM: 430MG

# BLUEBERRY BANANA MUFFINS

**MAKES 12 MUFFINS | PREP TIME:** 15 MINUTES **| COOK TIME:** 20 MINUTES

While their sweetness and batter consistency may vary, the only real visible difference between cupcakes and muffins is frosting. So, enjoying a fresh, pillowy muffin in the morning is kind of like having cake for breakfast, and why would anyone say no to that? Use frozen blueberries if fresh aren't available—just add them to the batter directly from the freezer (no need to thaw them first).

¾ cup soy milk

1 tablespoon apple cider vinegar

1½ cups whole wheat or all-purpose flour

½ cup sugar (see Tip)

1½ teaspoons baking powder

1 teaspoon baking soda

1 teaspoon ground cinnamon

½ teaspoon salt

1¼ cups mashed overripe bananas (about 3 medium)

1 teaspoon pure vanilla extract

1 cup fresh blueberries

¼ cup chopped almonds

1. Preheat the oven to 350°F. Line a 12-cup muffin tin with liners.

2. In a small bowl, combine the soy milk and vinegar. Set aside for about 10 minutes (it's okay if the soy milk curdles).

3. Meanwhile, in a large bowl, whisk together the flour, sugar, baking powder, baking soda, cinnamon, and salt. Add the soy milk mixture, bananas, and vanilla and stir just until combined (be careful not to over-mix). Fold in the blueberries and almonds.

4. Divide the mixture evenly among the wells of the prepared muffin tin. Bake for 20 to 25 minutes, until a toothpick inserted into the center of a muffin comes out clean. Let cool and serve.

**Ingredient Tip:** When buying granulated sugar, I recommend looking for an organic sugar, such as Sucanat or coconut palm sugar, for the best flavor.

**PER SERVING (1 MUFFIN):** CALORIES: 141; FAT: 2G; SATURATED FAT: 0G; CHOLESTEROL: 0G; PROTEIN: 3G; FIBER: 2G; SODIUM: 211MG

# TOFU RANCHEROS

**SERVES 4 | PREP TIME:** 10 MINUTES | **COOK TIME:** 20 MINUTES

The tofu scramble is a rite of passage for newbie vegans, and I can still remember my first one. It was memorable in that it was made with a boxed mix and not very good. This rancheros-style scramble is unforgettable because it's packed with bold flavor. Serve your scramble as is or with cooked brown rice, Refried Beans (page 232), and guacamole alongside.

1 teaspoon neutral-flavored vegetable oil

½ cup diced yellow onion (about ½ small onion)

2 poblano or Anaheim peppers, seeded and chopped

1 jalapeño pepper, seeded and diced

1 garlic clove, minced

1 (14-ounce) package extra-firm tofu, drained and pressed (see Tip)

1 (14-ounce) can diced tomatoes, drained

2 tablespoons nutritional yeast

2 teaspoons chili powder

1 teaspoon ground cumin

¼ teaspoon salt

¼ teaspoon freshly ground black pepper

8 (6-inch) corn tortillas, warmed

¼ cup chopped fresh cilantro

1. In a large skillet, heat the oil over medium-high heat until it shimmers. Add the onion and cook, stirring frequently, until it begins to brown, about 5 minutes. Stir in the poblano and jalapeño peppers and the garlic and cook for another 5 minutes, until fragrant and softened.

2. Crumble the tofu into the skillet, then add the tomatoes, nutritional yeast, chili powder, cumin, salt, and black pepper. Cook, stirring frequently, until the mixture is hot and bubbling, about 10 minutes.

3. To serve, place two tortillas on each plate and top with a large spoonful of the tofu mixture. Garnish with the cilantro.

**Ingredient Tip:** To press your tofu, drain off any liquid and then wrap the tofu in a clean kitchen towel and set it on a plate. Place something heavy on top of the tofu, such as a cast-iron pan or a few heavy books, and set it aside for about 20 minutes or refrigerate it overnight. There are several newfangled tofu presses on the market, but they're not necessary.

**PER SERVING:** CALORIES: 256; FAT: 9G; SATURATED FAT: 1G; CHOLESTEROL: 0G; PROTEIN: 16G; FIBER: 7G; SODIUM: 603MG

# CHICKPEA FLOUR OMELETS

GLUTEN-FREE, SOY-FREE, ONE-PAN/ONE-POT

**SERVES 2 | PREP TIME:** 15 MINUTES | **COOK TIME:** 25 MINUTES

If you're not familiar with chickpea flour, allow me to introduce you! It's simply a gluten-free flour that's made with ground chickpeas. Sometimes called garbanzo bean flour, besan, or gram flour, chickpea flour possesses a magical binding quality, and it can be used to mimic eggs. Omelets were my jam before I went veg, and I'm thankful that chickpea flour exists so that I can now make an egg-free version.

1 cup chickpea flour

1 cup water

¼ cup nutritional yeast

½ teaspoon baking soda

½ teaspoon onion powder

½ teaspoon garlic powder

½ teaspoon ground turmeric

½ teaspoon salt

¼ teaspoon freshly ground black pepper

1½ tablespoons neutral-flavored vegetable oil, divided

2 cups sliced mushrooms

2 scallions, sliced

1 garlic clove, minced

¼ cup Say Cheese! Sauce (page 228) or store-bought nondairy cheese sauce

> **Substitution Tip:**
> If you don't like mushrooms, give zucchini or broccoli a try. Add a little spinach or kale, too, if you like.

1. In a medium bowl, combine the chickpea flour, water, nutritional yeast, baking soda, onion powder, garlic powder, turmeric, salt, and pepper. Stir until the batter is smooth. Set aside for 10 minutes while you prepare the filling.

2. In a large skillet, heat 1 tablespoon of the oil over medium-high heat until it shimmers. Add the mushrooms and scallions. Cook, stirring occasionally, for about 5 minutes, until the vegetables begin to soften. Add the garlic and cook for another minute or two, until fragrant. Transfer the mixture to a bowl and set aside.

3. In the same pan, drizzle half the remaining oil. Pour in half the batter and cook, undisturbed, for about 5 minutes, until the edges begin to brown and the center bubbles slightly. Carefully flip it over. Top it with half of the mushroom mixture and cook for 3 to 4 minutes. Fold the omelet so the mushrooms are on the inside. Transfer the omelet to a serving plate and keep warm. Drizzle the remaining ¼ tablespoon oil over the pan and repeat with the remaining batter and mushroom mixture to make a second omelet.

4. To serve, drizzle the cheese sauce over the omelets.

PER SERVING: CALORIES: 240; FAT: 9G; SATURATED FAT: 1G; CHOLESTEROL: 0G; PROTEIN: 15G; FIBER: 6G; SODIUM: 1,350MG

# BREAKFAST SANDWICHES

KID-FRIENDLY, 30-MINUTE MEAL

**SERVES 4 | PREP TIME:** 10 MINUTES

Pics of breakfast sandwiches always please the Instagram crowd. It's easy to see why: They're loaded with chewy baked tofu, crisp tempeh bacon, and drippy nondairy sauce, so you can almost taste them through your phone screen. Use whatever flavor of baked tofu you like here, as any of them will create a 'gram-worthy sammie. #breakfastgoals

½ cup **Cashew Aioli (page 222) or vegan mayonnaise**

1 tablespoon **nutritional yeast**

1 teaspoon **Dijon mustard**

⅛ teaspoon **ground turmeric**

**Pinch freshly ground black pepper**

4 **English muffins, split and toasted**

1 batch **Baked Tofu, Three Ways (page 230), or 14 ounces store-bought baked tofu, sliced**

1 batch **Tempeh Bac'un (page 233), or 8 ounces store-bought tempeh bacon, cooked according to the package instructions**

1 **avocado, pitted, peeled, and sliced**

1 **tomato, sliced**

2 cups loosely **packed arugula**

1. In a small bowl, whisk together the cashew aioli, nutritional yeast, mustard, turmeric, and pepper. Set aside.

2. Place 4 English muffin halves on a large plate or cutting board. On each half, place a few slices each of the tofu, tempeh bac'un, avocado, and tomato. Top with some of the arugula and then drizzle each with about 2 tablespoons of aioli mixture. Top each sandwich with the remaining muffin half and serve.

> **Substitution Tip:** You can make your sandwiches on bagels or croissants instead of English muffins. You can also wrap the sandwich fillings in large tortillas for breakfast burritos, or stuff them into pitas to give the sandwiches a little Mediterranean flair.

PER SERVING: CALORIES: 474; FAT: 28G; SATURATED FAT: 3G; CHOLESTEROL: 0G; PROTEIN: 25G; FIBER: 9G; SODIUM: 598MG

# TOFU FLORENTINE

KID-FRIENDLY, ONE-PAN/ONE-POT

**SERVES 4 | PREP TIME:** 25 MINUTES | **COOK TIME:** 12 MINUTES

"Florentine" is a posh way to say "with spinach." Classic eggs Florentine consists of poached eggs and sautéed spinach perched on top of toast, topped with Mornay sauce. And since Mornay is just a fancy cheese sauce, I consider this to be a fancy-schmancy breakfast dish without all the fuss. Serve it on your finest china or a paper plate—it's delicious either way.

3 tablespoons reduced-sodium soy sauce or tamari

3 tablespoons apple cider vinegar

2 tablespoons nutritional yeast

½ teaspoon salt

½ teaspoon ground turmeric

¼ teaspoon freshly ground black pepper

2 teaspoons vegetable oil

1 (14-ounce) package extra-firm tofu, drained, pressed (see Tip, page 18), and cut into ½-inch-thick slabs

5 ounces baby spinach, coarsely chopped (about 8 cups)

4 slices of your favorite bread, toasted

½ cup Say Cheese! Sauce (page 228) or store-bought nondairy cheese sauce

2 teaspoons chopped fresh chives

1. In a small bowl, whisk together the soy sauce, vinegar, nutritional yeast, salt, turmeric, and pepper.

2. Place the tofu slabs in a shallow dish and pour the soy mixture over them. Cover and set aside to marinate for 10 to 15 minutes.

3. In a large skillet, heat the oil over medium-high heat until it shimmers. Place the marinated tofu in the pan and cook for about 5 minutes on each side, until browned. Transfer the tofu to a plate and set aside.

4. In the same pan, cook the spinach for a minute or two, until it turns bright green and wilts.

5. To serve, place a piece of toast on each plate. Pile some of the spinach on top. Add some tofu. Drizzle with cheese sauce and garnish with the chives.

**Substitution Tip:** If you'd like to make tofu Benedict, skip the spinach and place a few slices of tempeh bacon on each piece of toast in its place. I like to add a few slices of tomato, too. You can toast English muffins instead of bread, if you like.

PER SERVING: CALORIES: 499; FAT: 29G; SATURATED FAT: 3G; CHOLESTEROL: 0G; PROTEIN: 28G; FIBER: 10G; SODIUM: 732MG

# SOUTHWEST BREAKFAST SKILLET

NUT-FREE, SOY-FREE, KID-FRIENDLY

**SERVES 4 | PREP TIME:** 10 MINUTES | **COOK TIME:** 30 MINUTES

Forget armchair traveling. I'm into fork-and-knife traveling. You can take a trip to the American Southwest without leaving your home by digging into this Tex-Mex-inspired skillet. Made with comforting potatoes, peppers, beans, and spices, it's the ultimate lazy Sunday morning meal, but it makes a great brinner, too. Crank up the heat with a few drizzles of hot sauce. Yee-haw!

3 cups diced red potatoes (about 2 medium)

1 teaspoon salt, divided

2 teaspoons vegetable oil

1 cup diced red onion (about 1 small)

1 red bell pepper, seeded and chopped

1 jalapeño pepper, seeded and chopped

1 (15-ounce) can black beans, drained and rinsed

1 teaspoon chili powder

½ teaspoon garlic powder

¼ teaspoon freshly ground black pepper

¼ teaspoon red pepper flakes (optional)

1 tablespoon fresh lime juice

1 avocado, pitted, peeled, and chopped

1. Place the potatoes in a large pot with enough water to cover them by 2 inches. Add ½ teaspoon of the salt to the water. Bring the water to a boil over medium-high heat and cook the potatoes for 6 to 8 minutes, until fork-tender. Drain the potatoes and set aside.

2. In a large skillet, heat the oil over medium-high heat until it shimmers. Add the onion and cook until it begins to soften, about 5 minutes.

3. Add the potatoes, bell pepper, and jalapeño to the pan and cook, stirring frequently, until the vegetables soften and the potato browns, 7 to 10 minutes.

4. Stir in the beans, chili powder, garlic powder, remaining ½ teaspoon salt, the black pepper, and the red pepper flakes (if using). Cook until the beans are warmed through, about 5 minutes more.

5. Remove the pan from the heat. Stir in the lime juice and top with the avocado to serve.

**Substitution Tip:** Mix things up by swapping out the peppers for other vegetables, such as mushrooms and zucchini. Chickpeas can be used in place of the black beans. And Italian seasoning mix can take the place of the chili powder.

**PER SERVING:** CALORIES: 305; FAT: 11G; SATURATED FAT: 2G; CHOLESTEROL: 0G; PROTEIN: 10G; FIBER: 14G; SODIUM: 336MG

# CARROT CAKE PANCAKES

**SERVES 4 | PREP TIME:** 10 MINUTES | **COOK TIME:** 15 MINUTES

Grated carrots and raisins make these flapjacks seem a little more like dessert than breakfast, but they actually add a little boost of nutrition, and picky eaters probably won't even notice them. Pretty sneaky, huh? Serve your stack with a dollop of dairy-free cream cheese for an extra-luxurious breakfast.

1½ cups whole wheat or all-purpose flour

1 tablespoon baking powder

¼ teaspoon baking soda

1 teaspoon ground cinnamon

¼ teaspoon ground ginger

¼ teaspoon ground nutmeg

¼ teaspoon salt

1¾ cups Almond Milk (page 214) or store-bought nondairy milk

2 teaspoons vegetable oil, plus more for the griddle

2 tablespoons pure maple syrup

1 teaspoon pure vanilla extract

1 cup grated carrots (about 3 medium)

¼ cup raisins

¼ cup chopped walnuts

1. In a large bowl, whisk together the flour, baking powder, baking soda, cinnamon, ginger, nutmeg, and salt.

2. In a small bowl, whisk together the almond milk, oil, maple syrup, and vanilla.

3. Pour the wet mixture into the dry mixture and stir until just combined (be careful not to overmix). Fold in the carrots, raisins, and walnuts. Set aside.

4. Lightly oil a large griddle or skillet and place it over medium-high heat. When the griddle is hot, spoon about ½ cup of the batter onto it and cook for 2 to 3 minutes, until the edges look dry and small bubbles appear in the middle. Flip and cook on the second side for another minute or two. Transfer the pancake to a plate and repeat with the remaining batter. Serve.

> **Technique Tip:** Grating carrots sounds like a lot of work, but it takes only a few minutes with a box grater. And if you happen to have a grating attachment for your food processor, it can be done in a matter of seconds.

**PER SERVING:** CALORIES: 349; FAT: 10G; SATURATED FAT: 1G; CHOLESTEROL: 0G; PROTEIN: 10G; FIBER: 4G; SODIUM: 307MG

# LEMON RICOTTA PANCAKES WITH BLUEBERRY SAUCE

KID-FRIENDLY, 30-MINUTE MEAL

**SERVES 4 | PREP TIME:** 5 MINUTES | **COOK TIME:** 20 MINUTES

I know you're probably thinking, "Cheese in a pancake? What *was* she thinking?" Hear me out: Ricotta adds creamy texture, a bit of tang, and a boost of protein, taking simple flapjacks to new heights of flavor. A few bites, and your taste buds will be off on a culinary tour of Italy. Don't skip the blueberry sauce, as it's the ultimate pancake accoutrement.

FOR THE BLUEBERRY SAUCE

**2 cups fresh blueberries**

**3 tablespoons pure maple syrup**

**2 tablespoons water, plus more as needed**

**2 tablespoons fresh lemon juice**

**2 teaspoons cornstarch**

FOR THE PANCAKES

**1½ cups whole wheat or all-purpose flour**

**3 tablespoons sugar**

**1 tablespoon baking powder**

**¼ teaspoon baking soda**

**¼ teaspoon salt**

**1 cup Tofu Ricotta (page 229) or store-bought nondairy ricotta**

**1½ cups Almond Milk (page 214) or store-bought nondairy milk**

**1 tablespoon grated lemon zest**

**⅓ cup fresh lemon juice**

**1 teaspoon pure vanilla extract**

**Vegetable oil, for the griddle**

1. **Make the blueberry sauce:** In a medium saucepan, combine the blueberries, maple syrup, and water. Bring to a boil over medium-high heat, then reduce the heat to low. Stir in the lemon juice and cornstarch. Simmer, stirring, until the mixture thickens slightly. If the mixture gets too thick, stir in a little more water 1 tablespoon at a time. Remove the pan from the heat and cover it to keep warm while you prepare the pancakes.

2. **Make the pancakes:** In a large bowl, whisk together the flour, sugar, baking powder, baking soda, and salt.

3. In a medium bowl, mix together the ricotta, almond milk, lemon zest, lemon juice, and vanilla (the almond milk may curdle, which is okay).

4. Pour the wet mixture into the dry mixture and stir to combine (don't overmix the batter).

5. Lightly oil a large griddle or skillet and place it over medium-high heat. When the griddle is hot, spoon about ½ cup of the batter onto it and cook for 2 to 3 minutes, until the edges look dry and small bubbles appear in the middle. Flip and cook on the second side for another minute or two. Transfer the pancake to a plate and repeat with the remaining batter.

6. Serve the pancakes hot, topped with the warm blueberry sauce.

PER SERVING: CALORIES: 472; FAT: 11G; SATURATED FAT: 4G; CHOLESTEROL: 19G; PROTEIN: 15G; FIBER: 4G; SODIUM: 343MG

# BROCCOLI AND SUN-DRIED TOMATO QUICHE

**SERVES 5 | PREP TIME:** 20 MINUTES | **COOK TIME:** 55 MINUTES

Would you believe that I've never had a nonvegan quiche? Growing up, I didn't actually know what they were. I now know that they're kind of like a baked egg pie. Quiche is an easy dish to veganize using tofu, and I just can't get enough of it now. Serve this dish for brunch, and I can guarantee that all your friends will eat quiche.

FOR THE CRUST

½ cup neutral-flavored vegetable oil, plus more for the pie pan

1 cup whole wheat flour

½ cup quick-cooking rolled oats

½ teaspoon baking powder

½ teaspoon salt

½ teaspoon freshly ground black pepper

½ cup plain unsweetened Almond Milk (page 214) or store-bought nondairy milk

FOR THE FILLING

1 teaspoon neutral-flavored vegetable oil

5 cups chopped broccoli (cut into very small florets)

2 garlic cloves, minced

1 (14-ounce) package firm tofu, drained and pressed (see Tip, page 18)

3 tablespoons fresh lemon juice

3 tablespoons water or vegetable stock

3 tablespoons nutritional yeast

1 tablespoon cornstarch

1. **Make the crust:** Preheat the oven to 350°F. Lightly brush a 9-inch pie or tart pan with a little oil.

2. Place the flour, oats, baking powder, salt, and pepper in a food processor and process until the oats are finely ground.

3. In a medium bowl, whisk together the nondairy milk and vegetable oil. Add it to the food processor and mix until it forms a dough.

4. Press the dough into your prepared pie pan, spreading it out evenly as you go. Trim away any excess dough. Set aside until ready to use.

5. **Make the filling:** In a large skillet, heat the oil over medium-high heat until it shimmers. Sauté the broccoli and garlic until the broccoli turns bright green and the garlic is fragrant, about 5 minutes. Set aside.

6. Crumble the tofu into a food processor or blender, then add the lemon juice, water, nutritional yeast, cornstarch, thyme, garlic powder, onion powder, turmeric, pepper, and salt and blend until the mixture is thick and resembles ricotta cheese.

7. Transfer the tofu mixture to a bowl and fold in the sautéed broccoli and sun-dried tomatoes.

8. Fill the crust with the mixture and smooth the top with the back of a spatula or spoon. Dust the filling with paprika (if using). Bake for 45 to 50 minutes, until the filling is firm and golden brown.

½ teaspoon dried thyme

½ teaspoon garlic powder

½ teaspoon onion powder

½ teaspoon ground turmeric

½ teaspoon freshly ground black pepper

½ teaspoon salt

¼ cup minced sun-dried tomatoes

Paprika, for dusting (optional)

9. Let the quiche cool for 5 minutes before slicing and serving.

**Substitution Tip:** You can swap out the broccoli and sun-dried tomatoes for pretty much any vegetable you'd like. Try spinach and mushrooms or zucchini and red bell peppers. This recipe tastes delish with a few slices of tempeh bacon crumbled in, too.

PER SERVING: CALORIES: 530; FAT: 32G; SATURATED FAT: 4G; CHOLESTEROL: 0G; PROTEIN: 24G; FIBER: 10G; SODIUM: 754MG

## The Not-So-Incredible, No-Longer-Edible Egg

I gave up eggs before I fully plunged into veganism. One day I was about to eat a hard-boiled egg, and it suddenly dawned on me what that egg actually was. Just thinking about putting it in my mouth gave me the heebie-jeebies.

For many people, breakfast revolves around eggs, and it might seem difficult to make a morning meal once they're off the menu. Tofu is a super-easy replacement for eggs. It can be scrambled or fried and served up the same way eggs would be. If you're missing that pungent, slightly sulfurous flavor eggs have, add a little kala namak (Indian black salt, which is actually pinkish gray) to your tofu. Chickpea flour also acts as a nice egg stand-in, especially in omelets (see page 19) and frittatas (see page 28). I've found that eggs aren't really necessary in baked goods, but when I need a binder, I like to use chia seeds, flaxseed, or aquafaba (the liquid from a can of chickpeas).

# RED PEPPER AND SPINACH MINI FRITTATAS

NUT-FREE, GLUTEN-FREE, SOY-FREE

**MAKES 12 MINI FRITTATAS | PREP TIME:** 10 MINUTES | **COOK TIME:** 45 MINUTES

If I had to pick my favorite type of meal, it would be brunch. Brunch is the best of both worlds—a little bit of breakfast, a little bit of lunch. Frittatas are my brunch food of choice. They are pretty much just quiches without the crust, and these mini frittatas are akin to savory muffins. I like to make them for brunch potlucks with friends, but they're great for breakfast on the go, too.

1 teaspoon neutral-flavored vegetable oil, plus more (optional) for the muffin tin

2 cups chickpea flour

2 cups water

¼ cup nutritional yeast

1 teaspoon ground turmeric

1 teaspoon baking powder

½ teaspoon onion powder

½ teaspoon garlic powder

½ teaspoon salt

¼ teaspoon freshly ground black pepper

½ cup diced yellow onion (about ½ small)

1 small red bell pepper, seeded and chopped (about 1 cup)

2 cups tightly packed spinach, chopped

1 garlic clove, minced

1. Preheat the oven to 400°F. Lightly oil a 12-cup muffin tin or line it with paper liners.

2. In a large bowl, combine the chickpea flour, water, nutritional yeast, turmeric, baking powder, onion powder, garlic powder, salt, and black pepper. Set aside while you prepare the vegetables.

3. In a large skillet, heat the oil over medium-high heat until it shimmers. Add the onion, and cook for about 5 minutes, until it begins to soften. Add the bell pepper and cook for another 5 minutes. Then add the spinach and garlic, and cook for another 2 minutes or so, until the spinach wilts.

4. Stir the cooked vegetables into the chickpea flour mixture.

5. Divide the mixture evenly between the prepared muffin cups. Bake for 20 to 25 minutes, until a toothpick inserted into the center of a frittata comes out clean.

6. Remove the pan from the oven and let cool for about 10 minutes before removing the frittatas to serve.

**Variation Tip:** If you'd rather have one large frittata, bake the mixture in a lightly oiled 9-inch pie pan for 45 minutes.

**Substitution Tip:** You don't need to stick with red pepper and spinach as your frittata fillings—go crazy with veggies and use whatever you have a hankering for. Try 1 cup sliced mushrooms and 2 cups tightly packed kale, or 1 cup chopped zucchini and 2 cups tightly packed arugula.

**PER SERVING (2 FRITTATAS):** CALORIES: 164; FAT: 3G; SATURATED FAT: 0G; CHOLESTEROL: 0G; PROTEIN: 10G; FIBER: 5G; SODIUM: 579MG

Roasted Red Pepper
Hummus (page 34)
and Veggie Chips
(page 36)

# CHAPTER THREE

# SNACK ATTACK

## SNACKS, SMALL PLATES, AND SIDES

# CREAMY QUESO DIP

SOY-FREE

**SERVES 6 TO 8 | PREP TIME:** 10 MINUTES | **COOK TIME:** 20 MINUTES

I was totally addicted to queso dip in my pre-vegan days. I would buy jars of premade dip, nuke it in the microwave for a minute or two, and chow down with a bag of tortilla chips. But what's a girl to do once she's ditched dairy? Make her own queso with vegetables, that's what! It's always a big hit at parties, but I'll understand if you don't want to share.

1 medium russet potato, peeled and chopped

1 medium carrot, chopped

1 garlic clove

¼ cup raw cashews

1 (14-ounce can) diced tomatoes, drained

¼ cup nutritional yeast

2 teaspoons cornstarch

1 teaspoon chili powder

½ teaspoon ground cumin

½ teaspoon salt

1. Place the potato, carrot, garlic, and cashews in a large pot and add enough water to cover the vegetables by 2 inches.

2. Bring the water to a boil over medium-high heat, then reduce the heat to medium. Simmer for about 15 minutes, until the vegetables are fork-tender. Drain the vegetables, reserving 1 cup of the cooking water (set the pot aside).

3. Transfer the vegetables and reserved cooking water to a blender. Add the tomatoes, nutritional yeast, cornstarch, chili powder, cumin, and salt and blend until smooth and creamy.

4. Return the mixture to the pot. Bring to a boil over medium-high heat, stirring occasionally. Reduce the heat to medium and simmer the queso until it has thickened slightly, about 5 minutes. Serve warm.

**Technique Tip:** If you like a little chunkiness to your queso, don't blend the tomatoes into the dip. Instead, add them to the pot with the blended ingredients in step 4.

**PER SERVING:** CALORIES: 105; FAT: 3G; SATURATED FAT: 1G; CHOLESTEROL: 0G; PROTEIN: 5G; FIBER: 3G; SODIUM: 648MG

# FRENCH ONION DIP

GLUTEN-FREE, SOY-FREE

**SERVES 6 TO 8 | PREP TIME:** 15 MINUTES | **COOK TIME:** 30 MINUTES

We vegans can be pretty resourceful when it comes to mimicking our favorite pre-vegan dairy products. We have cashew cheese and nut milk. What's next? A creamy dip made with cauliflower? Yes, actually. Cooked cauliflower blends up so smooth and creamy that no one will know they're secretly eating healthy food when they indulge on this rich dip. Serve it with Veggie Chips (page 36) for the ultimate snack.

2 teaspoons neutral-flavored vegetable oil

1 large yellow onion, diced

2 cups cauliflower florets

½ cup raw cashews

2 tablespoons fresh lemon juice

1 tablespoon apple cider vinegar

½ teaspoon garlic powder

½ teaspoon onion powder

½ teaspoon salt

1 teaspoon finely chopped fresh dill

2 tablespoons finely chopped fresh chives

2 tablespoons finely chopped fresh parsley leaves

1. In a large skillet, heat the oil over medium heat until it shimmers. Add the onion and cook, stirring occasionally, for 20 to 30 minutes, until it turns brown and caramelizes.

2. Meanwhile, place the cauliflower and cashews in a large pot and add enough water to cover them by 2 inches. Bring the water to a boil over medium-high heat, then reduce the heat to medium-low. Simmer for about 15 minutes, until the cauliflower is fork-tender.

3. Drain the cauliflower and cashews, reserving the cooking water. Let cool slightly.

4. Transfer one-third of the reserved cooking water to a blender. Add the cauliflower, cashews, lemon juice, vinegar, garlic powder, onion powder, and salt and blend until smooth and creamy; if the mixture is too thick, add more cooking water 1 tablespoon at a time.

5. Pour the mixture into a medium bowl and gently fold in the cooked onion and fresh herbs. Cover and refrigerate for at least 1 hour before serving.

**Time-Saving Tip:** Yes, caramelizing onion can take a long time, but the resulting flavor is the big prize. If you're short on time, you can skip step 1 and use 2 tablespoons dried minced onion in place of the fresh onion.

PER SERVING: CALORIES: 106; FAT: 7G; SATURATED FAT: 1G; CHOLESTEROL: 0G; PROTEIN: 3G; FIBER: 2G; SODIUM: 170MG

# ROASTED RED PEPPER HUMMUS

NUT-FREE, GLUTEN-FREE, SOY-FREE, KID-FRIENDLY

**SERVES 6 TO 8 | PREP TIME:** 5 MINUTES | **COOK TIME:** 1 HOUR 30 MINUTES

Look, I know this seems like a lengthy recipe for something as simple as a chickpea dip. You'll just have to trust me when I say that the payoff is worth the time. (And most of that time is hands-off, so there's really nothing to complain about.) Boiling dried chickpeas with a touch of baking soda is the key to silky-smooth hummus. Once you've given it a try, you'll never go back to canned beans.

½ cup dried chickpeas

½ teaspoon baking soda

½ cup chopped roasted red pepper

3 tablespoons tahini

2 tablespoons fresh lemon juice

1 tablespoon ice-cold water

1 garlic clove, minced

½ teaspoon salt

1 teaspoon extra-virgin olive oil, for serving (optional)

1 teaspoon ground sumac or paprika, for serving (optional)

1. Place the chickpeas and baking soda in a medium pot with enough water to cover the beans plus 2 inches. Bring the water to a boil over medium-high heat. Reduce the heat to medium-low, partially cover the pot, and simmer for 1 hour to 1 hour 30 minutes, until the chickpeas begin to fall apart (the chickpea skins might float to the top of the water; skim them if possible, but if you can't get them all, that's okay).

2. Drain the chickpeas and transfer them to a food processor. Process until they form a paste. Add the roasted red pepper, tahini, lemon juice, water, garlic, and salt. Process until smooth and creamy.

3. Transfer the hummus to a bowl. Top with the olive oil (if using) and sumac (if using). Serve.

**Time-Saving Tip:** Chickpeas will cook quicker if they've been soaked ahead of time—and they'll also be more digestible. Soak them in about 2 cups water (enough to cover them completely) for 4 to 8 hours, then drain and rinse.

**Technique Tip:** If you're feeling ambitious and you'd like to roast your own red pepper rather than using jarred, position an oven rack about 4 inches from the top and preheat the oven to 450°F. Cut a pepper in half and remove the stem, seeds, and membrane. Place the pepper halves on a baking sheet, cut-side down. Roast until the skins are dark, for 15 to 20 minutes. Remove the pepper halves from the oven and place them in a paper bag for 10 minutes to steam (this makes it easier to remove their skins). Peel off the skins. Store the roasted peppers in an airtight container in the refrigerator for up to a week.

**PER SERVING:** CALORIES: 113; FAT: 5G; SATURATED FAT: 1G; CHOLESTEROL: 0G; PROTEIN: 5G; FIBER: 3G; SODIUM: 273MG

# BAKED AVOCADO FRIES

SOY-FREE, KID-FRIENDLY

**SERVES 4** | **PREP TIME:** 15 MINUTES | **COOK TIME:** 20 MINUTES

I know that baking avocado might seem weird, but I haven't steered you wrong yet, have I? This recipe was inspired by avocado fries I tried at a local taco place. I had no idea that such a thing existed until I saw them on the menu. Their version was delicious, but all the oil they used to fry the avocado gave me a bellyache. Trust me when I tell you baking these "fries" is much better for the stomach.

½ cup all-purpose flour

½ teaspoon garlic powder

½ teaspoon onion powder

½ teaspoon salt

¼ teaspoon freshly ground black pepper

1 cup Almond Milk (page 214) or store-bought nondairy milk

2 teaspoons cornstarch

1½ cups panko bread crumbs

2 large avocados, pitted, peeled, and cut into 16 wedges

Chipotle-Lime Dressing (page 219), for serving

1. Preheat the oven to 400°F. Line a baking sheet with parchment paper.

2. Set up a workstation with 3 medium bowls and place the prepared baking sheet at the end. In the first bowl, combine the flour, garlic powder, onion powder, salt, and pepper. In the second bowl, combine the almond milk and cornstarch. Place the bread crumbs in the last bowl. Dredge each of the avocado slices in the flour mixture, dunk them in the almond milk, then dip them into the bread crumbs, coating them well. Arrange the slices in a single layer on the prepared baking sheet.

3. Bake for 10 minutes, flip the fries, and bake for another 5 to 10 minutes, until golden brown and crisp. Serve.

**Technique Tip:** Toss the avocado slices in 1 tablespoon fresh lime juice to keep them from turning brown.

PER SERVING: CALORIES: 372; FAT: 17G; SATURATED FAT: 3G; CHOLESTEROL: 0G; PROTEIN: 10G; FIBER: 10G; SODIUM: 521MG

# VEGGIE CHIPS

NUT-FREE, GLUTEN-FREE, SOY-FREE, KID-FRIENDLY

**SERVES 4 | PREP TIME:** 15 MINUTES | **COOK TIME:** 30 MINUTES

Most potato chips are vegan, so why make your own? I think a better question is, why not? I find I'm less tempted to overindulge when I make chips at home. Plus, I like the variety of using different types of veggies. Potatoes are nice and all, but sometimes it's fun to switch things up and use beets and parsnips instead. Spice up your chips with garlic powder, cayenne pepper, or even chili powder. I'm a fan of noochy chips myself (see the variation below). Serve these chips with Roasted Red Pepper Hummus (page 34) or French Onion Dip (page 33).

**1 pound starchy root vegetables, such as potatoes, sweet potatoes, beets, rutabaga, and/or parsnips**

**1 tablespoon neutral-flavored vegetable oil**

**½ teaspoon salt**

**¼ teaspoon freshly ground black pepper**

1. Preheat the oven to 375°F. Line two baking sheets with parchment paper.

2. Cut the vegetables into thin slices, about ⅛ inch thick. Transfer the slices to a large bowl. Add the oil, salt, and pepper. Gently toss to coat.

3. Arrange the slices in a single layer on the prepared baking sheets. Bake for 20 to 30 minutes, until the chips begin to brown and crisp (keep an eye on them to make sure they don't burn), flipping them once about halfway through. Serve.

**Technique Tip:** Some food processors come with a slicing attachment, which can prep your veggies for these chips in a matter of seconds. A mandoline is also handy for thinly slicing vegetables.

**Variation Tip:** For noochy chips, sprinkle the vegetables with 1 tablespoon nutritional yeast in step 2.

**PER SERVING:** CALORIES: 118; FAT: 4G; SATURATED FAT: 0G; CHOLESTEROL: 0G; PROTEIN: 2G; FIBER: 3G; SODIUM: 239MG

# POLENTA FRIES

NUT-FREE, SOY-FREE, KID-FRIENDLY

**SERVES 4 | PREP TIME:** 10 MINUTES, PLUS CHILLING TIME | **COOK TIME:** 35 MINUTES

I think we can all agree that the best fries are crisp on the outside and creamy in the middle. Sure, potatoes can deliver when it comes to the crisp/creamy ratio, but baked polenta knocks it out of the park. These fries pair well with Spicy Tahini Dressing (page 215), Ranch Dressing (page 217), or the old standby: ketchup.

3½ cups vegetable stock

1½ cups quick-
    cooking polenta

3 tablespoons
    nutritional yeast

4 tablespoons olive
    oil, divided

1 teaspoon dried parsley

1 teaspoon dried oregano

1 teaspoon garlic powder

1 teaspoon salt

½ teaspoon onion powder

½ teaspoon freshly ground
    black pepper

1. Line a baking sheet with parchment paper.

2. In a large pot, bring the stock to a boil over medium-high heat. Slowly whisk in the polenta. Reduce the heat to medium and cook, stirring frequently, until the mixture is thick and smooth and pulls away from the pot, 5 to 10 minutes. Whisk in the nutritional yeast, 2 tablespoons of the oil, the parsley, oregano, garlic powder, salt, onion powder, and pepper.

3. Pour the mixture onto the prepared baking sheet. Use a rubber spatula to spread it out to about ¾ inch thick. Refrigerate for about 30 minutes, until it's firm.

4. About 10 minutes before you are ready to cook the fries, preheat the oven to 450°F.

5. Once the polenta has set, remove it from the refrigerator and slice it into fries, about ¾ inch thick.

6. Line the baking sheet with a clean piece of parchment paper and arrange the fries on it, making sure they don't overlap. Brush the fries with the remaining 2 tablespoons oil.

7. Bake the fries for 10 minutes, then flip them and bake for another 10 to 15 minutes, until crisp and golden brown. Serve.

**Time-Saving Tip:** If you're feeling impatient, you can use a tube of premade herbed polenta and skip ahead to step 4.

**PER SERVING:** CALORIES: 422; FAT: 15G; SATURATED FAT: 2G; CHOLESTEROL: 0G; PROTEIN: 8G; FIBER: 4G; SODIUM: 901MG

# STUFFED MUSHROOMS

NUT-FREE, SOY-FREE

**MAKES 16 STUFFED MUSHROOMS | PREP TIME:** 15 MINUTES | **COOK TIME:** 35 MINUTES

I usually make stuffed mushrooms as an appetizer for holiday gatherings and parties. One year I just didn't feel like it, so I decided to skip them. My guests all but staged a revolt, since they had come to expect them at our annual soirees. No one wants to deal with a group of hungry vegans, so I haven't made that mistake again. I usually make a double batch and keep my own stash hidden to munch on after they've left.

1 tablespoon neutral-flavored vegetable oil, plus more (optional) for the baking dish

16 large cremini or button mushrooms

2 small shallots, minced (about ½ cup)

2 garlic cloves, minced

½ cup fresh parsley leaves, chopped

1 teaspoon dried basil

1 teaspoon dried thyme

½ teaspoon freshly ground black pepper

½ teaspoon salt

¼ cup unseasoned dried bread crumbs

2 tablespoons nutritional yeast

2 tablespoons vegetable stock

1. Preheat the oven to 400°F. Line a baking sheet with parchment paper or lightly oil a baking dish.

2. Carefully remove the stems from the mushrooms and set the caps aside. Using a sharp knife or food processor, mince the stems.

3. In a medium skillet, heat the oil over medium-high heat until it shimmers. Add the shallots and cook for about 5 minutes, until they begin to brown.

4. Add the garlic and mushroom stems. Cook until the mushroom stems are very soft, about 10 minutes. Stir in the parsley, basil, thyme, pepper, and salt.

5. Remove the pan from the heat and mix in the bread crumbs, nutritional yeast, and stock.

6. Stuff the mushroom caps with the mixture and carefully place them stuffed-side up on the prepared baking sheet. Bake until the mushrooms are tender and the stuffing is hot, 15 to 20 minutes. Serve.

> **Variation Tip:** To jazz up your mushrooms a little, you can add ½ cup crumbled cooked Tempeh Bac'un (page 233) to the stuffing mixture.

PER SERVING (4 MUSHROOMS): CALORIES: 102; FAT: 4G; SATURATED FAT: 3G; CHOLESTEROL: 0G; PROTEIN: 6G; FIBER: 2G; SODIUM: 558MG

# CORN FRITTERS

GLUTEN-FREE, SOY-FREE, KID-FRIENDLY, ONE-PAN/ONE-POT

**MAKES 10 FRITTERS | PREP TIME:** 10 MINUTES **| COOK TIME:** 20 MINUTES

"Fritter" is a funny word. Go ahead and say it a few times: Fritter. Fritter. Fritter. When I hear the word "fritter," my ears automatically perk up, like a cat hearing the treat jar open. Fritters are foods that have been battered and fried, and I'm down with that. Well, with vegan fritters, anyway, as nonvegan varieties are often battered with eggs. Here I use chickpea flour and flax meal to bind everything together.

½ cup Almond Milk (page 214) or store-bought nondairy milk

½ cup cornmeal

½ cup chickpea flour

1 tablespoon baking powder

1 tablespoon flax meal (ground flaxseed)

½ teaspoon ground cumin

½ teaspoon dried thyme

½ teaspoon salt

¼ teaspoon freshly ground black pepper

1½ cups corn kernels (fresh, canned, or thawed frozen; see Tip)

1 jalapeño pepper, seeded and finely chopped

1 scallion, finely sliced

2 garlic cloves, minced

1 tablespoon chopped fresh chives

1 tablespoon neutral-flavored vegetable oil

1. In a large bowl, whisk together the almond milk, cornmeal, chickpea flour, baking powder, flax meal, cumin, thyme, salt, and pepper. Fold in the corn, jalapeño, scallion, garlic, and chives.

2. In large skillet, heat the oil over medium-high heat until it shimmers. Using a ¼-cup measuring cup, shape the mixture into patties. Carefully place the patties in the pan. (Depending on the size of your pan, you may need to cook the fritters in two batches.) Cook for 4 to 5 minutes, until the fritters are golden brown and crisp. Flip the fritters and cook for another 4 to 5 minutes. Serve.

**Ingredient Tip:** If using canned or thawed frozen corn kernels, place them in a bowl and pat them dry with a paper towel before adding them to the batter in step 1.

**Technique Tip:** If you'd prefer baked fritters, skip the oil and bake them on a parchment paper–lined baking sheet at 400°F for 25 to 30 minutes, flipping them once halfway through.

**PER SERVING (2 FRITTERS):** CALORIES: 182; FAT: 5G; SATURATED FAT: 0G; CHOLESTEROL: 0G; PROTEIN: 6G; FIBER: 4G; SODIUM: 301MG

# POTATO ANGELS

GLUTEN-FREE, SOY-FREE, KID-FRIENDLY

**MAKES 24 POTATO ANGELS | PREP TIME:** 15 MINUTES **| COOK TIME:** 15 MINUTES

When I was little, deviled eggs always made an appearance at gatherings, especially those that took place in the spring. I wouldn't touch them, though. What had been done to them to make them so satanic? It turns out that "deviled" just means it's spiced or seasoned. Potatoes are used instead of eggs here, and they're much kinder, almost heavenly, in nature.

**12 small potatoes (about 2 inches in diameter)**

**¾ teaspoon salt, divided**

**¼ cup Cashew Aioli (page 222) or vegan mayonnaise**

**2 teaspoons Dijon mustard**

**2 teaspoons nutritional yeast**

**½ teaspoon ground turmeric**

**½ teaspoon kala namak (Indian black salt; see Tip)**

**¼ teaspoon freshly ground black pepper**

**½ teaspoon sweet paprika**

1. Place the potatoes in a large pot with enough water to cover them by 2 inches. Add ½ teaspoon of the salt to the water. Bring the water to a boil over medium-high heat. Reduce the heat to medium and simmer the potatoes for about 10 minutes, until fork-tender.

2. Drain and rinse the potatoes, then set aside to cool.

3. Using a sharp knife, cut the potatoes in half. Using a melon baller or small spoon, scoop out the center of each potato half, placing the flesh in a medium bowl. Set the potato halves aside.

4. Add the aioli, mustard, nutritional yeast, turmeric, kala namak, pepper, and remaining ¼ teaspoon salt to the bowl with the potato flesh and mash well to combine.

5. Spoon the mixture into the potato halves and sprinkle with the paprika to serve.

> **Ingredient Tip:** Kala namak is also known as Indian black salt, even though it's actually pinkish gray. It's used in a lot of South Asian and Southeast Asian cooking. The smell is reminiscent of sulfur, and it has a bit of an eggy taste to it. It can be found in Indian grocery stores as well as online.

**PER SERVING (2 POTATO ANGELS):** CALORIES: 150; FAT: 2G; SATURATED FAT: 0G; CHOLESTEROL: 0G; PROTEIN: 4G; FIBER: 4G; SODIUM: 185MG

# POTATO PANCAKES

NUT-FREE, SOY-FREE, KID-FRIENDLY, ONE-PAN/ONE-POT

**MAKES 10 POTATO PANCAKES | PREP TIME:** 10 MINUTES | **COOK TIME:** 20 MINUTES

Pretty much every European culture has its own version of the potato pancake. They're also known as *latkes, rösti, kartoffelpuffer, raggmunk, draniki, deruny,* and *boxties*. I call them *yummy*, as they're delicious no matter what name they go by. Potato pancakes are usually served topped with applesauce or sour cream, but why not give a little French Onion Dip (page 33) a try?

3 medium russet potatoes (about 1 pound total), peeled and grated

1 scallion, thinly sliced

¼ cup all-purpose flour

1 tablespoon cornstarch

½ teaspoon baking powder

1 teaspoon salt

¼ teaspoon freshly ground black pepper

2 tablespoons neutral-flavored vegetable oil

1.  Place the grated potatoes in a colander and squeeze out as much excess water as you can.

2.  Transfer the drained potatoes to a large bowl. Add the scallion, flour, cornstarch, baking powder, salt, and pepper. Stir well.

3.  In a large skillet, heat the oil over medium-high heat until it shimmers. Using a ¼-cup measuring cup, scoop the batter in mounds in the pan. Using the back of the cup or a spatula, flatten the mounds until about ¼ inch thick. (Depending on the size of your pan, you may be able to cook about 5 pancakes at a time.) Cook for 4 to 5 minutes, until golden brown and crisp. Flip and cook the other side for another 4 to 5 minutes, until golden brown and crisp. Transfer the potato pancakes to a plate lined with a paper towel to drain off any excess oil. Repeat with the remaining potato batter. Serve.

> **Technique Tip:** For extra-crispy pancakes, soak the grated potatoes in ice-cold water for 15 minutes, then drain them and squeeze out any excess water.

**PER SERVING (2 PANCAKES):** CALORIES: 178; FAT: 6G; SATURATED FAT: 4G; CHOLESTEROL: 0G; PROTEIN: 3G; FIBER: 2G; SODIUM: 356MG

# NOT YO' ORDINARY NACHOS

KID-FRIENDLY, ONE-PAN/ONE-POT

**SERVES 4 | PREP TIME:** 20 MINUTES

When I first started making nachos back in the olden days (meaning the '90s), I would melt cheese on tortilla chips, toss on a few jalapeño slices, and call it a day. While they *were* technically nachos, they weren't very appealing. I now load up my tortilla chips with beans, avocado, and tomato, and I've been known to make a meal out of it. If you'd like to jazz up your nachos even more, add salsa, hot sauce, and nondairy sour cream.

1 (15-ounce) can black beans, drained and rinsed

1 teaspoon chili powder

½ teaspoon ground cumin

½ teaspoon dried oregano

½ teaspoon garlic powder

½ teaspoon onion powder

½ teaspoon salt

¼ teaspoon cayenne pepper

¼ teaspoon freshly ground black pepper

1 (8-ounce) bag tortilla chips

¼ cup diced red onion (about ¼ onion)

1 avocado, pitted, peeled, and diced

1 large tomato, diced

1 jalapeño pepper, thinly sliced

1 cup Say Cheese! Sauce (page 228), Creamy Queso Dip (page 32), or store-bought nondairy cheese sauce, warmed

¼ cup pitted black olives, chopped

¼ cup chopped fresh cilantro

1. In a medium bowl, combine the black beans, chili powder, cumin, oregano, garlic powder, onion powder, salt, cayenne, and black pepper. Toss until well coated.

2. Spread out the tortilla chips on a large plate or platter. Pile on the seasoned beans, onion, avocado, tomato, and jalapeño. Drizzle with the cheese sauce and top with the olives and cilantro to serve.

> **Substitution Tip:** Make nacho fries by replacing the tortilla chips with 1 batch of Polenta Fries (page 38) or a cooked 16-ounce bag of frozen French fries.

PER SERVING: CALORIES: 543; FAT: 24G; SATURATED FAT: 3G; CHOLESTEROL: 0G; PROTEIN: 16G; FIBER: 16G; SODIUM: 846MG

# 'TATER SKINS

**MAKES 12 POTATO SKINS | PREP TIME:** 15 MINUTES | **COOK TIME:** 1 HOUR

If there's a better vehicle for cheese and bac'un than the potato skin, I haven't found it. Potato skins are like little edible bowls of goodness, and much like potato chips, it's hard to eat just one. Go on—I dare you to try. Add a dollop of French Onion Dip (page 33) or nondairy sour cream for a little extra indulgence.

**4 teaspoons neutral-flavored vegetable oil, divided**

**6 medium potatoes (see Tip)**

**1 teaspoon salt, divided**

**1 teaspoon freshly ground black pepper, divided**

**1½ cups Say Cheese! Sauce (page 228) or store-bought nondairy cheese sauce, warmed**

**1 batch Tempeh Bac'un (page 233), or 16 ounces cooked store-bought tempeh bacon, crumbled**

**2 scallions, sliced**

1. Preheat the oven to 400°F. Line a baking sheet with parchment paper.

2. Brush 2 teaspoons of the oil onto the potatoes. Sprinkle them with ½ teaspoon each of salt and pepper. Arrange the potatoes in a single layer on the prepared baking sheet. Bake for 30 to 45 minutes, until the skins are crispy and browned.

3. Remove the pan from the oven (leave the heat on) and let the potatoes cool slightly. Once cool, slice them in half. Using a spoon, scoop out the centers (reserving the flesh for another use; see below), leaving about ½ inch of potato around the skins.

4. Brush the remaining 2 teaspoons oil on the inside of the potatoes and sprinkle with the remaining salt and pepper. Bake the potato skins for another 10 to 15 minutes, or until the edges are crisp and brown.

5. To serve, drizzle each potato skin with 2 tablespoons of warmed cheese sauce and top with tempeh bac'un and scallions.

**Ingredient Tip:** Use the flesh from the potatoes to make Broccoli Tots (page 48); you'll need about 3 cups of potato for the tots. Since the potato is already cooked, you'll just need to make sure you cook your broccoli. You can also use the leftover potato to make mashed potatoes: Just mash them with a little Almond Milk (page 214) and olive oil, then season them with salt and black pepper.

**PER SERVING (2 POTATO SKINS):** CALORIES: 444; FAT: 27G; SATURATED FAT: 5G; CHOLESTEROL: 0G; PROTEIN: 14G; FIBER: 9G; SODIUM: 1,266MG

# CHIC'UN NUGGETS

SOY-FREE, KID-FRIENDLY

**MAKES 12 NUGGETS | PREP TIME:** 10 MINUTES | **COOK TIME:** 30 MINUTES

Kids these days grow up chowin' down on chicken nuggets, but nuggets weren't that big a thing when I was young. I think we have a certain fast-food chain that introduced them nationwide in the '80s to blame for their popularity. I'm not opposed to food in nugget form, but I prefer this kinder version made with chickpeas. Serve them with your favorite dippin' sauce.

½ cup quick-cooking rolled oats

1 (14-ounce) can chickpeas, drained (liquid reserved), but not rinsed (see Tip)

¼ cup chickpea flour

1 teaspoon dried thyme

½ teaspoon ground sage

½ teaspoon ground rosemary

½ teaspoon salt

½ teaspoon garlic powder

¼ teaspoon freshly ground black pepper

½ cup plain unsweetened Almond Milk (page 214) or store-bought nondairy milk

1 tablespoon cornstarch

¾ cup panko bread crumbs

1. Preheat the oven to 400°F. Line a baking sheet with parchment paper.

2. Place the oats in a food processor and process into a fine flour. Add the chickpeas and ¼ cup of the liquid reserved from the can (see Tip), the chickpea flour, thyme, sage, rosemary, salt, garlic powder, and pepper. Pulse until the mixture is crumbly.

3. Set up a workstation with 2 medium bowls and place the prepared baking sheet at the end. In the first bowl, whisk together the almond milk and corn-starch. Place the panko in the second bowl.

4. Take a heaping tablespoon of the chickpea mix-ture and, using your hands, shape it into a nugget. Dip the nugget into the almond milk mixture, then dredge it in the panko, coating it well. Set the breaded nugget on the prepared baking sheet. Repeat with the remaining chickpea mixture, arrang-ing the nuggets in a single layer on the pan.

5. Bake for 15 minutes, flip the nuggets, and bake for another 15 minutes, or until they're golden brown and firm. Serve.

**Ingredient Tip:** There's no need to rinse your chickpeas when making this recipe. The liquid from canned beans is known as aquafaba, and it has a magical binding property, similar to that of eggs.

**PER SERVING (3 NUGGETS):** CALORIES: 248; FAT: 4G; SATURATED FAT: 1G; CHOLESTEROL: 1G; PROTEIN: 12G; FIBER: 7G; SODIUM: 355MG

# CRABBY CAKES

SOY-FREE, KID-FRIENDLY

**MAKES 14 CAKES | PREP TIME:** 15 MINUTES | **COOK TIME:** 30 MINUTES

For reasons unknown, some people think vegans eat fish. I've had tuna sandwiches offered to me for lunch, and I've seen grilled salmon in the veg section of restaurant menus. Fish don't grow on trees, y'all! Jackfruit does grow on trees, though, and when seasoned with a little seaweed, it makes a great replacement for seafood. You can eat this appetizer as is, or you can put the jackfruit cakes on mini buns and serve them as sliders.

### FOR THE JACKFRUIT CAKES

**2 tablespoons flax meal (ground flaxseed)**

**6 tablespoons water**

**1 teaspoon neutral-flavored vegetable oil**

**2 scallions, sliced**

**1 celery stalk, finely chopped**

**2 garlic cloves, minced**

**1 (20-ounce) can young jackfruit, drained and rinsed**

**1 (14-ounce) can hearts of palm, drained and rinsed**

**¾ cup panko bread crumbs, divided**

**1 tablespoon cornstarch**

**1 tablespoon Old Bay seasoning**

**1 tablespoon kelp flakes (see Tip)**

**1 teaspoon Dijon mustard**

1. Preheat the oven to 400°F. Line a baking sheet with parchment paper.

2. **Make the jackfruit cakes:** In a small bowl, stir together the flax meal and water. Set aside to gel.

3. In a medium skillet, heat the oil over medium heat until it shimmers. Add the scallions, celery, and garlic and cook until softened, about 5 minutes.

4. Pull the jackfruit and hearts of palm apart into small shreds (you can do this by hand, by mashing them with a potato masher, or by giving them a few pulses in a food processor).

5. Transfer the jackfruit and hearts of palm to a large bowl. Add the flax egg, cooked vegetables, ¼ cup of the panko, the cornstarch, Old Bay seasoning, kelp flakes, and mustard. Stir well.

6. Using a ¼-cup measuring cup, shape the mixture into patties.

7. Place the remaining panko in a shallow dish. Dredge each patty through the panko, coating well.

8. Arrange the patties in a single layer on the prepared baking sheet. Bake for 10 minutes. Flip the cakes, and bake for another 10 to 15 minutes, or until golden brown and firm.

½ cup **Cashew Aioli (page 222) or** vegan mayonnaise

**3 tablespoons sweet relish** or chopped dill pickles

**1 teaspoon fresh** lemon juice

9. **Meanwhile, make the tartar sauce:** In a small bowl, stir together the cashew aioli, sweet relish, and lemon juice.

10. Serve the crab cakes topped with the tartar sauce.

> **Ingredient Tip:** Kelp is a type of seaweed. It can usually be found in flake form in shaker jars in the Asian section of grocery stores. If you can't find kelp flakes, any type of seaweed flakes can be used instead, including nori, dulse, or arame.

> **Troubleshooting Tip:** The smaller the jackfruit and hearts of palm are shredded, the better your Crabby Cakes will hold together. Large chunks may cause the cakes to fall apart.

PER SERVING (2 CAKES): CALORIES: 238; FAT: 8G; SATURATED FAT: 1G; CHOLESTEROL: 0G; PROTEIN: 5G; FIBER: 3G; SODIUM: 261MG

## Meat Substitutes

Most vegans give up meat not because they don't like the taste, but rather for reasons of compassion, health, and concern for the planet. Thankfully, vegan substitutes for meat are easy to come by. Most grocery stores carry plant-based versions of burgers, chicken, bacon, sausages, and even holiday roasts. Fast-food joints are getting in on the vegan game, too. Those products are good every once in a while, but keep in mind that they can often contain extra fat and sodium. It's easy to make your own "meat" at home, using simple ingredients such as tofu, tempeh, seitan, or even beans.

# BROCCOLI TOTS

GLUTEN-FREE, SOY-FREE, KID-FRIENDLY

**SERVES 4 TO 6 | PREP TIME:** 15 MINUTES | **COOK TIME:** 50 MINUTES

Tots are the quintessential potato-delivery system. With their crunchy exterior and soft, pillowy centers, they're a great way to hide veggies from picky eaters, too. Sure, the broccoli is visible, but it doesn't interfere with the taste. You know what they say: 'Taters gonna 'tate.

**2 medium russet potatoes,** peeled and diced (about 3 cups)

**1 teaspoon salt, divided**

**2 cups broccoli florets,** chopped into small pieces

**2 tablespoons plain** unsweetened Almond Milk (page 214) or store-bought nondairy milk

**2 tablespoons** nutritional yeast

**1 tablespoon potato starch** or cornstarch

**½ teaspoon onion powder**

**½ teaspoon garlic powder**

**¼ teaspoon freshly ground** black pepper

**Substitution Tip:** Cauliflower or kale can be used in place of the broccoli.

1. Preheat the oven to 425°F. Line a baking sheet with parchment paper.

2. Place the potatoes in a large pot with enough water to cover them by 2 inches. Add ½ teaspoon of the salt. Bring to a rolling boil over medium-high heat, then cook the potatoes until fork-tender, 15 to 20 minutes. About 3 minutes before the potatoes are done, add the broccoli to the pot.

3. Drain the potatoes and broccoli in a fine-mesh sieve and pat them dry with a paper towel.

4. Transfer the potatoes and broccoli to a large bowl. Add the almond milk, nutritional yeast, potato starch, onion powder, garlic powder, and pepper. Using a potato masher or large fork, mash everything together until the mixture has the consistency of mashed potatoes.

5. Using a melon baller or large spoon, roll the mixture into short cylinders, about 1 inch in diameter.

6. Arrange the tots in a single layer on the prepared baking sheet. Bake for 15 minutes. Flip the tots and bake for another 15 minutes, or until golden brown and crisp. Serve.

**Troubleshooting Tip:** If your tots aren't holding together, it means the broccoli pieces are too large. Use your hands to break up any large pieces that are left after you've mashed everything together.

**PER SERVING:** CALORIES: 130; FAT: 0G; SATURATED FAT: 0G; CHOLESTEROL: 0G; PROTEIN: 6G; FIBER: 3G; SODIUM: 698MG

# BUFFALO TEMPEH

**SERVES 4 | PREP TIME:** 10 MINUTES, PLUS MARINATING TIME **| COOK TIME:** 20 MINUTES

There's a saying in these parts: If you can't stand the heat, stay away from the tempeh. And by "these parts," I mean my house. We like our tempeh spicy, so Buffalo "wings" are a favorite. I've been told that I'm committing Buffalo heresy by dipping mine in Ranch Dressing (page 217) instead of blue cheese, but I'm okay with that.

¾ cup hot sauce

3 tablespoons vegetable stock

3 tablespoons olive oil

2 (8-ounce) packages tempeh, cut into 1¾-by-3-inch strips

½ cup plain unsweetened Almond Milk (page 214) or store-bought nondairy milk

1 tablespoon cornstarch

¾ cup all-purpose flour

1 teaspoon dried thyme

1 teaspoon garlic powder

1 teaspoon onion powder

½ teaspoon salt

¾ cup panko bread crumbs

1. In a small bowl, whisk together the hot sauce, stock, and oil.

2. Place the tempeh in a shallow dish and pour the hot sauce mixture over it. Gently toss to coat. Cover and set aside to marinate for an hour to overnight (refrigerate if overnight). Remove the tempeh and reserve the remaining marinade.

3. Preheat the oven to 400°F. Line a baking sheet with parchment paper.

4. Set up a workstation with 3 medium bowls and place the prepared baking sheet at the end. In the first bowl, combine the almond milk and cornstarch. In the second bowl, combine the flour, thyme, garlic powder, onion powder, and salt. Place the panko in the third bowl.

5. Dip each tempeh piece into the milk mixture, dredge it in the flour mixture, then toss it in the panko mixture, coating it well. Place each piece on the prepared baking sheet, being careful not to overlap them.

6. Bake for 10 minutes, flip each piece, and bake for another 10 minutes, or until golden brown and crisp. Toss the cooked tempeh with the remaining marinade. Serve.

**Substitution Tip:** If you'd prefer barbecue tempeh, skip the hot sauce, vegetable stock, and olive oil and use 1 cup barbecue sauce instead. If the sauce seems too thick to marinate your tempeh, you can thin it down with a little water or stock.

PER SERVING: CALORIES: 473; FAT: 24G; SATURATED FAT: 4G; CHOLESTEROL: 0G; PROTEIN: 26G; FIBER: 2G; SODIUM: 1,321MG

# POPCORN TOFU

KID-FRIENDLY

**SERVES 4 | PREP TIME:** 15 MINUTES | **COOK TIME:** 30 MINUTES

My family didn't eat seafood growing up, so the first time I heard about popcorn shrimp, I thought it was either something battered in popped corn kernels or it was a snack for movie night. It turns out that "popcorn" just means it's bite-size. That hasn't stopped me from munching away on a bowl of this tofu while watching Netflix on Friday nights, though. These little nuggets are great on a sandwich, too.

¾ cup Cashew Aioli (page 222) or vegan mayonnaise

½ cup cornmeal

½ cup unseasoned bread crumbs

2 tablespoons nutritional yeast

1 teaspoon garlic powder

1 teaspoon onion powder

1 teaspoon sweet paprika

½ teaspoon mustard powder

½ teaspoon salt

¼ teaspoon freshly ground black pepper

1 (14-ounce) package extra-firm tofu, drained, pressed (see Tip, page 18), and cut into 1½-inch cubes

1. Preheat the oven to 400°F. Line a baking sheet with parchment paper.

2. Set up a workstation with 2 medium bowls and place the prepared baking sheet at the end. Place the cashew aioli in the first bowl. In the other bowl, combine the cornmeal, bread crumbs, nutritional yeast, garlic powder, onion powder, paprika, mustard powder, salt, and pepper.

3. Coat the tofu cubes in the aioli, then coat them in the bread crumb mixture. Arrange them in a single layer on the prepared baking sheet.

4. Bake for 15 minutes, then flip the pieces and bake for another 15 minutes, or until the tofu is crisp and golden brown. Serve.

**Technique Tip:** When making recipes like this one where something needs to be dipped in a liquid and then in flour or bread crumbs, I like to use one hand for the wet ingredients and the other hand for the dry. This helps keep my hands from getting too messy.

**PER SERVING:** CALORIES: 374; FAT: 21G; SATURATED FAT: 2G; CHOLESTEROL: 0G; PROTEIN: 18G; FIBER: 3G; SODIUM: 944MG

# OVEN-FRIED OKRA

GLUTEN-FREE, SOY-FREE

**SERVES 4 | PREP TIME:** 15 MINUTES **| COOK TIME:** 25 MINUTES

Here in the United States, fried okra is a Southern thing, so it's hard to come by in the Northeast, where I live. A few years ago, I spotted it on the menu at a vegan soul food restaurant and decided to give it a try. I was immediately hooked. How have other parts of the country not learned of its addictive goodness by now? I'm now on a mission to spread this deliciousness to other parts of the world. Try them, and you'll be hooked, too.

1 cup plain unsweetened Almond Milk (page 214) or store-bought nondairy milk

¾ cup chickpea flour

1 cup cornmeal

1 teaspoon garlic powder

1 teaspoon onion powder

½ teaspoon salt

¼ teaspoon sweet paprika

¼ teaspoon cayenne pepper

¼ teaspoon freshly ground black pepper

12 ounces okra, trimmed and halved lengthwise (about 4 cups)

1. Preheat the oven to 425°F. Line a baking sheet with parchment paper.

2. Set up a workstation with 2 medium bowls and place the prepared baking sheet at the end. In the first bowl, mix together the almond milk and chickpea flour. In the second bowl, mix together the cornmeal, garlic powder, onion powder, salt, paprika, cayenne, and black pepper.

3. Dip each piece of okra in the almond milk mixture, then dredge it in the cornmeal mixture. Arrange the okra in a single layer on the prepared baking sheet.

4. Bake for 10 minutes, then flip the pieces and bake for another 10 to 15 minutes, until golden brown and crisp. Serve.

> **Time-Saving Tip:** If you happen to have an air fryer, you can use it to cook your okra faster. Air-fry the okra at 400°F for about 15 minutes, giving the basket a good shake about halfway through.

**PER SERVING:** CALORIES: 278; FAT: 3G; SATURATED FAT: 0G; CHOLESTEROL: 0G; PROTEIN: 10G; FIBER: 7G; SODIUM: 284MG

# TAHINI GREENIES

NUT-FREE, GLUTEN-FREE, SOY-FREE, KID-FRIENDLY, ONE-PAN/ONE-POT

**SERVES 4 | PREP TIME:** 10 MINUTES **| COOK TIME:** 12 MINUTES

If a spoonful of sugar makes the medicine go down, then I reckon a tasty sauce will help the kale go down. I've had people tell me they don't like kale, but it's because they've eaten it steamed or—*gasp*—boiled. Kale is far more flavorful when sautéed with garlic and onion and then tossed in a savory sauce. If this recipe won't win over the kale haters, nothing will.

2 teaspoons neutral-flavored vegetable oil

½ cup diced yellow onion (about ½ onion)

2 garlic cloves, minced

1 pound kale or Swiss chard, leaves stemmed and chopped (about 8 cups)

¼ cup tahini

2 tablespoons fresh lemon juice

2 tablespoons water

½ teaspoon salt

1 tablespoon toasted sesame seeds

1. In a large skillet, heat the oil over medium-high heat until it shimmers. Add the onion and cook for 5 minutes, or until it softens and begins to brown. Add the garlic and cook for another minute or two, until fragrant. Add the kale and cook, stirring often, until it wilts and turns bright green, about 5 minutes.

2. Meanwhile, in a small bowl, whisk together the tahini, lemon juice, water, and salt.

3. Remove the kale from the heat and stir in the tahini mixture, tossing to coat well. Sprinkle on the sesame seeds to serve.

**Technique Tip:** Depending on the size of your pan, it may be difficult to cook all the kale at once. You can cook a little bit at first, adding more once it wilts. Kitchen tongs make it easier to toss the kale around in the pot.

**PER SERVING:** CALORIES: 185; FAT: 12G; SATURATED FAT: 2G; CHOLESTEROL: 0G; PROTEIN: 8G; FIBER: 6G; SODIUM: 306MG

# MISO-GLAZED EGGPLANT

NUT-FREE, GLUTEN-FREE, ONE-PAN/ONE-POT

**SERVES 4 | PREP TIME:** 5 MINUTES | **COOK TIME:** 13 MINUTES

If you're like me and you can't decide between sweet and salty when choosing what to eat, you need this recipe in your life. It was inspired by the Japanese dish *nasu dengaku*, and it's super easy to make. When broiled, eggplant has a melt-in-your mouth, almost creamy texture, and the miso-agave glaze caramelizes on top of it, transforming the vegetable into pure culinary bliss.

**Vegetable oil, for the baking sheet**

**¼ cup mellow white miso paste**

**3 tablespoons unseasoned rice vinegar**

**3 tablespoons agave nectar**

**4 Japanese eggplant, stems trimmed (see Tip)**

**2 tablespoons sesame oil**

**1 scallion, sliced**

**1 tablespoon toasted sesame seeds**

1. Preheat the broiler. Lightly oil a baking sheet.

2. In a small bowl, whisk together the miso, vinegar, and agave.

3. Cut the eggplant in half lengthwise. Using a sharp knife, score the flesh in a grid pattern, without cutting all the way through the skin.

4. Place the eggplant on the prepared baking sheet and broil for 3 to 5 minutes. Then flip them over and broil for another 3 to 5 minutes. Keep an eye on your eggplant to make sure it doesn't burn.

5. Remove from the oven and, with the cut sides up, spoon the miso mixture onto each eggplant half. Broil for another 2 to 3 minutes, until the miso mixture bubbles.

6. Top the eggplant halves with scallions and sesame seeds to serve.

**Ingredient Tip:** Japanese eggplant are small, slim eggplant with dark purple skin. They have a milder flavor than globe eggplant, the large variety we're used to cooking with. If you can't find Japanese eggplant, look for small globe eggplant, 6 to 8 inches long and just a few inches wide.

**Troubleshooting Tip:** I usually line my baking sheets with parchment paper; however, it shouldn't be used in ovens hotter than 450°F, or it will burn. In order to reduce fire risk, don't use parchment paper when using your broiler. You can use aluminum foil in its place, if you like.

PER SERVING: CALORIES: 217; FAT: 9G; SATURATED FAT: 1G; CHOLESTEROL: 0G; PROTEIN: 5G; FIBER: 10G; SODIUM: 661MG

# BALSAMIC ROASTED 'SHROOMS

NUT-FREE

**SERVES 4 | PREP TIME:** 10 MINUTES | **COOK TIME:** 40 MINUTES

Mushrooms: You either love them or hate them. I love them, but my affection for them came later in life. You see, when I was growing up, the only type of 'shrooms we had were the ones that came in a can. They were limp and slimy, and I was *not* a fan. Roasting fresh mushrooms elevates this misunderstood veggie from slime to divine. I've converted a few self-professed mushroom haters with this recipe.

**4 garlic cloves, minced**

**3 tablespoons balsamic vinegar**

**1 tablespoon reduced-sodium soy sauce or tamari**

**1 tablespoon olive oil**

**½ teaspoon dried thyme**

**½ teaspoon dried parsley**

**½ teaspoon salt**

**¼ teaspoon freshly ground black pepper**

**2 pounds cremini or white button mushrooms (see Tip)**

1. Preheat the oven to 400°F. Line a baking sheet with parchment paper.

2. In a small bowl, whisk together the garlic, balsamic vinegar, soy sauce, olive oil, thyme, parsley, salt, and pepper.

3. Place the mushrooms in a large bowl and pour the vinegar mixture over top. Gently toss the mushrooms to coat them evenly.

4. Spread the mushrooms in a single layer on the prepared baking sheet. Roast for 30 to 40 minutes, flipping them at about the halfway point. The mushrooms are done when they're tender and nicely browned. Serve.

**Ingredient Tip:** To clean mushrooms, wipe off any dirt with a damp kitchen towel. If your mushrooms are on the larger side, you can slice them in half, but I like to roast them whole.

PER SERVING: CALORIES: 98; FAT: 4G; SATURATED FAT: 1G; CHOLESTEROL: 0G; PROTEIN: 8G; FIBER: 2G; SODIUM: 557MG

# BROCCOLI IN CHEESE SAUCE

GLUTEN-FREE, SOY-FREE, KID-FRIENDLY, ONE-PAN/ONE-POT

**SERVES 4 | PREP TIME:** 10 MINUTES | **COOK TIME:** 20 MINUTES

When I was a kid, broccoli was my favorite vegetable. My mom would heat up a bag of frozen broccoli and toss it in cheese sauce made from a powdered mix. Powdered cheese sauce is kinda gross, but hey, it got me to eat my veggies. This is my adult take on that beloved childhood dish. I roast my broccoli because it's more flavorful than steaming or sautéing, and I like when the little edges get brown and crisp.

5 cups chopped broccoli (cut into bite-size florets)

2 teaspoons neutral-flavored vegetable oil

½ teaspoon salt

¼ teaspoon freshly ground black pepper

2 cups Say Cheese! Sauce (page 228) or store-bought nondairy cheese sauce, warmed

1. Preheat the oven to 425°F. Line a baking sheet with parchment paper.

2. Place the broccoli in a large bowl. Add the vegetable oil, salt, and pepper, and toss until well coated. Spread out the broccoli in a single layer on the prepared baking sheet. Roast for 15 to 20 minutes, or until the broccoli starts to crisp and turn brown.

3. Transfer the cooked broccoli to a serving bowl, Add the warm cheese sauce and gently toss until well coated to serve.

**Substitution Tip:** Cauliflower or Brussels sprouts can be used instead of the broccoli.

PER SERVING: CALORIES: 174; FAT: 7G; SATURATED FAT: 1G; CHOLESTEROL: 0G; PROTEIN: 10G; FIBER: 6G; SODIUM: 971MG

# MAPLE-MUSTARD BRUSSELS SPROUTS

GLUTEN-FREE, SOY-FREE, KID-FRIENDLY, ONE-PAN/ONE-POT

**SERVES 4 | PREP TIME:** 10 MINUTES | **COOK TIME:** 18 MINUTES

I've said it before and I'll say it again: Brussels sprouts don't get the props they deserve. I get it. I spent many years hating them. Once I realized how to properly cook Brussels sprouts (please don't stick a bag of frozen sprouts in the microwave and call it a side dish), I realized how wasted those years were, and I'm trying to make up for them now. Sweet, tangy maple-mustard sauce takes away the sprouts' bitter edge in this dish.

3 tablespoons pure maple syrup

2 tablespoons Dijon mustard

4 teaspoons neutral-flavored vegetable oil, divided

2 medium shallots, thinly sliced (about ½ cup)

1 pound Brussels sprouts, halved (about 4 cups)

½ teaspoon salt

¼ cup pecans, toasted and chopped

1. In a small bowl, whisk together the maple syrup and Dijon mustard.

2. In a large skillet, heat the oil over medium-high heat until it shimmers. Add the shallots and cook, stirring frequently, for about 5 minutes, until they have begun to brown. Remove the shallots from the pan and set aside on a plate.

3. To the same pan, add the remaining oil and then arrange the Brussels sprouts in a single layer. Sprinkle them with the salt. Cook, undisturbed, for 5 minutes or until the cut sides brown. Continue cooking for another 5 minutes, stirring frequently, until the Brussels sprouts brown all over.

4. Return the cooked shallots to the pan along with the maple mustard mixture and the pecans. Cook for another 2 to 3 minutes, stirring frequently to coat the vegetables in the sauce before serving.

**Substitution Tip:** If you're really opposed to sprouts, you can use broccoli or cauliflower in their place.

PER SERVING: CALORIES: 183; FAT: 10G; SATURATED FAT: 1G; CHOLESTEROL: 0G; PROTEIN: 5G; FIBER: 5G; SODIUM: 349MG

# LEMON-GARLIC HASSELBACK POTATOES

NUT-FREE, GLUTEN-FREE, SOY-FREE, KID-FRIENDLY, ONE-PAN/ONE-POT

**SERVES 4 | PREP TIME:** 15 MINUTES | **COOK TIME:** 1 HOUR 15 MINUTES

I think we can all agree that the best parts of a roasted potato are the crispy edges. And these pretty 'taters have edges for days. They also have the soft and creamy centers we know and love from baked potatoes, so they're really the best of both worlds. Plus, they look all fancy-pants on the plate, so they're sure to wow your dining companions, whether that's your friends, your family, or your cats.

3 tablespoons neutral-flavored vegetable oil, divided, plus more for the baking dish

4 large Yukon Gold or russet potatoes

½ teaspoon salt

¼ teaspoon freshly ground black pepper

1 teaspoon grated lemon zest

2 tablespoons fresh lemon juice

1 teaspoon Dijon mustard

4 garlic cloves, minced

1 tablespoon chopped fresh rosemary leaves

1. Preheat the oven to 425°F. Lightly oil a baking dish.

2. Using a knife, cut vertical slits in the potatoes, about ¼ inch apart from one another, stopping about ½ inch from the bottom.

3. Place the potatoes cut-side up in the prepared baking dish. Brush them with half the oil and sprinkle with the salt and pepper. Bake for 45 minutes.

4. Meanwhile, in a small bowl, whisk together the remaining oil, lemon zest, lemon juice, mustard, garlic, and rosemary.

5. Remove the potatoes from the oven and brush on about half of the lemon juice mixture (the potato slices should have started to peel away from one another, so try to get the mixture between them). Bake for another 15 minutes.

6. Remove the potatoes from the oven and brush on the remaining lemon juice mixture. Bake for another 15 minutes, until the potatoes have browned and the edges are crisp. Serve.

**Troubleshooting Tip:** It can be a little tough to slice the potatoes without cutting all the way through them. I like to place my potatoes between the handles of two wooden spoons to act as a guard so I can't cut all the way through to the bottom.

PER SERVING: CALORIES: 384; FAT: 11G; SATURATED FAT: 1G; CHOLESTEROL: 0G; PROTEIN: 8G; FIBER: 8G; SODIUM: 269MG

# SUMMER ROLLS

NUT-FREE, KID-FRIENDLY, ONE-PAN/ONE-POT

**MAKES 8 ROLLS | PREP TIME:** 20 MINUTES

Summer rolls, also known as fresh spring rolls, are a Vietnamese appetizer. They're pretty much just salad in a wrapper, and wrapped food is always much more fun to eat than those in bowls. You can customize your rolls to suit your tastes (and the contents of your fridge). I sometimes make them with shredded cabbage and romaine lettuce. Serve your rolls with Spicy Peanut Sauce (page 221) or Carrot-Ginger Dressing (page 216) for dipping.

8 (10-inch) rice paper spring roll wrappers

1 cup shredded carrots (about 2 medium)

1 cup thinly sliced cucumber (about ½ medium)

1 red bell pepper, seeded and thinly sliced

1 avocado, pitted, peeled, and sliced

1 batch Baked Tofu, Three Ways (page 230) or 16 ounces store-bought baked tofu, cut into thin strips

1. Fill a large bowl with warm water. Have a plastic cutting board or ceramic plate ready to assemble your spring rolls.

2. Submerge a wrapper in the warm water for about 30 seconds, until it becomes soft and pliable.

3. Place the softened wrapper on your cutting board or plate. Place some of the vegetable and avocado slices and a few tofu strips on the bottom third of the wrapper.

4. Gently fold the bottom of the wrapper over the filling, then fold over the sides. Carefully roll the spring up, keeping it tight. Repeat with the remaining ingredients. Serve.

**Technique Tip:** Summer rolls require a little patience, as the rice paper wrappers are delicate and can tear easily. Don't overstuff them, as they'll definitely rip. Make sure the surface you're rolling them on isn't porous, such as a wooden cutting board, because the wrappers will stick. You can work on parchment paper, too.

**PER SERVING (2 ROLLS):** CALORIES: 280; FAT: 14G; SATURATED FAT: 2G; CHOLESTEROL: 0G; PROTEIN: 16G; FIBER: 6G; SODIUM: 54MG

Arugula and
Farro Salad, page 75

# CHAPTER FOUR

# LETTUCE EAT

## SALADS AND SLAWS

# PESTO IS THE BESTO PASTA SALAD

SOY-FREE, KID-FRIENDLY

**SERVES 6 | PREP TIME:** 20 MINUTES | **COOK TIME:** 15 MINUTES

Where are my fellow pesto lovers at? Pesto is often my sauce of choice on pasta, and that goes for cold pasta salads as well as hot dinner entrées. Pasta salad is often thought of as a warm-weather dish, but I like to make it year-round; it keeps me in a summertime frame of mind. If you happen to have vegan mozzarella or fresh basil on hand, go ahead and toss in some. I sometimes add a little steamed broccoli, too.

8 ounces dried bite-size pasta, such as rotini or farfalle

1 cup cooked chickpeas

½ cup sun-dried tomatoes, sliced

¼ cup pitted kalamata olives, sliced

1 cup Popeye Pesto (page 225) or store-bought dairy-free pesto

1. Cook the pasta according to the package instructions. Drain, rinse, and set aside to cool for about 10 minutes.

2. Transfer the cooked pasta to a large bowl. Add the chickpeas, sun-dried tomatoes, and olives. Gently mix in the pesto before serving.

**Time-Saving Tip:** Life is too short to pit olives. When buying kalamatas, make sure they're already pitted.

**Substitution Tip:** A cup of halved fresh cherry tomatoes can be used in place of the sun-dried tomatoes.

PER SERVING: CALORIES: 424; FAT: 25G; SATURATED FAT: 4G; CHOLESTEROL: 0G; PROTEIN: 12G; FIBER: 4G; SODIUM: 428MG

# CLASSIC MACARONI SALAD

SOY-FREE, KID-FRIENDLY

**SERVES 6 | PREP TIME:** 20 MINUTES | **COOK TIME:** 15 MINUTES

Macaroni salad conjures up memories of the summertime barbecues of my childhood. We'd enjoy it alongside corn on the cob, burgers, and cold lemonade, with ice pops for dessert. As an adult, I find myself craving the combination of tangy dressing and cold pasta the second the mercury rises above 70°F. Don't wait until the hot weather hits to make this dish, though, as it's a terrific companion to burgers and sandwiches any day of the year.

**8 ounces dried elbow macaroni**

**½ cup Cashew Aioli (page 222) or vegan mayonnaise**

**2 tablespoons fresh lemon juice**

**1 tablespoon Dijon mustard**

**1 garlic clove, minced**

**½ teaspoon salt**

**¼ teaspoon freshly ground black pepper**

**2 small carrots, diced**

**1 small red bell pepper, seeded and diced**

**2 celery stalks, sliced**

**2 scallions, sliced**

**½ cup green peas**

**¼ cup chopped fresh flat-leaf parsley leaves**

1. Cook the pasta according to the package instructions. Drain, rinse, and set aside to cool for about 10 minutes.

2. Meanwhile, in a small bowl, whisk together the cashew aioli, lemon juice, mustard, garlic, salt, and black pepper.

3. Transfer the pasta to a large bowl. Add the carrots, bell pepper, celery, scallions, peas, and parsley and toss to combine. Gently stir in the dressing before serving.

> **Substitution Tip:** It's easy to sub out any of the ingredients in this salad for other veggies to suit your tastes or the contents of your fridge. For a taste of the Southwest, use chopped tomatoes instead of carrots, avocado instead of celery, corn instead of peas, diced red onion instead of scallions, and cilantro instead of parsley. Sub lime juice for the lemon juice in the dressing, add ½ teaspoon chili powder, and a pinch of red pepper flakes. Black beans and chopped jalapeño can be added, too.

**PER SERVING:** CALORIES: 233; FAT: 7G; SATURATED FAT: 1G; CHOLESTEROL: 0G; PROTEIN: 8G; FIBER: 3G; SODIUM: 363MG

# RANCH POTATO SALAD

**SERVES 6 | PREP TIME:** 20 MINUTES **| COOK TIME:** 20 MINUTES

This ain't your mama's mayo-laden potato salad! This is its tangy, fun-loving relative, made with zesty ranch dressing and tempeh bacon, and it's sure to be the life of the party when it accompanies you to potlucks and cookouts. Enjoy it throughout the year as a side to your sandwiches instead of a boring garden salad. Sprinkle on a little shredded nondairy cheddar, if you happen to have it.

3 pounds red potatoes, halved or quartered (see Tip)

½ teaspoon salt

1 batch Tempeh Bac'un (page 233), or 8 ounces store-bought tempeh bacon

2 celery stalks, sliced

4 scallions, sliced

1 cup Ranch Dressing (page 217) or store-bought dairy-free ranch dressing

¼ cup chopped fresh chives

1. Place the potatoes in a large pot and add water to cover by 2 inches. Add the salt. Bring the water to a boil over medium-high heat. Reduce the heat to medium and simmer the potatoes until fork-tender, about 15 minutes. Drain and rinse the potatoes. Set aside to cool for about 10 minutes.

2. Transfer the potatoes to a large bowl. Add the tempeh bac'un, celery, and scallions. Gently stir in the dressing. Top with the chives before serving.

**Ingredient Tip:** Waxy potatoes, such as red, new, or fingerling, work best in potato salad because they don't have as much starch as other varieties and they hold their shape well when boiled. I keep the peel on my potatoes in recipes like this because it saves time, and the skins do contain nutrients. You can peel yours if you prefer.

**PER SERVING:** CALORIES: 359; FAT: 16G; SATURATED FAT: 2G; CHOLESTEROL: 0G; PROTEIN: 9G; FIBER: 6G; SODIUM: 1,204MG

# SPICY TAHINI SLAW

NUT-FREE, GLUTEN-FREE, SOY-FREE, 30-MINUTE MEAL, ONE-PAN/ONE-POT

**SERVES 6 | PREP TIME:** 15 MINUTES

I'm from New Jersey, which is proudly home to more diners than any other state. The one thing you can count on when you eat at a diner is a side of limp, soupy coleslaw. I really love coleslaw, but I find the diner version to be a culinary crime. I've created a legit homemade version that includes kale, and I've used spicy tahini instead of mayo, because tahini makes everything better.

2 cups shredded curly
    kale leaves

2 cups shredded
    green cabbage

2 cups shredded
    purple cabbage

2 carrots, grated
    or shredded

¾ cup Spicy Tahini
    Dressing (page 215)

Salt

**Freshly ground black pepper**

Place the kale, cabbage, and carrots in a large bowl. Gently stir in the dressing. Season with salt and pepper. Serve.

**Substitution Tip:** For a more traditional coleslaw, you can use Cashew Aioli (page 222) or vegan mayo instead of the Spicy Tahini Dressing.

**Technique Tip:** When "shredding" kale, I remove the stems, then stack the leaves and roll them into a tight tube. I then cut through the leaves to create fine slices or shreds. Kale and cabbage can also be shredded with the slicing attachment on a food processor.

PER SERVING: CALORIES: 120; FAT: 8G; SATURATED FAT: 1G; CHOLESTEROL: 0G; PROTEIN: 4G; FIBER: 4G; SODIUM: 199MG

# KIMCHI SLAW

**SERVES 6 | PREP TIME:** 15 MINUTES

Since kimchi is spicy fermented cabbage, it may give the appearance of being vegan, but it often contains hidden fish- or shrimp-based ingredients. There are a few vegan varieties of kimchi available, but I prefer to make my own so I can control the ingredients. This slaw comes together quickly and isn't fermented, so it's technically not kimchi, but it has all the flavors we know and love from the traditional dish. Crank up the heat with more sriracha, if you dare.

¼ cup unseasoned
rice vinegar

2 tablespoons
reduced-sodium soy
sauce or tamari

2 tablespoons toasted
sesame oil

1 tablespoon sriracha

1 tablespoon grated peeled
fresh ginger

1 garlic clove, minced

4 cups shredded napa
cabbage (see Tip)

1 cup shredded
purple cabbage

1 cup mung bean sprouts

4 scallions, sliced

2 carrots, grated
or shredded

2 tablespoons toasted
sesame seeds

1. In a small bowl, whisk together the vinegar, soy sauce, sesame oil, sriracha, ginger, and garlic. Set the dressing aside.

2. Place the cabbage, mung bean sprouts, scallions, and carrots in a large bowl. Gently fold in the dressing. Top with the sesame seeds before serving.

**Ingredient Tip:** Napa cabbage is a type of Chinese cabbage that's sweeter than regular green cabbage. A head is oblong in shape, and the leaves are frilly on their edges. If napa cabbage is difficult to find, savoy cabbage or bok choy can be used in its place.

PER SERVING: CALORIES: 96; FAT: 6G; SATURATED FAT: 1G; CHOLESTEROL: 0G; PROTEIN: 3G; FIBER: 3G; SODIUM: 385MG

# TEX-MEX QUINOA SALAD

NUT-FREE, SOY-FREE

**SERVES 6 | PREP TIME:** 15 MINUTES **| COOK TIME:** 20 MINUTES

Quinoa may look like birdseed, but when cooked up and mixed with veggies and beans, it's the base of a scrumptious salad. And remember: If birdseed can be salad, you can be anything you put your mind to. Quinoa has a natural coating called saponin, which can be quite bitter; give your grains a good rinse in a fine-mesh sieve before cooking to get rid of it.

**1 cup uncooked quinoa, rinsed**

**2 cups vegetable stock or water**

**¼ cup extra-virgin olive oil**

**2 tablespoons fresh lime juice**

**½ teaspoon chili powder**

**½ teaspoon garlic powder**

**½ teaspoon salt**

**¼ teaspoon freshly ground black pepper**

**Pinch cayenne pepper**

**1 (15-ounce) can black beans, drained and rinsed**

**1 cup cherry tomatoes, halved**

**1 cup fresh or thawed frozen corn kernels**

**1 small red bell pepper, seeded and diced**

**1 avocado, pitted, peeled, and diced**

**½ cup diced red onion**

**½ cup chopped fresh cilantro**

1. In a medium pot, combine the quinoa and stock. Bring to a boil over medium-high heat, then reduce the heat to low. Cover the pot and cook the quinoa for about 15 minutes, until all the liquid has been absorbed. Set aside to cool slightly.

2. Meanwhile, in a small bowl, whisk together the oil, lime juice, chili powder, garlic powder, salt, black pepper, and cayenne. Set the dressing aside.

3. Transfer the quinoa to a large bowl. Add the black beans, tomatoes, corn, bell pepper, avocado, onion, and cilantro. Gently fold in the dressing before serving.

> **Time-Saving Tip:** Quinoa is the quickest cooking of all whole grains, but if you don't feel like waiting, you can buy frozen precooked quinoa in most grocery stores. Make sure you defrost it or heat it up before making your salad.

PER SERVING: CALORIES: 293; FAT: 11G; SATURATED FAT: 2G; CHOLESTEROL: 3G; PROTEIN: 10G; FIBER: 10G; SODIUM: 296MG

# GREEN GODDESS CUCUMBER SALAD

NUT-FREE, GLUTEN-FREE, SOY-FREE, 30-MINUTE MEAL

**SERVES 6 | PREP TIME:** 20 MINUTES

While I share my home with way more houseplants than I care to admit, I have a total black thumb when it comes to outdoor gardening. I find myself relying on the kindness of friends for fresh, home-grown produce. Thankfully, many of them oblige, and during the summer months, my fridge often overflows with juicy cukes. When life (or a friend) gives you cucumbers, make cucumber salad.

**4 medium English cucumbers, thinly sliced**

**1 teaspoon salt, plus more for seasoning**

**½ cup thinly sliced red onion (about ½ onion)**

**½ cup Green Goddess Dressing (page 218)**

**Freshly ground black pepper**

**2 tablespoons chopped fresh chives**

1. Place the cucumbers in a colander and sprinkle them with the salt. Let stand for about 10 minutes. Gently pat them dry with a paper towel.

2. Transfer the cucumbers to a medium bowl. Add the onion. Gently fold in the dressing. Season with salt and pepper. Top with the chives before serving.

> **Substitution Tip:** For a more traditional cucumber salad, use ½ cup Balsamic Dijon Vinaigrette (page 220) instead of the Green Goddess Dressing.

**PER SERVING:** CALORIES: 107; FAT: 6G; SATURATED FAT: 0G; CHOLESTEROL: 0G; PROTEIN: 3G; FIBER: 3G; SODIUM: 409MG

# BRING HOME THE BACON BLT SALAD

NUT-FREE, 30-MINUTE MEAL

**SERVES 4 | PREP TIME:** 20 MINUTES

When I was old enough to use the stove, bacon was one of the first things I learned how to cook. Bacon, lettuce, and tomato sandwiches were a high school mainstay. After kicking meat to the curb, I was still able to enjoy my favorite sandwich, thanks to tempeh bacon. This salad has the flavors of my old friend the BLT, but in a much healthier form.

¼ cup tahini

¼ cup water

1 tablespoon Dijon mustard

1 tablespoon apple cider vinegar

1 teaspoon garlic powder

½ teaspoon salt

6 cups chopped romaine lettuce (about 1 large head)

2 large tomatoes, diced

1 avocado, pitted, peeled, and diced

1 batch Tempeh Bac'un (page 233), or 8 ounces store-bought tempeh bacon, cooked according to the package instructions, chopped

1. In a blender, combine the tahini, water, mustard, vinegar, garlic powder, and salt and blend until smooth and creamy (the dressing can also be whisked together by hand in a small bowl).

2. In a large bowl, combine the lettuce, tomatoes, avocado, and tempeh bac'un. Gently fold in the dressing to serve.

> **Variation Tip:** Feel free to add your favorite BLT fixin's to your salad. Thinly sliced onion, crunchy croutons (see the Kale, Caesar! recipe on page 71 to make your own), and shredded carrots are great additions.

PER SERVING: CALORIES: 389; FAT: 33G; SATURATED FAT: 5G; CHOLESTEROL: 0G; PROTEIN: 12G; FIBER: 9G; SODIUM: 1,134MG

# IT'S ALL GREEK TO ME SALAD

NUT-FREE, GLUTEN-FREE, SOY-FREE, 30-MINUTE MEAL, ONE-PAN/ONE-POT

**SERVES 4 | PREP TIME:** 20 MINUTES

If you can't take a trip to the Mediterranean, let the Mediterranean come to you in the form of a savory meal. Purists may scoff at this recipe, as Greek salad isn't traditionally made with leafy greens, but I've added lettuce and spinach to make this version more of a meal than a side. If you're a naysayer, feel free to omit them. Add a little nondairy feta, if you feel so inclined.

4 cups loosely packed chopped romaine lettuce

2 cups loosely packed chopped baby spinach

1 medium English cucumber, chopped

2 cups cherry tomatoes, halved

1 green bell pepper, seeded and chopped

½ cup thinly sliced red onion (about ½ onion)

½ cup Balsamic Dijon Vinaigrette (page 220)

⅓ cup pitted kalamata olives

In a large bowl, combine the lettuce, spinach, cucumber, tomatoes, bell pepper, and onion. Add the dressing and toss to coat. Top with the olives to serve.

> **Substitution Tip:** If you're in the mood for a creamy dressing, use my Spicy Tahini Dressing (page 215) instead of the Balsamic Dijon Vinaigrette. Also, although they're not traditional to Greek salad, I sometimes like to add chopped artichoke hearts, cooked chickpeas, and peperoncini to my meal.

PER SERVING: CALORIES: 81; FAT: 3G; SATURATED FAT: 0G; CHOLESTEROL: 0G; PROTEIN: 2G; FIBER: 4G; SODIUM: 471MG

# KALE, CAESAR!

SOY-FREE, KID-FRIENDLY, 30-MINUTE MEAL

**SERVES 4 | PREP TIME:** 10 MINUTES | **COOK TIME:** 20 MINUTES

The vegan police would probably break down my door and take away my vegan membership card if I didn't include a kale salad recipe in this book. Kale can be a little tough to chew when it's raw, but that can be easily remedied by giving it a nice massage with some of the dressing. The acid in the dressing helps to break down the leaves' tough fibers, so roll up those sleeves and get ready to shiatsu your salad!

3 slices whole-grain bread, cut into cubes

1 tablespoon neutral-flavored vegetable oil

1 teaspoon Italian seasoning

¼ teaspoon garlic powder

½ cup Cashew Aioli (page 222) or vegan mayonnaise

2 tablespoons water

2 teaspoons capers, drained

½ teaspoon Dijon mustard

6 cups chopped curly kale leaves (about 1 large bunch)

2 tablespoons nutritional yeast

1. Preheat the oven to 350°F. Line a baking sheet with parchment paper.

2. Put the cubed bread in a medium bowl and drizzle it with the oil. Sprinkle it with the Italian seasoning and garlic powder.

3. Spread out the bread in a single layer on the prepared baking sheet. Bake for 15 to 20 minutes, until the croutons have browned and crisped, flipping the cubes once after about 7 minutes.

4. Meanwhile, in a small bowl, stir together the aioli, water, capers, and mustard.

5. Put the kale in a large bowl. Pour on about half the dressing. Using clean hands, massage the dressing into the kale until it just begins to wilt. Add the rest of the dressing to the bowl and toss to coat.

6. Toss the croutons into the salad and sprinkle with the nutritional yeast to serve.

> **Substitution Tip:** For a more traditional Caesar, use 6 cups chopped romaine lettuce instead of the kale—no massage required.

PER SERVING: CALORIES: 210; FAT: 14G; SATURATED FAT: 1G; CHOLESTEROL: 0G; PROTEIN: 7G; FIBER: 3G; SODIUM: 690MG

# TACO SALAD

**SERVES 4 | PREP TIME:** 15 MINUTES | **COOK TIME:** 12 MINUTES

I'm a firm believer in the motto "Live every day like it's Taco Tuesday." I mean, pretty much everything tastes better when it's folded into a tortilla. And for those days when you want something a little lighter, there's taco salad. Add a little drizzle of Say Cheese! Sauce (page 228) or shredded nondairy cheese for a little somethin' extra.

**2 teaspoons neutral-flavored vegetable oil**

**¼ cup diced red onion (about ¼ onion)**

**2 garlic cloves, minced**

**1 (15-ounce) can brown lentils, drained and rinsed**

**½ teaspoon chili powder**

**½ teaspoon onion powder**

**1 teaspoon garlic powder**

**½ teaspoon ground cumin**

**½ teaspoon salt**

**¼ teaspoon freshly ground black pepper**

**¼ teaspoon cayenne pepper (optional)**

**6 cups chopped romaine lettuce (about 1 large head)**

**2 large tomatoes, diced**

**1 avocado, pitted, peeled, and diced**

**1 cup fresh or thawed frozen corn kernels**

**½ cup Chipotle-Lime Dressing (page 219)**

**1 cup crumbled tortilla chips**

1. In a large skillet, heat the oil over medium-high heat until it shimmers. Add the onion and cook until it begins to soften, about 5 minutes. Add the garlic and cook for another minute or two, until fragrant.

2. Add the lentils, chili powder, onion powder, garlic powder, cumin, salt, black pepper, and cayenne (if using) to the pan. Cook for about 5 minutes more, until the lentils are heated through. If the pan dries out, add a little water. Remove the pan from the heat.

3. In a large bowl, combine the lettuce, tomatoes, avocado, corn, and lentil mixture. Gently stir in the dressing. Top the salad with the tortilla chips to serve.

**Substitution Tip:** I like using lentils in this recipe because they have a hearty, meaty texture. Black beans or pinto beans would work just as well, though.

PER SERVING: CALORIES: 387; FAT: 15G; SATURATED FAT: 4G; CHOLESTEROL: 0G; PROTEIN: 13G; FIBER: 15G; SODIUM: 679MG

# STRONG TO THE FINISH SPINACH SALAD

GLUTEN-FREE, 30-MINUTE MEAL, ONE-PAN/ONE-POT

**SERVES 4 | PREP TIME:** 10 MINUTES

Lettuce gets all the glory when it comes to salads, but I think it's high time we look to other leafy greens. Spinach has always been a favorite of mine, so I've used it in this recipe, which was inspired by the flavors of Asian ginger cashew chicken salad. Chickpeas are always a safe bet when veganizing recipes, but you can use a chopped Chic'un Patty (page 234) or two as well.

1 (5-ounce) package baby spinach

1 (15-ounce) can chickpeas, drained and rinsed

1 cup shredded purple cabbage

2 carrots, shredded or grated

2 scallions, sliced

½ cup cashews, toasted

½ cup Carrot-Ginger Dressing (page 216) or store-bought dairy-free carrot ginger dressing

In a large bowl, combine the spinach, chickpeas, cabbage, carrots, scallions, and cashews. Gently fold in the dressing before serving.

**Substitution Tip:** Try arugula or baby kale in place of the spinach. To change the flavor profile, use ½ cup Spicy Peanut Sauce (page 221) instead of the Carrot-Ginger Dressing.

PER SERVING: CALORIES: 258; FAT: 10G; SATURATED FAT: 2G; CHOLESTEROL: 0G; PROTEIN: 9G; FIBER: 7G; SODIUM: 481MG

# ARUGULA AND FARRO SALAD

SOY-FREE

**SERVES 4 | PREP TIME:** 10 MINUTES **| COOK TIME:** 30 MINUTES

This salad is the farro-ist of them all. (Get it? Farro and "the fairest of them all." Thank you—I'm here all night!) Farro is an ancient grain that's part of the wheat family. It has a hearty, chewy texture that lends itself well not only to hot dishes, but also to salads such as this one. I don't think we vegans cook with it enough, and I'm hoping to right that wrong.

1 medium sweet potato, diced (about 2 cups)

1 teaspoon neutral-flavored vegetable oil

½ teaspoon salt

¼ teaspoon freshly ground black pepper

½ cup uncooked farro

5 ounces arugula (about 8 cups)

1 apple, cored and chopped

½ cup Balsamic Dijon Vinaigrette (page 220) or store-bought vinaigrette

¼ cup pecans, toasted and chopped

1. Preheat the oven to 350°F. Line a baking sheet with parchment paper.

2. Put the sweet potato in a medium bowl. Add the oil, salt, and pepper and toss until well coated. Spread out the sweet potato in a single layer on the prepared baking sheet. Bake for 30 minutes, or until fork-tender and browned, flipping the pieces after 15 minutes.

3. Meanwhile, cook the farro according to the package instructions.

4. Put the arugula in a large bowl. Add the apple, cooked sweet potato, and cooked farro and toss to combine. Add the dressing and stir gently to coat. Top with the pecans to serve.

**Time-Saving Tip:** Farro can take anywhere from 15 to 45 minutes to cook, depending on the type you use. If you're in no hurry, you can use whole farro, but if you're feeling impatient, try the pearled or semi-pearled variety.

PER SERVING: CALORIES: 198; FAT: 8G; SATURATED FAT: 1G; CHOLESTEROL: 0G; PROTEIN: 4G; FIBER: 6G; SODIUM: 630MG

# PEANUT MANGO TANGO SALAD

30-MINUTE MEAL, ONE-PAN/ONE-POT

**SERVES 4 | PREP TIME:** 15 MINUTES

If you've never paired mangos with peanut sauce, we need to fix that ASAP. This recipe was inspired by a Thai restaurant favorite, and I've added my own little touches to the dish with the addition of baked tofu and cucumbers. Feel free to add your own touches, too. Diced avocado or slices of red bell pepper would be excellent additions.

4 cups chopped butter
   lettuce (about
   1 medium head)

2 cups tightly packed
   shredded napa cabbage

1 cup diced Teriyaki Baked
   Tofu (page 230), or
   8 ounces store-bought
   baked tofu, diced

2 ripe mangos, pitted,
   peeled, and diced

1 carrot, shredded or grated

1 medium English
   cucumber, chopped

½ cup chopped
   fresh cilantro

½ cup Spicy Peanut Sauce
   (page 221) or
   store-bought
   peanut dressing

2 scallions, sliced

¼ cup roasted unsalted
   peanuts, chopped

Place the lettuce, cabbage, tofu, mangos, carrot, cucumber, and cilantro in a large bowl, and toss to combine. Gently fold in the dressing. Top with the scallions and peanuts to serve.

**Technique Tip:** Mangos have long, flat seeds that run down their centers. The fruit's flesh clings to the pit, so it can be difficult to see where the fruit stops and the pit starts. To cut your mango, stand it upright on one end on a cutting board, holding it with one hand. You can see the indents around the pit on the top. Slice the flesh away from either side of the pit. Being careful not to cut through the skin, make crosshatched cuts about 1 inch apart in each mango half, then use a spoon to scoop the mango cubes out of the skin; discard the skin.

**PER SERVING:** CALORIES: 333; FAT: 15G; SATURATED FAT: 2G; CHOLESTEROL: 0G; PROTEIN: 14G; FIBER: 6G; SODIUM: 511MG

Butternut
Tahini
Soup,
page 81

# CHAPTER FIVE

# BOWLS OF COMFORT

## SOUPS, STEWS, AND CHILIS

# CREAMY COCONUT SOUP

NUT-FREE, 30-MINUTE MEAL, ONE-PAN/ONE-POT

**SERVES 4 | PREP TIME:** 10 MINUTES | **COOK TIME:** 20 MINUTES

This recipe is based on *tom kha kai*, a coconut milk–based, creamy chicken soup from Thailand. Some of its traditional ingredients can be difficult to find in regular grocery stores, so I've swapped in ingredients that are readily available. This soup is the perfect blend of creamy, tangy, spicy, and salty. It doesn't take long to cook, so you'll be slurpin' it down in no time. Serve it as is or with cooked jasmine rice.

2 teaspoons neutral-flavored vegetable oil

2 cups chopped shiitake mushrooms (about 5 ounces)

2 garlic cloves, minced

1 tablespoon minced peeled fresh ginger

1 lemongrass stalk, cut into 1-inch pieces (about 3 tablespoons)

4 Chic'un Patties (page 234) or 16 ounces store-bought seitan, chopped

4 cups vegetable stock

1 (14-ounce) can full-fat coconut milk

2 tablespoons reduced-sodium soy sauce or tamari

½ teaspoon red pepper flakes

¼ cup chopped fresh cilantro leaves

2 tablespoons fresh lime juice

1. In a large stockpot, heat the oil over medium heat until it shimmers. Add the mushrooms, garlic, ginger, and lemongrass. Cook, stirring frequently, for 5 minutes, or until the vegetables have softened.

2. Increase the heat to medium-high. Add the chic'un patties, stock, coconut milk, soy sauce, and red pepper flakes to the pot. Bring to a boil, then reduce the heat to medium. Simmer the soup, stirring occasionally, for 15 minutes to let the flavors come together.

3. Remove the pot from the heat. Stir in the cilantro and lime juice Divide the soup evenly among 4 bowls to serve.

**Substitution Tip:** If you'd like to make this recipe gluten-free, use 16 ounces cubed baked tofu instead of the seitan. Teriyaki Baked Tofu (page 230) works really well here.

PER SERVING: CALORIES: 452; FAT: 36G; SATURATED FAT: 21G; CHOLESTEROL: 0G; PROTEIN: 25G; FIBER: 1G; SODIUM: 529MG

# BUTTERNUT TAHINI SOUP

NUT-FREE, KID-FRIENDLY, 30-MINUTE MEAL, ONE-PAN/ONE-POT

**SERVES 4 | PREP TIME:** 5 MINUTES **| COOK TIME:** 25 MINUTES

Ah, tahini, how do I love thee? Let me count the ways. I love you in savory hummus, in creamy salad dressings, and paired with chocolate in sweet desserts. And let's not forget hearty soups. My beloved sesame paste adds a velvety richness to this recipe. Serve this soup as is or with cooked brown rice.

1 teaspoon neutral-flavored vegetable oil

2 garlic cloves, minced

1 (1-inch) piece fresh ginger, peeled and minced

4 cups vegetable stock

3 cups chopped peeled butternut squash (½-inch pieces; from about 2 pounds of squash)

2 cups tightly packed spinach, chopped

½ teaspoon salt

¼ teaspoon freshly ground black pepper

½ cup warm water

¼ cup mellow white miso paste

¼ cup tahini

2 scallions, sliced

2 tablespoons toasted sesame seeds

1. In a large pot, heat the oil over medium heat until it shimmers. Add the garlic and ginger. Cook for a minute or two, until just starting to brown.

2. Add the stock and squash to the pot and increase the heat to medium-high. Bring the mixture to a boil, then reduce the heat to medium. Simmer the soup until the squash is fork-tender, about 15 minutes. Stir in the spinach, salt, and pepper and cook for another minute or two, until the spinach turns bright green and wilts.

3. Meanwhile, in a small bowl, whisk together the warm water, miso, and tahini.

4. Remove the pot from the heat and stir in the miso-tahini mixture. Top with the scallions and sesame seeds. Divide the soup evenly among 4 bowls to serve.

**Troubleshooting Tip:** High heat will cause tahini to separate, so don't add the tahini to the soup too early in the cooking process.

**Variation Tip:** For a creamy soup, blend it directly in the pot with an immersion blender before topping it with the scallions and sesame seeds.

**PER SERVING:** CALORIES: 212; FAT: 12G; SATURATED FAT: 2G; CHOLESTEROL: 0G; PROTEIN: 7G; FIBER: 6G; SODIUM: 932MG

# MAC 'N' CHEESE SOUP

SOY-FREE, KID-FRIENDLY, 30-MINUTE MEAL

**SERVES 4 | PREP TIME:** 5 MINUTES | **COOK TIME:** 20 MINUTES

I don't know about you, but I was addicted to that blue box of macaroni and cheese mix as a kid. I couldn't get enough of that florescent orange, powder-based sauce. And I especially loved when it was served alongside broccoli, as broccoli with cheese sauce was another favorite (you can find my veganized version on page 55). This soup has all the tastes I loved as a kid, with nary a packet of brightly colored powder in sight.

1½ cups dried
    elbow macaroni

2 cups broccoli florets, cut
    into small pieces

¼ cup neutral-flavored oil

½ cup diced yellow onion
    (about ½ onion)

2 garlic cloves, minced

6 tablespoons
    all-purpose flour

4 cups plain unsweetened
    Almond Milk (page 214)
    or store-bought
    nondairy milk

½ cup nutritional yeast

1 tablespoon fresh
    lemon juice

1 teaspoon Dijon mustard

1 teaspoon onion powder

½ teaspoon salt

¼ teaspoon freshly ground
    black pepper

1. Cook the pasta according to the package instructions. About 3 minutes before the pasta is done, add the broccoli to the pot. Drain well.

2. Meanwhile, in a large pot, heat the oil over medium-high heat until it shimmers. Add the onion and cook, stirring frequently, for about 5 minutes, until it begins to soften. Add the garlic and cook for another minute or two, until fragrant.

3. Reduce the heat to medium. Add the flour to the pot and stir to coat the vegetables. Cook for about 2 minutes, until the flour forms a paste.

4. Slowly whisk in the almond milk. Stir in the nutritional yeast, lemon juice, mustard, onion powder, salt, and pepper. Simmer, whisking occasionally, until the mixture thickens, 5 to 10 minutes.

5. Stir in the cooked pasta and broccoli. Divide the soup evenly among 4 bowls to serve.

**Troubleshooting Tip:** If the soup gets too thick, add a little water or vegetable stock ¼ cup at a time until it reaches your desired consistency.

PER SERVING: CALORIES: 509; FAT: 20G; SATURATED FAT: 2G; CHOLESTEROL: 0G; PROTEIN: 20G; FIBER: 6G; SODIUM: 732MG

# LASAGNA SOUP

NUT-FREE, KID-FRIENDLY, ONE-PAN/ONE-POT

**SERVES 4 | PREP TIME:** 5 MINUTES **| COOK TIME:** 35 MINUTES

What's not to love about lasagna? With its layers of chewy noodles, creamy ricotta and tangy tomato sauce, it's a comfort-food classic. The one thing I don't love about it is the time it takes to assemble. And then there's the time it takes to bake. But this soup has all the best parts of lasagna with none of the wait. When I want lasagna, I want it now!

2 teaspoons neutral-flavored vegetable oil

1 medium yellow onion, diced

2 cups chopped cremini or white button mushrooms (about 8 ounces)

2 garlic cloves, minced

4 cups vegetable stock

1 (28-ounce) can crushed tomatoes

2 tablespoons tomato paste

1 teaspoon dried oregano

1 teaspoon dried basil

8 dried lasagna noodles, broken into 2-inch pieces

4 cups tightly packed baby spinach, chopped

1 cup Tofu Ricotta (page 229) or store-bought nondairy ricotta

1. In a large pot, heat the oil over medium-high heat until it shimmers. Add the onion and cook, stirring frequently, until it begins to soften, about 5 minutes. Add the mushrooms and cook until they soften and brown, about 5 minutes more. Add the garlic and cook for another minute or two, until fragrant.

2. Add the stock, crushed tomatoes, tomato paste, oregano, and basil to the pot. Bring the mixture to a boil, then reduce the heat to medium. Simmer the soup for about 10 minutes.

3. Add the noodles and cook, stirring often, for another 10 minutes or so, until they are al dente.

4. Stir in the spinach and cook for another minute or two, until it turns bright green and wilts.

5. Divide the soup evenly among 4 bowls and top with the ricotta to serve.

**Variation Tip:** Tired of tomato-based soups? Try white lasagna soup instead! Soak 1 cup raw cashews in water for 2 hours, then drain and transfer to a blender, then add 1 cup vegetable stock, 1 tablespoon fresh lemon juice, and ½ teaspoon salt and blend until smooth and creamy. Omit the crushed tomatoes and tomato paste from the soup and add the cashew mixture in step 2.

**Troubleshooting Tip:** To keep the lasagna noodles from exploding all over your kitchen as you break them, place them in a plastic bag and hit the bag a few times with a wooden spoon.

**PER SERVING:** CALORIES: 308; FAT: 5G; SATURATED FAT: 1G; CHOLESTEROL: 0G; PROTEIN: 12G; FIBER: 8G; SODIUM: 299MG

# TORTILLA SOUP

NUT-FREE, SOY-FREE

**SERVES 6 | PREP TIME:** 10 MINUTES | **COOK TIME:** 35 MINUTES

Taco Salad (page 72) is one of my go-to lunches in warmer weather. But what are taco lovers to do when the temperature takes a dive and it's too chilly for salad? We turn that salad into a soup, that's what we do! Don't worry, it still has all my taco favorites—peppers, beans, and corn, with lots of spices and seasonings. Serve it with your favorite taco toppings.

4 (6-inch) corn tortillas, cut into ½-by-3-inch strips

4 teaspoons neutral-flavored vegetable oil, divided

1 teaspoon salt, divided

1 medium yellow onion, diced

3 garlic cloves, minced

2 jalapeño peppers, seeded and diced

2 bell peppers, seeded and diced

4 cups vegetable stock

1 (28-ounce) can diced tomatoes

1 (15-ounce) can black beans, drained and rinsed

1 cup fresh or thawed frozen corn kernels

2 teaspoons chili powder

1 teaspoon ground cumin

1 teaspoon garlic powder

1. Preheat the oven to 400°F. Line a baking sheet with parchment paper.

2. Put the tortilla strips in a medium bowl and drizzle with 2 teaspoons of the oil. Sprinkle with ½ teaspoon of the salt. Toss to coat well.

3. Arrange the tortilla strips in a single layer on the prepared baking sheet. Bake for 5 to 10 minutes, until crisp (be careful not to burn them).

4. Meanwhile, in a large pot, heat the remaining 2 teaspoons oil over medium-high heat until it shimmers. Add the onion and cook, stirring frequently, until it begins to soften, about 5 minutes. Add the garlic, jalapeño, and bell pepper and cook until they soften, about 5 minutes more.

5. Add the stock, diced tomatoes, black beans, corn, chili powder, cumin, garlic powder, red pepper flakes, black pepper, and remaining ½ teaspoon salt to the pot. Bring to a boil, then reduce the heat to medium. Simmer, stirring occasionally, for 15 minutes, or until the vegetables are tender.

¼ teaspoon red
   pepper flakes

¼ teaspoon freshly ground
   black pepper

2 teaspoons fresh lime juice

1 avocado, pitted, peeled,
   and diced

2 scallions, sliced

¼ cup chopped
   fresh cilantro

6. Remove the pot from the heat and stir in the lime juice. Divide the mixture evenly among 6 bowls. Top with the tortilla strips, avocado, scallions, and cilantro to serve.

**Time-Saving Tip:** Instead of making the tortilla strips, you can use 2 cups broken store-bought tortilla chips.

**Variation Tip:** Omnivore tortilla soup is often made with chicken, so why not add Chic'un Patties (page 234) to your dish? Thinly slice 2 patties and add them to the pot in step 5.

PER SERVING: CALORIES: 255; FAT: 10G; SATURATED FAT: 1G; CHOLESTEROL: 0G; PROTEIN: 9G; FIBER: 13G; SODIUM: 514MG

# PHO SHO' NOODLE SOUP

NUT-FREE

**SERVES 4 | PREP TIME:** 10 MINUTES | **COOK TIME:** 40 MINUTES

*Pho* (which is actually pronounced *fuh*) is a Vietnamese noodle soup with spiced broth. I never know how to consume noodle-y soups like this one. The noodles slip out of the spoon and you can't eat broth with chopsticks. Eating soup with a fork is just weird. In the end, I find myself messily sucking it down using a combination of all three.

8 cups water

1 large yellow
   onion, quartered

4 garlic cloves

4 star anise pods

1 tablespoon whole
   black peppercorns

1 (3-inch) cinnamon stick

1 teaspoon whole cloves

8 ounces uncooked
   rice noodles

½ cup reduced-sodium soy
   sauce or tamari

2 tablespoons unseasoned
   rice vinegar

2 cups chopped shiitake
   mushrooms (about
   5 ounces)

4 baby bok choy,
   quartered lengthwise

1 cup shelled edamame

2 scallions, sliced

1 jalapeño pepper, sliced

1 cup mung bean sprouts

1 lime, cut into wedges

1. In a large pot, combine the water, onion, garlic, anise, peppercorns, cinnamon, and cloves. Bring to a boil over medium-high heat, then reduce the heat to medium. Simmer for 30 minutes, or until the liquid is infused with flavor.

2. Meanwhile, cook the rice noodles according to the package instructions.

3. Strain the stock through a fine-mesh sieve set over a large bowl (discard the solids), then return it to the pot. Add the soy sauce, vinegar, mushrooms, bok choy, and edamame to the pot. Cook over medium-high heat for about 10 minutes, until the vegetables are tender. Add the noodles to the pot, then remove from the heat.

4. Divide the soup evenly among 4 bowls. Top with the scallions, jalapeño, and bean sprouts and serve with the lime wedges alongside.

**Technique Tip:** If you'd rather not pour the hot liquid through a strainer, you can use a slotted spoon to remove the aromatics from the pot. You just need a little patience and diligence to make sure you get them all.

**Substitution Tip:** Diced Baked Tofu, Three Ways (page 230) made with sriracha or teriyaki marinade can be used instead of the edamame. You can also sub in 16 ounces cubed cooked seitan.

**PER SERVING:** CALORIES: 334; FAT: 3G; SATURATED FAT: 0G; CHOLESTEROL: 0G; PROTEIN: 15G; FIBER: 7G; SODIUM: 2,133MG

# CURRIED CAULIFLOWER SOUP

NUT-FREE, SOY-FREE

**SERVES 4 | PREP TIME:** 15 MINUTES | **COOK TIME:** 30 MINUTES

Creamy and curried are my all-time favorite types of soup. They're velvety smooth, with a spicy bite, and I just can't resist them. I could probably write an entire cookbook dedicated to them. Until then, we'll have to settle for this cauliflower version. The beauty of cauliflower is that once you've cooked it until softened, it blends into a rich, luxe cream, without a drop of dairy in sight.

2 teaspoons neutral-flavored vegetable oil

1 medium yellow onion, diced

2 garlic cloves, minced

2 teaspoons grated peeled fresh ginger

2 tablespoons red curry paste (see Tip)

½ teaspoon ground turmeric

½ teaspoon salt

¼ teaspoon freshly ground black pepper

4 cups cauliflower florets (about 1 medium head)

4 cups vegetable stock

1 (14-ounce) can full-fat coconut milk

1 tablespoon fresh lime juice

¼ cup chopped fresh cilantro

1. In a large pot, heat the oil over medium-high heat until it shimmers. Add the onion and cook, stirring frequently, until it begins to soften, about 5 minutes. Add the garlic, ginger, curry paste, turmeric, salt, and pepper. Cook for another minute or two, until the mixture is fragrant.

2. Add the cauliflower, stock, and coconut milk to the pot. Bring the mixture to a boil, then reduce the heat to medium. Simmer the soup until the cauliflower is tender, about 15 minutes.

3. Remove the pot from the heat. Puree the soup with an immersion blender (or carefully transfer the soup to an upright blender and blend until smooth and creamy, then return it to the pot).

4. Return the pot to medium heat and cook the soup until heated through, about 5 minutes. Remove the pot from the heat. Stir in the lime juice and top with the cilantro Divide the soup evenly among 4 bowls to serve.

**Ingredient Tip:** Be sure to read the label when buying curry paste, as some contain fish-based ingredients.

**Variation Tip:** For a roasted version of this soup, preheat the oven to 400°F and line a baking sheet with parchment paper. Toss the cauliflower florets with 1 tablespoon oil and sprinkle with a little salt and pepper. Roast until tender, about 20 minutes. Skip step 2, and blend the cauliflower with the cooked onion mixture, coconut milk, and vegetable stock using an immersion blender or in an upright blender.

**PER SERVING:** CALORIES: 269; FAT: 24G; SATURATED FAT: 19G; CHOLESTEROL: 0G; PROTEIN: 5G; FIBER: 5G; SODIUM: 281MG

# CHICKPEA AND RICE SOUP

NUT-FREE, SOY-FREE, KID-FRIENDLY, ONE-PAN/ONE-POT

**SERVES 6 | PREP TIME:** 15 MINUTES | **COOK TIME:** 1 HOUR

Noodles tend to be the ingredient of choice when it comes to making sick-day soups, but I've always secretly preferred rice. I favor its hearty, chewy texture over that of soft pasta. If I found myself craving a bowl of comforting, rice-filled soup when I was young, I would grab a can from the pantry. These days I just throw a bunch of ingredients into a pot. It takes a little more effort than working a can opener, but not much.

2 teaspoons neutral-flavored vegetable oil

1 medium yellow onion, diced

2 carrots, diced

3 celery stalks, chopped

3 garlic cloves, minced

½ teaspoon dried thyme

½ teaspoon ground sage

½ teaspoon dried oregano

½ teaspoon dried rosemary

6 cups vegetable stock

¾ cup uncooked brown rice

2 (15-ounce) cans chickpeas, drained and rinsed

4 cups tightly packed chopped kale

½ teaspoon salt

¼ teaspoon freshly ground black pepper

1. In a large pot, heat the oil over medium-high heat until it shimmers. Add the onion, carrot, and celery and cook, stirring frequently, until they begin to soften, about 5 minutes. Add the garlic, thyme, sage, oregano, and rosemary and cook for another minute or two, until fragrant.

2. Add the stock and rice to the pot. Bring the mixture to a boil, then reduce the heat to medium. Cover the pot and simmer for 35 to 45 minutes, until the rice is fully cooked.

3. Add the chickpeas and kale to the pot and season with the salt and pepper. Cook, stirring frequently, until the kale has wilted, about 5 minutes more. Divide the soup evenly among 4 bowls to serve.

**Time-Saving Tip:** If desired, you can add 2 cups cooked brown rice to your soup to speed things up. Cut the amount of vegetable stock down to 4 cups, and skip step 2. You can also use uncooked white rice, which will take only 10 to 15 minutes to cook in step 2.

PER SERVING: CALORIES: 344; FAT: 6G; SATURATED FAT: 1G; CHOLESTEROL: 0G; PROTEIN: 12G; FIBER: 11G; SODIUM: 573MG

# ESCAROLE AND WHITE BEAN SOUP

**SERVES 4 | PREP TIME:** 5 MINUTES **| COOK TIME:** 25 MINUTES

Most people reach for the kale or spinach when purchasing leafy greens, but what about escarole? Many walk right past it in the produce aisle, not sure of what to do with it, but it's deserving of some of that leafy-green affection, too. Escarole looks like lettuce, so should it be served in salad? It's a little bitter, so I prefer to add it to hot dishes. Think of this simple beans-and-greens soup as Escarole Cooking 101.

- 2 teaspoons neutral-flavored vegetable oil
- 1 leek, white and pale green parts only, sliced (see Tip)
- 4 garlic cloves, minced
- 1 medium head escarole, coarsely chopped (about 10 cups)
- 4 cups vegetable stock
- 2 (15-ounce) cans cannellini beans, drained and rinsed
- ½ teaspoon dried thyme
- ½ teaspoon dried oregano
- ½ teaspoon salt
- ½ teaspoon red pepper flakes (optional)
- 2 teaspoons fresh lemon juice
- 2 tablespoons nutritional yeast

1. In a large pot, heat the oil over medium-high heat until it shimmers. Add the onion and cook, stirring frequently, until it begins to soften, about 5 minutes. Add the garlic and escarole and cook until the escarole softens, 2 to 3 minutes more.

2. Add the stock, cannellini beans, thyme, oregano, salt, and red pepper flakes (if using) to the pot. Bring the mixture to a boil, then reduce the heat to medium. Simmer, stirring occasionally, for 15 minutes to let the flavors develop.

3. Remove the pot from the heat. Stir in the lemon juice. Divide the soup evenly among 4 bowls. Sprinkle with the nutritional yeast to serve.

**Ingredient Tip:** Leeks tend to be dirty, with grit trapped between their layers, so be sure to clean them well. The best way to do this is to slice them, place the slices in a bowl of water, and let them soak for a few minutes. Scoop the leek slices out with a slotted spoon or fine-mesh sieve and give them a good rinse before adding them to your soup.

**PER SERVING:** CALORIES: 260; FAT: 4G; SATURATED FAT: 0G; CHOLESTEROL: 0G; PROTEIN: 17G; FIBER: 16G; SODIUM: 928MG

# EGGPLANT AND OKRA STEW

SOY-FREE, ONE-PAN/ONE-POT

**SERVES 4 | PREP TIME:** 15 MINUTES | **COOK TIME:** 40 MINUTES

If you've never added peanut butter to a stew, you're in for a real treat here. It adds a lush richness, and it pairs well with coconut milk for a creamy texture. This recipe was inspired by West African groundnut stew or peanut stew. There are many variations on the peanut stew theme, but tomatoes and a paste made from ground peanuts are always part of the mix. Feel free to throw in whatever you have a hankering for.

2 teaspoons neutral-flavored vegetable oil

1 medium red onion, diced

3 garlic cloves, minced

1 teaspoon grated peeled fresh ginger

2 cups vegetable stock

2 medium sweet potatoes, diced (about 2 cups)

1 medium eggplant, diced (about 3 cups)

1 (14-ounce) can full-fat coconut milk

1 (15-ounce) can diced tomatoes, drained

1 (15-ounce) can chickpeas, drained and rinsed

1½ teaspoons ground cumin

1 teaspoon salt

1 teaspoon dried basil

½ teaspoon cayenne pepper

½ teaspoon sweet paprika

½ teaspoon freshly ground black pepper

2 cups sliced okra (see Tip)

½ cup creamy natural peanut butter

¼ cup roasted peanuts, chopped

1. In a large pot, heat the oil over medium-high heat until it shimmers. Add the onion and cook, stirring frequently, until it begins to soften, about 5 minutes. Add the garlic and ginger, and cook for another minute or two, until fragrant.

2. Add the stock, sweet potatoes, eggplant, coconut milk, tomatoes, chickpeas, cumin, salt, basil, cayenne, paprika, and black pepper to the pot. Bring the mixture to a boil, then reduce the heat to medium. Cover the pot and cook, stirring occasionally, for 15 minutes, to let the flavors develop.

3. Add the okra and stir in the peanut butter. Cover the pot again and simmer the soup, stirring occasionally, for 10 to 15 minutes, until the vegetables are fork-tender.

4. Divide the mixture evenly among 4 bowls. Top with the peanuts to serve.

**Ingredient Tip:** Okra is notoriously slimy, which is part of what makes it good for thickening stews like this one. If you're adverse to its gloopy texture, there are a couple ways to avoid it. The first way is to wash your uncut okra pods really well under running water, then make sure they're really dry before slicing. Another way to deslime your okra is to soak the uncut pods in a mixture of 4 cups water and 1 cup distilled white vinegar for about an hour (again, make sure you dry them well before slicing).

**PER SERVING:** CALORIES: 681; FAT: 48G; SATURATED FAT: 23G; CHOLESTEROL: 0G; PROTEIN: 21G; FIBER: 17G; SODIUM: 805MG

# SEITAN STEW

NUT-FREE, SOY-FREE, ONE-PAN/ONE-POT

**SERVES 6** | **PREP TIME:** 10 MINUTES | **COOK TIME:** 45 MINUTES

Did you know that "stewing" is actually an old-timey way to slow cook meat? It was often done in a cauldron over an open flame. This dish, which is based on Irish stew, is made with seitan rather than meat, and the cauldron is optional.

2 teaspoons neutral-flavored vegetable oil

1 red onion, diced

4 Chic'un Patties (page 234) or 16 ounces store-bought seitan, cut into bite-size pieces

3 cups sliced cremini or white button mushrooms (about 12 ounces)

2 garlic cloves, minced

¼ cup all-purpose flour

6 medium red-skinned potatoes (about 1 pound total), diced

3 carrots, chopped

3 cups vegetable stock

1 cup dry red wine

2 tablespoons tomato paste

2 bay leaves

1 teaspoon dried thyme

1 teaspoon dried rosemary

½ teaspoon salt

¼ teaspoon freshly ground black pepper

¼ cup chopped fresh parsley leaves

1. In a large pot, heat the oil over medium-high heat until it shimmers. Add the onion and cook, stirring frequently, until it begins to soften, about 5 minutes. Add the chic'un patties and cook until they begin to brown, about 5 minutes. Add the mushrooms and garlic and cook until the mushrooms soften, about 5 minutes more.

2. Sprinkle the flour over the seitan and vegetables and stir to combine.

3. Add the potatoes, carrots, stock, wine, tomato paste, bay leaves, thyme, rosemary, salt, and pepper to the pot. Bring the mixture to a boil, then reduce the heat to medium. Cover the pot and cook, stirring occasionally, for 30 minutes, or until the potatoes and carrots are fork-tender.

4. Remove the pot from the heat and discard the bay leaves. Divide the stew evenly among 6 bowls. Top with the parsley to serve.

**Substitution Tip:** If you'd like to make this recipe gluten-free, 4 large portabella mushrooms can be substituted for the chic'un patties, and gluten-free all-purpose flour can be used instead of the wheat flour.

**Ingredient Tip:** You'd think fermented grapes would be vegan, wouldn't you? Well, wine isn't always vegan. Check Barnivore.com or ask the manufacturer to make sure the wine you're buying is vegan.

PER SERVING: CALORIES: 395; FAT: 10G; SATURATED FAT: 2G; CHOLESTEROL: 0G; PROTEIN: 22G; FIBER: 6G; SODIUM: 230MG

# RED BEAN GUMBO

NUT-FREE, SOY-FREE, ONE-PAN/ONE-POT

**SERVES 6 | PREP TIME:** 15 MINUTES | **COOK TIME:** 25 MINUTES

Traditionally, gumbo is cooked for at least 3 hours, and some people even let it simmer all day. I don't know about you, but I don't have that kind of time. This is a quick, meatless version of the Louisiana favorite. Purists may not approve of my speedy roux and brisk simmer, but the result of my hurried labor is a scrumptious stew, so I'm okay with that.

¼ cup neutral-flavored vegetable oil

¼ cup all-purpose flour

1 medium yellow onion, diced (about 1 cup)

3 celery stalks, chopped

2 green bell peppers, seeded and chopped

5 garlic cloves, minced

4 cups vegetable stock

1 (14-ounce) can diced tomatoes

2 (15-ounce) cans kidney beans, drained and rinsed

2 cups sliced okra

2 teaspoons dried thyme

1 teaspoon sweet paprika

1 teaspoon garlic powder

1 teaspoon dried oregano

½ teaspoon cayenne pepper

½ teaspoon onion powder

½ teaspoon salt

¼ teaspoon freshly ground black pepper

3 cups cooked rice

2 scallions, sliced

1. Make a roux: In a large pot, heat the oil over medium heat. Add the flour and cook, stirring continually, for 10 minutes, or until the mixture turns golden brown.

2. Add the onion, celery, bell peppers, and garlic to the pot. Cook, stirring frequently, for another 10 minutes, or until the vegetables soften.

3. Add the stock and stir until smooth. Add the tomatoes, kidney beans, okra, thyme, paprika, garlic powder, oregano, cayenne, onion powder, salt, and black pepper. Increase the heat to medium-high and bring the mixture to a boil. Reduce the heat to medium and simmer, uncovered, for 10 to 15 minutes, or until the vegetables soften.

4. Divide the gumbo evenly among 6 bowls. Top each with ½ cup of the rice and garnish with the scallions to serve.

**Substitution Tip:** Gumbo is traditionally made with sausage. Feel free to swap out one can of the beans for 14 ounces sliced vegan sausage.

**PER SERVING:** CALORIES: 364; FAT: 11G; SATURATED FAT: 1G; CHOLESTEROL: 0G; PROTEIN: 11G; FIBER: 10G; SODIUM: 409MG

# QUINOA CHILI

NUT-FREE, SOY-FREE, ONE-PAN/ONE-POT

**SERVES 6 | PREP TIME:** 5 MINUTES | **COOK TIME:** 40 MINUTES

When I was first starting out in the world of veganism, chili was my go-to dish to serve my nonvegan friends. Tofu and tempeh seemed weird to them, but chili was one food that we could all agree upon, those bowls of warm, beany goodness uniting us. Top your chili with a few spoonfuls of nondairy sour cream and shredded vegan cheddar cheese, if you happen to have them on hand.

2 teaspoons neutral-flavored vegetable oil

1 medium red onion, diced

3 garlic cloves, minced

2 medium sweet potatoes, diced

4 cups vegetable stock

¾ cup uncooked quinoa, rinsed

1 (28-ounce) can diced tomatoes

1 (8-ounce) can tomato paste

1 (15-ounce) can black beans, drained and rinsed

1 (15-ounce) can pinto beans, drained and rinsed

2 teaspoons chili powder

1 teaspoon ground cumin

1 teaspoon dried oregano

½ teaspoon smoked paprika

½ teaspoon salt

¼ teaspoon freshly ground black pepper

¼ teaspoon cayenne pepper

2 scallions, sliced

1 avocado, pitted, peeled, and diced

1. In a large pot, heat the oil over medium-high heat until it shimmers. Add the onion and cook, stirring frequently, until it begins to soften, about 5 minutes. Add the garlic and cook for another minute or two, until fragrant.

2. Add the sweet potato, stock, quinoa, diced tomatoes, tomato paste, black beans, pinto beans, chili powder, cumin, oregano, smoked paprika, salt, black pepper, and cayenne to the pot. Bring the mixture to a boil, then reduce the heat to medium. Cover the pot and simmer, stirring occasionally, for 30 minutes, or until the chili has thickened and the sweet potatoes are tender.

3. Divide the mixture evenly among 6 bowls. Top with the scallions and avocado to serve.

**Substitution Tip:** Pretty much any vegetable can be used in place of (or in addition to) the sweet potatoes. Try zucchini and summer squash, bell peppers, or mushrooms. You can also add corn kernels, jalapeño peppers, and a little chipotle pepper in adobo.

PER SERVING: CALORIES: 364; FAT: 9G; SATURATED FAT: 1G; CHOLESTEROL: 0G; PROTEIN: 15G; FIBER: 14G; SODIUM: 474MG

# JACKFRUIT WHITE CHILI

NUT-FREE, SOY-FREE, ONE-PAN/ONE-POT

**SERVES 4 | PREP TIME:** 10 MINUTES | **COOK TIME:** 25 MINUTES

By now we're all familiar with zesty, tomato-based chilis, but have you met their calmer cousin, white chili? Just because white chili is milder doesn't mean it's any less tasty, and it's still packed with veggies, beans, and spices. White chili is not actually white, but rather a shade of yellowish beige ("beige chili" just doesn't have a nice ring to it, though). I like to incorporate a splash of green by adding poblano peppers and cilantro, because that's my style.

2 (20-ounce) cans young
    jackfruit, drained
    and rinsed

2 teaspoons neutral-flavored
    vegetable oil

1 medium yellow onion,
    diced (about 1 cup)

3 garlic cloves, minced

2 poblano or Anaheim
    peppers, seeded
    and diced

2 jalapeño peppers, seeded
    and diced

4 cups vegetable stock

2 (15-ounce) cans navy
    beans, drained
    and rinsed

1 cup fresh or thawed
    frozen corn kernels

2 teaspoons chili powder

1 teaspoon ground cumin

½ teaspoon salt

¼ teaspoon freshly ground
    black pepper

1 avocado, pitted, peeled,
    and diced

¼ cup chopped fresh
    cilantro leaves

1 lime, cut into wedges

1. Pull the jackfruit into shreds. You can do this by hand with a potato masher or in a food processor (pulse just a few times).

2. In a large pot, heat the oil over medium-high heat until it shimmers. Add the onion and cook, stirring frequently, until it begins to soften, about 5 minutes. Add the garlic, poblano and jalapeño peppers, and jackfruit, and cook until the peppers soften, about 5 minutes more.

3. Add the stock, beans, corn, chili powder, cumin, salt, and black pepper to the pot. Bring the mixture to a boil, then reduce the heat to medium. Simmer the chili for 15 minutes, or until it thickens.

4. Divide the chili evenly among 4 bowls. Top with the avocado and cilantro, and serve with the lime wedges alongside.

**Substitution Tip:** Any type of white bean will do in this recipe, so give great northern beans, cannellini beans, or even chickpeas a try. Four thinly sliced Chic'un Patties (page 234) can be used in place of the jackfruit.

**PER SERVING:** CALORIES: 681; FAT: 15G; SATURATED FAT: 2G; CHOLESTEROL: 0G; PROTEIN: 20G; FIBER: 13G; SODIUM: 567MG

## Use Your Bean

The recipes in this book call for canned beans, but you can certainly cook your own dried beans and legumes to use instead. Opening a can of beans is super convenient, but home-cooked beans are much tastier, and they can be prepped in advance and frozen to save time. One 14- or 15-ounce can of beans is equal to 1¾ cups cooked beans.

To cook dried beans, place them in a colander, check for and discard any debris (anything that's not a bean, basically!), and give them a good rinse under cool running water. To cut down on the cooking time and make the beans more digestible, they can be soaked for 4 to 8 hours, but it's not necessary. If you do soak the beans, drain them and give them another rinse afterward. (Lentils cook quickly, so they don't need to be soaked.)

Place 1 cup dried beans in a pot with 3 to 4 cups water, bring to a boil over medium-high heat, then reduce the heat to medium-low and simmer, uncovered, until they're tender, anywhere between 45 minutes and 2 hours (the exact time will depend on the type of bean and how old they are). Don't add salt to the water until the end, or it will cause the beans to toughen and take longer to cook.

| TYPE OF BEAN OR LEGUME (1 CUP DRIED) | WATER | COOKING TIME | YIELD |
|---|---|---|---|
| BLACK BEANS | 4 cups | 1 to 1¼ hours | 2¼ cups |
| BLACK-EYED PEAS | 3 cups | 1 hour | 2 cups |
| CANNELLINI BEANS | 3 cups | 45 minutes | 2½ cups |
| CHICKPEAS | 4 cups | 1 to 2 hours | 2 cups |
| GREAT NORTHERN BEANS | 3½ cups | 1½ hours | 2⅔ cups |
| KIDNEY BEANS | 3 cups | 1 hour | 2¼ cups |
| LENTILS, BROWN | 2¼ cups | 15 to 20 minutes | 2¼ cups |
| LENTILS, SPLIT RED | 3 cups | 5 to 10 minutes | 2½ cups |
| NAVY BEANS | 3 cups | 45 minutes to 1 hour | 2⅔ cups |
| PINTO BEANS | 3 cups | 1 to 1½ hours | 2¾ cups |

Chickpea Mushroom Burgers, page 111

# LUNCH BREAK

## SANDWICHES, WRAPS, AND BOWLS

# CURRIED CHICKPEA WRAP

SOY-FREE, 30-MINUTE MEAL

**SERVES 4 | PREP TIME:** 10 MINUTES

The humble chickpea can do a lot of heavy lifting come mealtime. In addition to being tossed directly into soups and stews right from the can, garbanzos (another name for the same bean) can be pureed into a creamy dip, roasted for a crunchy snack, or mashed up for a savory sandwich filling. Chickpea salad is probably the most vegan lunch option out there. I've used curry powder and cashews to spice up this version.

¼ cup Cashew Aioli (page 222) or vegan mayonnaise

2 teaspoons fresh lemon juice

2 teaspoons curry powder

½ teaspoon garlic powder

½ teaspoon salt

¼ teaspoon ground turmeric

¼ teaspoon freshly ground black pepper

1 (15-ounce) can chickpeas, drained and rinsed

2 celery stalks, chopped

2 scallions, sliced

1 carrot, finely diced

¼ cup chopped fresh cilantro leaves

¼ cup chopped raw cashews

2 cups tightly packed baby spinach

4 (10-inch) whole-grain wraps or tortillas

1. In a small bowl, combine the aioli, lemon juice, curry powder, garlic powder, salt, turmeric, and pepper.

2. In a large bowl, combine the chickpeas, celery, scallions, carrot, cilantro, and cashews. Add the aioli mixture. Stir everything together, lightly mashing the chickpeas as you go.

3. To assemble, place some of the spinach on each wrap and top it with the chickpea mixture, dividing it evenly. Roll up each wrap, tucking in the sides as you go. Serve.

**Variation Tip:** If you're not into curry, omit the curry powder and turmeric, and use ½ teaspoon each of dried dill, dried basil, and onion powder instead. Add 1 teaspoon whole-grain mustard, and sub in flat-leaf parsley for the cilantro.

PER SERVING: CALORIES: 333; FAT: 13G; SATURATED FAT: 2G; CHOLESTEROL: 0G; PROTEIN: 11G; FIBER: 7G; SODIUM: 836MG

# TEMPTING TEMPEH WRAPS

30-MINUTE MEAL, ONE-PAN/ONE-POT

**SERVES 4 | PREP TIME:** 10 MINUTES **| COOK TIME:** 10 MINUTES

When I worked in an office, I'd see my omnivore coworkers with the same sad-looking sandwiches for lunch, day in, day out—some sort of sliced meat, cheese, lettuce, and tomato on white bread. I'd plop myself down at the break room's community table with my whole-grain wrap filled with savory tempeh, crunchy fresh veggies, and spicy peanut sauce and watch their faces turn green with envy. Life's too short for boring sandwiches.

2 teaspoons neutral-flavored vegetable oil

2 teaspoons reduced-sodium soy sauce or tamari

1 (8-ounce) package tempeh, cut into 1-inch-thick slabs

½ cup Spicy Peanut Sauce (page 221) or store-bought peanut sauce

4 (10-inch) whole-grain wraps or tortillas

½ cup thinly sliced English cucumber (about ¼ cucumber)

1 carrot, grated or shredded

2 cups shredded purple cabbage

1 red bell pepper, seeded and thinly sliced

1. In a large skillet, heat the oil and soy sauce over medium-high heat. Add the tempeh and cook on the first side for 4 to 5 minutes, until golden brown. Flip the tempeh and cook for 4 to 5 minutes on the second side.

2. To assemble the wraps, spread 2 tablespoons of the peanut sauce on each wrap. Top with the tempeh, cucumber, carrot, cabbage, and bell pepper. Roll up each wrap, tucking in the sides as you go. Serve.

**Technique Tip:** The thinner you slice your tempeh, the crispier it will be. If you'd like a little crunch to your wrap, slice the tempeh into slabs that are ¼ to ½ inch thick.

**Substitution Tip:** If desired, 8 ounces super-firm tofu can be used in place of the tempeh.

PER SERVING: CALORIES: 393; FAT: 17G; SATURATED FAT: 3G; CHOLESTEROL: 0G; PROTEIN: 18G; FIBER: 4G; SODIUM: 921MG

# DOUBLE-DECKER CLUB SANDWICH

**SERVES 4 | PREP TIME:** 10 MINUTES

There was a rumor floating around the interwebs a few years ago that the "club" in club sandwich was an acronym for "chicken and lettuce under bacon." Sounds clever, except it's not true. This epic sandwich was probably first served at the Union Club in New York City, although the original version bears only a passing resemblance to today's incarnation, and it didn't actually contain any lettuce. If you'd like to deck out your sandwich even more, add slices of nondairy cheese, pickle chips, and thinly sliced red onion.

12 slices of your favorite bread, toasted

¼ cup Cashew Aioli (page 222) or vegan mayonnaise

16 Sammich Slices (page 235) or store-bought vegan sandwich slices

2 cups chopped romaine lettuce

2 large tomatoes, sliced

¼ cup whole-grain mustard

1 batch Tempeh Bac'un (page 233), or 8 ounces store-bought tempeh bacon, cooked according to the package instructions

1 large avocado, pitted, peeled, and sliced

1 cup broccoli sprouts or alfalfa sprouts

1. Place 4 slices of the toast on a plate or large cutting board. Spread about 1 teaspoon of the aioli on each. Top each with 4 sammich slices, ½ cup of the lettuce, and one-quarter of the tomatoes. Spread about 1 teaspoon of the mustard on each of 4 more pieces of toast, and place one on top of each sandwich, mustard-side down.

2. Spread the remaining aioli over the top of the toast, and top the sandwiches evenly with the tempeh bac'un, avocado, and sprouts. Spread the remaining mustard on one side of the remaining 4 slices of toast, and place one on top of each sandwich, mustard-side down.

3. Cut each sandwich into triangles and use a toothpick or sandwich pick to hold each triangle together. Serve.

> **Variation Tip:** Club sandwiches are traditionally double-decker, but if that's too much bread for your tastes, you can omit the middle slice.

PER SERVING: CALORIES: 627; FAT: 24G; SATURATED FAT: 3G; CHOLESTEROL: 0G; PROTEIN: 44G; FIBER: 9G; SODIUM: 1,621MG

# SEITAN PANINI

NUT-FREE, 30-MINUTE MEAL, ONE-PAN/ONE-POT

**SERVES 4 | PREP TIME:** 10 MINUTES | **COOK TIME:** 20 MINUTES

Paninis were all the rage in the '80s and '90s. Sandwiches with fancy grill marks found their way onto the menus of eateries everywhere, from fast-food joints to swanky restaurants. Paninis soon fell out of favor, and snazzy sandwich presses began littering the shelves of thrift stores across the nation. I've never been a follower of fashion, so with this spicy sandwich, I hereby declare that paninis are once again in style.

4 teaspoons neutral-flavored vegetable oil, divided

½ cup thinly sliced red onion (about ½ onion)

4 Chic'un Patties (page 234), sliced, or 4 cups sliced store-bought seitan

8 slices of your favorite bread

¼ cup Chipotle-Lime Dressing (page 219) or store-bought dairy-free chipotle dressing

2 large tomatoes, sliced

1 avocado, pitted, peeled, and sliced

1 cup loosely packed arugula

> **Substitution Tip:** Sandwich rolls or large flatbreads can be used in place of the bread.

1. In a large skillet, heat 2 teaspoons of the oil over medium-high heat until it shimmers. Add the onion and cook until it begins to brown, about 5 minutes. Add the chic'un patties and cook for about 5 minutes more, until they begin to brown and are heated through.

2. Spread the dressing over 4 slices of the bread. Top them evenly with the onion-chic'un mixture, tomatoes, avocado, and arugula. Top each sandwich with a second slice of bread.

3. In the same pan you used for the onion, heat the remaining 2 teaspoons oil over medium-high heat until it shimmers. Carefully place the sandwiches in the pan. Place a heavy object, such as another pan, on top of the sandwiches to weigh them down and cook for 4 to 5 minutes, until golden and crisp on the bottom. Carefully flip each sandwich, place the heavy object on top again, and cook for another 4 to 5 minutes, until golden and crisp on the second side. Serve.

> **Technique Tip:** Paninis are known for their grill marks, so you can cook these sandwiches on a grill or an indoor grill pan. If you happen to have a panini press, you're in luck—that's the perfect tool with which to make these sandwiches.

PER SERVING: CALORIES: 501; FAT: 25G; SATURATED FAT: 7G; CHOLESTEROL: 0G; PROTEIN: 29G; FIBER: 14G; SODIUM: 923MG

# BAC'UN CHIC'UN RANCH SANDWICH

30-MINUTE MEAL, ONE-PAN/ONE-POT

**SERVES 4 | PREP TIME:** 10 MINUTES | **COOK TIME:** 10 MINUTES

When word got out that I was writing this cookbook, I received a special request to make a vegan bacon chicken ranch sandwich. I've been meat-free since the early '90s, so I didn't even know such a thing existed. A quick Google search gave me the deets, and I went off to my laboratory (aka the kitchen) to conduct some experiments. My labor paid off, and now I don't know how I lived for so long without this amazing creation.

1 teaspoon neutral-flavored vegetable oil

4 Chic'un Patties (page 234) or store-bought vegan chicken patties

½ cup Ranch Dressing (page 217) or store-bought dairy-free ranch dressing

4 submarine sandwich rolls, cut in half and toasted

1 batch Tempeh Bac'un (page 233), or 8 ounces store-bought tempeh bacon, cooked according to the package instructions

2 large tomatoes, sliced

½ thinly sliced red onion (about ½ onion)

2 cups shredded romaine lettuce

½ cup Say Cheese! Sauce (page 228) or store-bought nondairy cheese sauce, or 4 slices nondairy cheddar cheese

1. In a large skillet or grill pan, heat the oil over medium-high heat until it shimmers. Add the chic'un patties and cook for about 5 minutes on each side.

2. Remove the patties from the pan and cut each into slices about 1 inch wide.

3. Spread about 2 tablespoons of the ranch on half of each roll. Divide the chic'un patty strips evenly among them, then top evenly with the tempeh bac'un, tomatoes, onion, and lettuce. Drizzle 2 tablespoons of the cheese sauce over each one. Close the sandwiches by placing the top half of the roll on each. Serve.

**Variation Tip:** If, much like George Costanza, you like your chic'un spicy, you can "Buffalo" it by adding 3 tablespoons of your favorite hot sauce or prepared vegan Buffalo sauce to the pan while it cooks in step 1.

PER SERVING: CALORIES: 595; FAT: 35G; SATURATED FAT: 5G; CHOLESTEROL: 0G; PROTEIN: 34G; FIBER: 9G; SODIUM: 1,745MG

# EGGPLANT PESTO SANDWICH

SOY-FREE, KID-FRIENDLY, ONE-PAN/ONE-POT

**SERVES 4 | PREP TIME:** 10 MINUTES **| COOK TIME:** 30 MINUTES

Did you know that science says eggplants are actually berries? Wild! I certainly wouldn't slice up a strawberry and bake it for a midday meal, but eggplants lend themselves nicely to sandwiches. Eggplant is often battered and breaded, but I think all that is unnecessary. The tasty aubergine only needs a little bit of seasoning, and it's good to go. (Although you *could* add some nondairy mozzarella, if you happen to have some on hand.)

3 tablespoons
  balsamic vinegar

3 tablespoons olive oil

1 garlic clove, minced

½ teaspoon salt

¼ teaspoon freshly ground
  black pepper

1 large eggplant, sliced
  crosswise into
  ¼-inch-thick rounds

4 round sandwich rolls,
  cut in half

½ cup Popeye Pesto
  (page 225) or
  store-bought
  dairy-free pesto

2 cups loosely
  packed arugula

1. Preheat the oven to 400°F. Line a baking sheet with parchment paper.

2. In a small bowl, whisk together the vinegar, olive oil, garlic, salt, and pepper.

3. Arrange the eggplant slices in a single layer on the prepared baking sheet. Brush each side with the vinegar mixture. Roast the eggplant for 20 to 30 minutes, until tender and golden brown, flipping the slices once after about 15 minutes.

4. Spread 2 tablespoons of the pesto over half of each roll. Top evenly with the baked eggplant slices and the arugula. Close the sandwiches by placing the top half of the roll on each. Serve.

**Substitution Tip:** Sliced cauliflower can be used in place of (or in addition to) the eggplant. Place a head of cauliflower stem-side down on a cutting board and slice it the same way you would a loaf of bread. Cut the larger pieces into smaller florets that will fit on your rolls. Season and roast the cauliflower as directed in step 3.

PER SERVING: CALORIES: 420; FAT: 29G; SATURATED FAT: 5G; CHOLESTEROL: 0G; PROTEIN: 9G; FIBER: 6G; SODIUM: 788MG

# TOFU AND KIMCHI SANDWICH

**SERVES 4 | PREP TIME:** 10 MINUTES

I like to think of this sandwich as a lazy person's bánh mì. I should warn you that it's hot as heck. If you want to turn down the heat, make your baked tofu with the teriyaki marinade rather than the sriracha version. You can cut back on the amount of sriracha you mix into your cashew aioli, too.

¼ cup Cashew Aioli (page 222) or vegan mayonnaise

1 tablespoon sriracha

4 sandwich rolls, cut in half

1 cup tightly packed baby spinach

½ cup thinly sliced radishes (about 4 medium)

½ cup thinly sliced English cucumber (about ¼ cucumber)

1 batch Sriracha Baked Tofu (page 230), or 16 ounces store-bought baked tofu, sliced into thin strips

3 cups Kimchi Slaw (page 66) or store-bought vegan kimchi

1. In a small bowl, whisk together the aioli and sriracha.

2. Spread the spicy aioli onto one half of each sandwich roll. Top with the baby spinach, radishes, cucumber, baked tofu, and slaw. Close the sandwiches by placing the top half of the roll on each. Serve.

> **Ingredient Tip:** Make sure you read the label if you're using store-bought kimchi, as it's often made with ingredients derived from fish or shrimp.

**PER SERVING:** CALORIES: 350; FAT: 17G; SATURATED FAT: 2G; CHOLESTEROL: 0G; PROTEIN: 25G; FIBER: 5G; SODIUM: 481MG

# SEITAN-UMMS

KID-FRIENDLY, 30-MINUTE MEAL, ONE-PAN/ONE-POT

**SERVES 4 | PREP TIME:** 10 MINUTES | **COOK TIME:** 15 MINUTES

When I was young, boxes of Steak-umm (thinly sliced beef) were staples in our freezer. We would fry the slices in a pan and eat them on rolls with melted cheese. They were the closest I came to Philly cheesesteaks growing up. I loved them, so I didn't care how unauthentic they were. These days, I often re-create that beloved meal of my youth using seitan-based Sammich Slices. When slicing your Sammich Slices for this recipe, cut them a little thicker than you would for a regular sandwich (I recommend ¼ inch thick).

3 teaspoons neutral-flavored vegetable oil, divided

1 medium yellow onion, thinly sliced

2 garlic cloves, minced

2 bell peppers, seeded and sliced into thin strips

16 Sammich Slices (page 235) or 8 ounces thinly sliced store-bought seitan

4 submarine sandwich rolls, cut in half

½ cup Say Cheese! Sauce (page 228) or store-bought nondairy cheese sauce, or 4 slices nondairy cheddar cheese

1. In a large skillet, heat 1½ teaspoons of the oil over medium-high heat until it shimmers. Add the onion and cook for about 5 minutes, until it begins to soften and brown. Add the garlic and bell peppers and cook for another 5 minutes, or until they begin to soften. Transfer the vegetables to a plate and cover to keep warm.

2. In the same pan, combine the remaining 1½ teaspoons oil and the sammich slices. Cook for 3 to 4 minutes, until the slices begin to brown. Flip the slices and cook for another 3 to 4 minutes.

3. Assemble the sandwiches by placing a few of the sammich slices on one half of each roll, then top evenly with the onion-pepper mixture. Spoon 2 tablespoons of the cheese sauce over each one. Close the sandwiches by placing the top half of the roll on each. Serve.

**Substitution Tip:** If you'd like to skip the seitan, you can use 4 sliced portabella mushrooms instead of the sammich slices. Cook them in the pan along with the bell peppers in step 1, and skip step 2.

PER SERVING: CALORIES: 613; FAT: 15G; SATURATED FAT: 2G; CHOLESTEROL: 0G; PROTEIN: 44G; FIBER: 10G; SODIUM: 1,712MG

# JACK 'N' GYRO

NUT-FREE, ONE-PAN/ONE-POT

**SERVES 4 | PREP TIME:** 15 MINUTES | **COOK TIME:** 30 MINUTES

Move over, cauliflower, because jackfruit is officially the "it" food in the vegan world right now. And rightly so. It has a mild taste and meatlike texture, so it's a good substitute for meat, especially in dishes in which the meat is "pulled." When buying jackfruit, look for the type packed in water or brine, not in syrup.

2 teaspoons neutral-flavored vegetable oil

1 (20-ounce) can young jackfruit, drained and rinsed

1 teaspoon dried oregano

1 teaspoon dried thyme

1 teaspoon ground cumin

½ teaspoon garlic powder

½ teaspoon onion powder

½ teaspoon salt

¼ teaspoon freshly ground black pepper

⅓ cup vegetable stock

2 tablespoons fresh lemon juice

1 tablespoon tomato paste

1 tablespoon reduced-sodium soy sauce or tamari

4 flatbreads or pitas, warmed

4 cups loosely packed chopped romaine lettuce

1 cup sliced English cucumber (about ½ cucumber)

1 tomato, sliced

½ cup thinly sliced red onion (about ½ onion)

½ cup Spicy Tahini Dressing (page 215)

1. Pull the jackfruit apart into shreds. You can do this by hand, by mashing it with a potato masher, or by giving it a few pulses in a food processor.

2. In a large pan, heat the oil over medium heat until it shimmers. Add the jackfruit, oregano, thyme, cumin, garlic powder, onion powder, salt, and pepper. Cook, stirring occasionally, for 20 minutes, or until the jackfruit browns and caramelizes.

3. Add the stock, lemon juice, tomato paste, and tamari to the pan, stirring to combine. Simmer the mixture for about 10 minutes, until the jackfruit has absorbed all the liquid in the pan.

4. To assemble the gyros, top each flatbread evenly with the romaine, cucumber, tomato, onion, and jackfruit mixture. Drizzle each with 2 tablespoons of the dressing. Serve.

**Substitution Tip:** If desired, 16 ounces shredded seitan can be used in place of the jackfruit.

PER SERVING: CALORIES: 335; FAT: 12G; SATURATED FAT: 1G; CHOLESTEROL: 0G; PROTEIN: 10G; FIBER: 7G; SODIUM: 770MG

# VEGETABLE BURRITOS

NUT-FREE, SOY-FREE, KID-FRIENDLY, 30-MINUTE MEAL, ONE-PAN/ONE-POT

**SERVES 4 | PREP TIME:** 15 MINUTES | **COOK TIME:** 15 MINUTES

There's been some debate in the culinary world as to which is better, tacos or burritos. I hate to admit—right here in my burrito recipe—that I'm on Team Taco, but I don't see how the two can't live together in tortilla-based harmony. Add a little extra oomph to your burritos with a dab of queso (see page 32), salsa, and nondairy sour cream.

2 teaspoons neutral-flavored vegetable oil

½ cup diced red onion (about ½ onion)

1 red bell pepper, seeded and chopped

1 green bell pepper, seeded and chopped

1 cup fresh, canned, or thawed frozen corn kernels

1 (15-ounce) can pinto beans, drained and rinsed

1 teaspoon chili powder

1 teaspoon ground cumin

¼ teaspoon salt

2 cups cooked rice, warm

4 large (10- to 12-inch) whole wheat or gluten-free tortillas, warmed

2 avocados, pitted, peeled, and sliced

1. In a large skillet, heat the oil over medium-high heat until it shimmers. Add the onion and cook, stirring frequently, until it has begun to soften and brown, about 5 minutes. Add the bell peppers and cook until they begin to soften, about 5 minutes more. Add the corn, pinto beans, chili powder, cumin, and salt and cook until everything is warmed all the way through, about 5 minutes more.

2. To assemble the burritos, spoon ¼ cup of the rice onto each tortilla. Follow with one-quarter of the vegetable-bean mixture and a few slices of the avocado. Roll up each tortilla, tucking in the sides as you go. Serve.

**Time-Saving Tip:** When I'm in an absolute rush to cook, I'll use a bag of frozen onions and peppers in this recipe rather than fresh veggies. Just follow the heating instructions on the package before mixing the vegetables with the corn and beans.

**PER SERVING:** CALORIES: 582; FAT: 23G; SATURATED FAT: 5G; CHOLESTEROL: 0G; PROTEIN: 16G; FIBER: 16G; SODIUM: 492MG

# LENTIL BURGERS

NUT-FREE, SOY-FREE, KID-FRIENDLY

**SERVES 4 | PREP TIME:** 10 MINUTES | **COOK TIME:** 25 MINUTES

Why make your own veggie burgers at home when you can just pop out to the store and pick up a box from the freezer section? Because making them at home can actually be *faster* than driving to the store and back, that's why. And have you looked at the ingredient list on a box of burgers? You need a science degree to understand it all. I'll take my bean patties without the ferrous sulfate and thiamine mononitrate, thank you very much.

1 cup quick-cooking rolled oats

1 (15-ounce) can brown lentils, drained and rinsed well

2 garlic cloves, minced

1 tablespoon tomato paste

1 teaspoon onion powder

½ teaspoon salt

½ teaspoon freshly ground black pepper

4 whole wheat or gluten-free burger buns

1 large tomato, sliced

4 large lettuce leaves

Other burger toppings of your choice

1. Preheat the oven to 400°F. Line a baking sheet with parchment paper.

2. In a food processor, pulse the oats into a coarse flour. Add the lentils, garlic, tomato paste, onion powder, salt, and pepper and pulse until well incorporated and the mixture resembles a chunky paste.

3. Using your hands, form the mixture into 4 patties and place them on the prepared baking sheet.

4. Bake the burgers for 20 to 25 minutes, until golden brown and firm, flipping them at the halfway point.

5. Serve the burgers on the buns, topped with the tomato slices, lettuce leaves, and any other favorite toppings.

**Time-Saving Tip:** These burgers freeze well, so they're great for meal-prepping. Once they've cooled, place a piece of parchment paper or wax paper between them and then pop them into a resealable freezer bag or airtight container before putting them in the freezer; they'll keep for up to 6 months. Once you're ready to eat them, thaw them on the counter, then reheat by baking them in the oven for a few minutes or panfrying them.

PER SERVING: CALORIES: 312; FAT: 4G; SATURATED FAT: 1G; CHOLESTEROL: 0G; PROTEIN: 16G; FIBER: 10G; SODIUM: 451MG

# CHICKPEA MUSHROOM BURGERS

NUT-FREE, SOY-FREE, KID-FRIENDLY

**SERVES 4 | PREP TIME:** 15 MINUTES | **COOK TIME:** 40 MINUTES

I wish I had known how to make veggie burgers when I first went veg. There was only one brand available at the time, and the burgers tasted very similar to the box they came in. (Not that I'm in the habit of chewing on cardboard.) Making homemade burgers seemed too daunting, but I've since learned that they're incredibly easy—and much tastier than those burgers of yore. Top these burgers with pickles, sliced onions, ketchup, mustard, or whatever your favorite fixin's are.

2 teaspoons neutral-flavored vegetable oil

¼ cup minced yellow onion

1 cup coarsely chopped white button mushrooms

2 garlic cloves, minced

1 (14-ounce) can chickpeas, drained and rinsed

⅓ cup tahini

⅓ cup chickpea flour

½ teaspoon dried thyme

½ teaspoon ground sage

½ teaspoon salt

¼ teaspoon freshly ground black pepper

4 whole wheat or gluten-free burger buns, toasted

1 large tomato, sliced

4 large lettuce leaves

Other burger toppings of your choice

1. Preheat the oven to 400°F. Line a baking sheet with parchment paper.

2. In a large skillet, heat the oil over medium-high heat until it shimmers. Add the onion and cook for about 5 minutes, until it begins to soften. Add the mushrooms and garlic and cook, stirring frequently, until the mushrooms have browned and softened, about 10 minutes. If there's any mushroom liquid left in the pan, drain it off.

3. In a large bowl, combine the cooked vegetables, chickpeas, tahini, chickpea flour, thyme, sage, salt, and pepper. Stir everything together, mashing the chickpeas as you go.

4. Using your hands, form the mixture into 4 patties and place them on the prepared baking sheet.

5. Bake the burgers for 20 to 30 minutes, until golden brown and firm, flipping them at the halfway point.

6. Serve the burgers on the buns, topped with the tomato slices, lettuce leaves, and any other favorite toppings.

**Time-Saving Tip:** Rather than mixing the burger ingredients by hand, you can throw them all in a food processor and pulse a few times to mix everything together.

**PER SERVING:** CALORIES: 387; FAT: 17G; SATURATED FAT: 2G; CHOLESTEROL: 0G; PROTEIN: 14G; FIBER: 8G; SODIUM: 597MG

# PORTABELLA CHIMICHURRI TACOS

NUT-FREE, GLUTEN-FREE, SOY-FREE, 30-MINUTE MEAL, ONE-PAN/ONE-POT

**MAKES 8 TACOS | PREP TIME:** 15 MINUTES **| COOK TIME:** 15 MINUTES

Some people think a taco isn't a taco unless its filling is made with meat. I was once asked what, as a vegan, I make tacos with. My response was, "Pretty much anything I can get my hands on." Sure, you can use spiced black beans or ground seitan, but why stop there? My philosophy is that if it can fit into a tortilla, turn it into a taco. And portabella mushrooms fit into tortillas beautifully.

2 teaspoons neutral-flavored vegetable oil

1 yellow onion, thinly sliced

2 green bell peppers, seeded and thinly sliced

8 portabella mushrooms, thinly sliced

1 cup Chimichurri (page 223) or store-bought chimichurri

8 small (6-inch) tortillas, warmed

1 avocado, pitted, peeled, and sliced

1 jalapeño pepper, seeded and thinly sliced (optional)

1. In large pan, heat the oil over medium-high heat until it shimmers. Add the onion and cook for about 5 minutes, until it begins to brown. Add the bell peppers and mushrooms to the pan and cook, stirring often, until they soften and brown, about 10 minutes. Stir in the chimichurri.

2. To assemble the tacos, spoon the mushroom mixture onto the tortillas, dividing it evenly. Top with the avocado and jalapeño (if using). Serve.

**Substitution Tip:** I prefer my tacos made with soft tortillas, but if crunch is your thing, use hard taco shells.

PER SERVING (2 TACOS): CALORIES: 611; FAT: 32G; SATURATED FAT: 5G; CHOLESTEROL: 0G; PROTEIN: 15G; FIBER: 11G; SODIUM: 645MG

# BRUSSELS SPROUT TACOS

SOY-FREE, 30-MINUTE MEAL, ONE-PAN/ONE-POT

**MAKES 8 TACOS | PREP TIME:** 10 MINUTES | **COOK TIME:** 20 MINUTES

I'm always met with rather rude comments when I post something about Brussels sprouts on social media, so I know they're not a favorite, even with the vegan crowd. Hear me out, though. There are two fast ways to get people to eat food they're iffy about: (1) Drench it in peanut sauce; or (2) put it in a taco. I've done both here. Yes, I know it's a strange combination, but it's one I stand by.

2 teaspoons neutral-flavored vegetable oil

1 pound Brussels sprouts, halved (see Tip)

1 red bell pepper, seeded and sliced

2 scallions, thinly sliced

1 cup Spicy Peanut Sauce (page 221) or store-bought peanut sauce

8 small (6-inch) tortillas, warmed

1 avocado, pitted, peeled, and sliced

¼ cup chopped roasted peanuts

¼ cup chopped fresh cilantro leaves

1. In a large skillet, heat the oil over medium-high heat until it shimmers. Add the Brussels sprouts, bell pepper, and scallions and cook, stirring often, until they soften and begin to brown, 15 to 20 minutes. Stir in the peanut sauce.

2. To assemble the tacos, divide the vegetable mixture among the tortillas and top with the avocado, peanuts, and cilantro. Serve.

**Ingredient Tip:** If your Brussels sprouts are on the larger side, quarter them so they don't take forever to cook.

**PER SERVING (2 TACOS):** CALORIES: 617; FAT: 31G; SATURATED FAT: 6G; CHOLESTEROL: 0G; PROTEIN: 18G; FIBER: 14G; SODIUM: 912MG

# FISH-FREE RICE BOWLS

ONE-PAN/ONE-POT

**SERVES 4 | PREP TIME:** 20 MINUTES **| COOK TIME:** 25 MINUTES

Have you ever tried to make your own sushi at home? I have. Always up for a challenge, I bought rolling mats, a bamboo paddle, and sheets of nori. I ended up with rice in my hair, nori stuck to my clothes, and a giant mess in my kitchen. In the end, I just threw everything into a big bowl and ate it with a fork. That's when I realized that rice bowls are just as delicious as my favorite rolls, with far less fuss.

2 cups uncooked sushi rice

2½ cups water

¼ cup unseasoned
rice vinegar

1 tablespoon agave nectar
or pure maple syrup

1 tablespoon
reduced-sodium soy
sauce or tamari

2 cups shelled edamame

2 carrots, grated
or shredded

2 nori sheets, cut into
thin strips

1 English cucumber,
thinly sliced

1 avocado, pitted, peeled,
and diced

2 scallions, sliced

1 cup Carrot-Ginger
Dressing (page 216) or
store-bought
ginger dressing

4 teaspoons toasted
sesame seeds

1. Place the rice in a fine-mesh sieve and rinse it under running water until the water runs clear.

2. In a medium pot, combine the rice and the water. Bring to a boil over medium-high heat, then reduce the heat to medium-low. Cover the pot and cook until all the liquid has been absorbed, 15 to 20 minutes. Remove the pot from the heat and let the rice steam (still covered) for about 10 minutes more.

3. Uncover the pot and gently stir the vinegar, agave, and soy sauce into the rice.

4. Divide the rice evenly among 4 bowls. Top with the edamame, carrots, nori, cucumber, avocado, and scallions. Drizzle each bowl with ¼ cup of the dressing and sprinkle with 1 teaspoon of the sesame seeds to serve.

**Substitution Tip:** Sushi rice is a white, short-grain glutinous rice that cooks up firm and sticky. If you'd rather use a whole grain, give short-grain brown rice a try. For brown rice, you'll need just 2 cups water and the cooking time will increase to about 45 minutes.

**PER SERVING:** CALORIES: 684; FAT: 19G; SATURATED FAT: 0G; CHOLESTEROL: 0G; PROTEIN: 20G; FIBER: 15G; SODIUM: 662MG

# CHIMICHURRI BOWLS

NUT-FREE, SOY-FREE

**SERVES 4 | PREP TIME:** 15 MINUTES | **COOK TIME:** 30 MINUTES

Is there anything cozier than a bowl of potatoes? How about a bowl of roasted sweet potatoes combined with beans, grains, and a spicy sauce? Now you're talkin'! This meal is pretty simple, but sometimes simple is all you need. Consider it the mealtime equivalent of your favorite sweater or a quiet night in. It's not too flashy, but it does the trick and it's there when you need it.

2 medium sweet potatoes, diced (about 4 cups)

2 teaspoons neutral-flavored vegetable oil

½ teaspoon salt

¼ teaspoon freshly ground black pepper

1¼ cups uncooked quinoa, rinsed

2½ cups vegetable stock or water

1 (15-ounce) can black beans, drained and rinsed

4 cups tightly packed baby spinach

1 avocado, pitted, peeled, and diced

1 cup Chimichurri (page 223) or store-bought chimichurri

1. Preheat the oven to 350°F. Line a baking sheet with parchment paper.

2. Place the sweet potato in a medium bowl and toss it with the oil, salt, and pepper. Arrange the sweet potato in a single layer on the prepared baking sheet. Bake for 30 minutes, or until the sweet potato is fork-tender and brown, flipping the pieces once after 15 minutes.

3. Meanwhile, in a medium pot, combine the quinoa and stock. Bring to a boil over medium-high heat, then reduce the heat to medium-low. Cover the pot and cook the quinoa for about 15 minutes, until all the liquid has been absorbed.

4. Divide the quinoa evenly among 4 bowls. Top with the roasted sweet potatoes, black beans, spinach, and avocado. Drizzle each bowl with ¼ cup of the chimichurri to serve.

**Substitution Tip:** Roasted butternut squash can be used in place of the sweet potatoes. Try grilled zucchini or summer squash in the warmer months. Popeye Pesto (page 225) can be used if chimichurri is too spicy for your tastes.

PER SERVING: CALORIES: 657; FAT: 32G; SATURATED FAT: 4G; CHOLESTEROL: 0G; PROTEIN: 19G; FIBER: 18G; SODIUM: 540MG

# HOLD THE TORTILLA BURRITO BOWL

NUT-FREE, GLUTEN-FREE, ONE-PAN/ONE-POT

**SERVES 4 | PREP TIME:** 15 MINUTES **| COOK TIME:** 45 MINUTES

Rolling tortillas to make burritos can be challenging. It takes practice and patience to get it right. It sometimes happens that I've finally tucked in the sides just right, only to find that the center has spilt open. What if you want all that burrito-y goodness without the hassle of tortilla origami? Pile all the filling ingredients into a big bowl, of course! Add queso (see page 32), salsa, guacamole, or nondairy sour cream for some *oomph*.

2½ cups water

1¼ cups uncooked brown rice, rinsed

¼ cup minced fresh cilantro leaves

2 tablespoons fresh lime juice

1 tablespoon fresh lemon juice

1 (15-ounce) can pinto beans, drained and rinsed

4 cups loosely packed shredded romaine lettuce

2 tomatoes, diced

1 avocado, pitted, peeled, and diced

1 cup fresh or thawed frozen corn kernels

1 cup Chipotle-Lime Dressing (page 219) or store-bought dairy-free chipotle dressing

¼ cup pickled jalapeño pepper slices

1. In a medium pot, combine the water and rice. Bring to a boil over medium-high heat, then reduce the heat to medium-low. Cover the pot and cook the rice for about 45 minutes, until all the water has been absorbed.

2. Remove the pot from the heat. Stir in the cilantro, lime juice, and lemon juice.

3. Divide the rice evenly among 4 bowls. Top with the pinto beans, lettuce, tomatoes, avocado, and corn. Drizzle each bowl with ¼ cup of the dressing and finish with a few jalapeño slices to serve.

**Substitution Tip:** Because of a variation in olfactory-receptor genes, cilantro tastes like soap to about 20 percent of the population (*ick!*). If you're in that group, you can use flat-leaf parsley in place of the cilantro.

PER SERVING: CALORIES: 534; FAT: 12G; SATURATED FAT: 2G; CHOLESTEROL: 1G; PROTEIN: 13G; FIBER: 10G; SODIUM: 824MG

# GREEN GODDESS BOWL

NUT-FREE, SOY-FREE, KID-FRIENDLY

**SERVES 4 | PREP TIME:** 15 MINUTES | **COOK TIME:** 20 MINUTES

I find myself drawn to the color green. I once got out of my green car carrying my green purse and wearing my favorite green dress, and I realized I must have looked like the crazy green lady to anyone watching me. When green veggies are piled into a bowl, however, no one bats an eye, so I frequently make meals devoted to my beloved hue. You, too, can get your green on with this healthy bowl.

5 cups chopped broccoli (cut into bite-size florets)

2 cups chopped green beans

2 teaspoons neutral-flavored vegetable oil

½ teaspoon garlic powder

½ teaspoon salt

¼ teaspoon freshly ground black pepper

3 cups water

1¼ cups uncooked semi-pearled farro

1 (15-ounce) can chickpeas, drained and rinsed

4 cups loosely packed baby kale

1 cup Green Goddess Dressing (page 218)

2 tablespoons chopped fresh chives

1. Preheat the oven to 425°F. Line a baking sheet with parchment paper.

2. In a large bowl, combine the broccoli and green beans. Add the oil, garlic powder, salt, and pepper and toss to coat well. Spread out the vegetables in an even layer on the prepared baking sheet. Roast for 15 to 20 minutes, until they begin to crisp and brown.

3. Meanwhile, in a medium pot, combine the water and farro. Bring to a boil over medium-high heat, then reduce the heat to medium-low. Cover the pot and cook the farro for about 20 minutes, until all the water has been absorbed.

4. Divide the cooked farro evenly among 4 bowls. Top with the roasted vegetables, chickpeas, and kale. Drizzle ¼ cup of the dressing over each bowl. Finish with the chives. Serve.

**Substitution Tip:** You can use just about any green veggie in place of the broccoli and green beans here. Brussels sprouts and asparagus would work well, as would zucchini and snap peas. Arugula, baby spinach, or even mixed baby greens can be used in place of the baby kale.

**PER SERVING:** CALORIES: 589; FAT: 21G; SATURATED FAT: 3G; CHOLESTEROL: 0G; PROTEIN: 20G; FIBER: 25G; SODIUM: 684MG

# Build-a-Bowl

Plates are so last century. Bowls are the future of food! You don't need a recipe to create your own meal in a bowl. It's easy to throw one together using ingredients you already have on hand, and bowl-based meals are a terrific way to dress up leftovers.

If you have a busy week ahead, spend a little time on Sunday prepping your bowls by cooking grains, roasting veggies, and whipping up a few sauces. When you're ready to eat, assemble your bowls by mixing and matching ingredients.

1. **Pick Your Grain.** Start your bowl with a starchy base. Any whole grain will do. Rice and quinoa are common grains, but you can also give millet, spelt, or bulgur a try. Pasta and starchy veggies like potato and butternut squash are great bowl bases, too.

2. **Pick Your Protein.** Just open a can of beans, and the protein portion of your bowl is taken care of. Chickpeas, black beans, and pinto beans are always good bets, but don't forget about edamame and lentils. Baked tofu, roasted seitan, and sautéed tempeh are also great sources of protein.

3. **Pick Your Vegetables.** Anything goes when it comes to bowls and veggies. You can use raw or cooked produce—or a combo of both. Make sure you include leafy greens like spinach or arugula, too.

4. **Pick Your Sauce.** My bowl philosophy boils down to this: Don't skimp on the sauce. See chapter 11 for some of my faves. Try Carrot-Ginger Dressing (page 216) or Spicy Peanut Sauce (page 221) on Asian-inspired bowls. Chimichurri (page 223) and Chipotle-Lime Dressing (page 219) both pair well with Tex-Mex-style dishes. Ranch Dressing (page 217) and Green Goddess Dressing (page 218) enhance just about any meal.

Spicy Green Bean Stir-Fry, page 124

# CHAPTER SEVEN

# EAT YOUR VEGGIES

## VEGETABLE MAINS

# THE GENERAL'S SPICY CAULIFLOWER

**SERVES 4 | PREP TIME:** 10 MINUTES | **COOK TIME:** 30 MINUTES

This recipe was inspired by General Tso's tofu, the Chinese take-out favorite. A little sweet and a little spicy, with a flavorful kick from ginger and garlic—what's not to love? I've used cauliflower rather than tofu here, because I've found that battering and baking cauliflower is a great way to get picky eaters to enjoy their veggies. Serve with steamed broccoli for an even more veg-centric dish.

1 cup whole wheat or all-purpose flour

½ teaspoon garlic powder

½ teaspoon onion powder

½ teaspoon salt

1 cup plain unsweetened Almond Milk (page 214) or store-bought nondairy milk

1 medium head cauliflower, cut into bite-size florets (about 4 cups)

1 teaspoon peanut oil

2 garlic cloves, minced

2 scallions, sliced

1 teaspoon minced peeled fresh ginger

1 teaspoon red pepper flakes

½ cup vegetable stock

⅓ cup reduced-sodium soy sauce or tamari

¼ cup unseasoned rice vinegar

2 tablespoons pure maple syrup

1 tablespoon tomato paste

1 tablespoon cornstarch

4 cups cooked brown rice

1 tablespoon toasted sesame seeds

1. Preheat the oven to 425°F. Line a baking sheet with parchment paper.

2. In a large bowl, whisk together the flour, garlic powder, onion powder, and salt. Slowly whisk in the almond milk.

3. Add the cauliflower to the flour mixture, tossing to coat all the florets well. Arrange the cauliflower in a single layer on the prepared baking sheet. Bake for 15 minutes, flip the pieces, and bake for another 15 minutes, or until golden brown and crisp.

4. Meanwhile, in a large skillet, heat the oil over medium heat until it shimmers. Add the garlic, scallions, ginger, and red pepper flakes. Cook for 2 to 3 minutes, until fragrant.

5. Meanwhile, in a small bowl, whisk together the stock, soy sauce, vinegar, maple syrup, tomato paste, and cornstarch. Add the sauce to the pan and cook, stirring occasionally, until thickened, about 5 minutes more.

6. Add the cooked cauliflower to the pan with the sauce and gently toss to coat the pieces well.

7. Divide the rice evenly among 4 plates. Top with the cauliflower and garnish with the sesame seeds. Serve.

**Variation Tip:** For sesame cauliflower, omit the tomato paste and red pepper flakes. Add 1 tablespoon toasted sesame oil and 2 tablespoons sesame seeds to the sauce. Top with extra sesame seeds and sliced scallions.

**PER SERVING:** CALORIES: 478; FAT: 5G; SATURATED FAT: 1G; CHOLESTEROL: 0G; PROTEIN: 16G; FIBER: 8G; SODIUM: 1,711MG

# EGGPLANT AND BROCCOLI IN GARLIC SAUCE

30-MINUTE MEAL, ONE-PAN/ONE-POT

**SERVES 4 | PREP TIME:** 10 MINUTES | **COOK TIME:** 13 MINUTES

When ordering Chinese takeout, I often go for something in garlic sauce. But what? The choice is quite often between broccoli and eggplant, and I love both, so it's hard to decide. Why not just combine the two and make it easier? This dish comes together faster than it would take to have dinner delivered, so there's no excuse not to make it. Throw in some cubed baked tofu (see page 230) if you'd like a little protein boost.

2 teaspoons peanut oil

5 cups chopped broccoli (cut into bite-size florets)

4 Japanese eggplants, cut into bite-size pieces (about 1 by 2 inches; see Tip)

½ cup vegetable stock

¼ cup reduced-sodium soy sauce or tamari

¼ cup unseasoned rice vinegar

1 tablespoon pure maple syrup

1 tablespoon cornstarch

1 tablespoon minced peeled fresh ginger

6 garlic cloves, minced

4 cups cooked brown rice

2 scallions, sliced

1. In a large skillet, heat the oil over medium-high heat until it shimmers. Add the broccoli and eggplant, and increase the heat to high. Cook, stirring frequently, for about 10 minutes, until the vegetables have softened.

2. Meanwhile, in a small bowl, whisk together the stock, soy sauce, vinegar, maple syrup, cornstarch, ginger, and garlic. Pour the sauce mixture into the pan and cook, stirring frequently, for 2 to 3 minutes, until the sauce thickens.

3. Divide the rice evenly among 4 plates. Top with the vegetables and garnish with the scallions. Serve.

**Ingredient Tip:** If you can't find Japanese eggplants, you can use just about any type. You'll need about 1½ pounds.

PER SERVING: CALORIES: 390; FAT: 5G; SATURATED FAT: 1G; CHOLESTEROL: 0G; PROTEIN: 13G; FIBER: 15G; SODIUM: 1,054MG

# SPICY GREEN BEAN STIR-FRY

30-MINUTE MEAL, ONE-PAN/ONE-POT

**SERVES 4 | PREP TIME:** 10 MINUTES | **COOK TIME:** 20 MINUTES

I like my stir-fries spicy. If it doesn't bring tears to my eyes, why even bother? It wasn't always this way, though. I used to be a lightweight, adding the tiniest amount of heat to recipes that called for it. Unwittingly, I built up my tolerance, and I can pile it on now. If you're adverse to heat like I used to be, reduce the amount of red pepper flakes or omit them altogether. Serve the stir-fry as is or with cooked brown rice or noodles.

1 teaspoon neutral-flavored vegetable oil

½ cup diced yellow onion (about ½ onion)

1 tablespoon minced peeled fresh ginger

3 garlic cloves, minced

1 (8-ounce) package tempeh, cut into 1-inch cubes

1 pound green beans, chopped

½ cup vegetable stock

3 tablespoons reduced-sodium soy sauce or tamari

1 tablespoon unseasoned rice vinegar

1 teaspoon red pepper flakes

1 teaspoon cornstarch

¼ cup cashews, toasted and chopped

1. In a large skillet, heat the oil over medium heat until it shimmers. Add the onion and cook until it begins to soften, about 5 minutes. Add the ginger and garlic, and cook for a minute or two, or until fragrant.

2. Add the tempeh and green beans to the pan, and increase the heat to medium-high. Cook, stirring frequently, for about 10 minutes, until the green beans soften and the tempeh browns.

3. Meanwhile, in a small bowl, whisk together the stock, soy sauce, vinegar, red pepper flakes, and cornstarch. Add the sauce mixture to the pan and cook for another minute or two, or until the sauce thickens.

4. Divide the stir-fry evenly among 4 bowls. Top with the toasted cashews. Serve.

**Technique Tip:** To toast the cashews, place a large, dry (no oil) skillet over medium-high heat. Once the pan is hot, add the nuts and cook, stirring frequently, until they are golden brown, 5 to 10 minutes. They can also be toasted on a baking sheet in a preheated 400°F oven for 5 to 10 minutes. Keep an eye on them, because they can burn easily.

PER SERVING: CALORIES: 225; FAT: 11G; SATURATED FAT: 2G; CHOLESTEROL: 0G; PROTEIN: 16G; FIBER: 4G; SODIUM: 769MG

# KEEP CALM AND CURRY ON

SOY-FREE, KID-FRIENDLY, ONE-PAN/ONE-POT

**SERVES 4 | PREP TIME:** 10 MINUTES | **COOK TIME:** 27 MINUTES

Because it's the perfect blend of easy-to-make and yummy-to-eat, curry is one of my go-to dishes on busy weeknights. You just throw some veggies in a pot along with curry paste and coconut milk and wait for them to do their magic. What could be easier than that? I've used sweet potatoes and green beans here, but you can mix things up and use cauliflower, mushrooms, zucchini, eggplant, or whatever vegetables strike your fancy.

- 2 teaspoons neutral-flavored vegetable oil
- 1 medium yellow onion, diced
- 2 garlic cloves, minced
- 1 tablespoon minced peeled fresh ginger
- 3 tablespoons green curry paste
- 1 (14-ounce) can full-fat coconut milk
- ½ cup vegetable stock
- 2 tablespoons creamy natural peanut butter
- 8 ounces green beans, cut into 1-inch pieces
- 1 large sweet potato, diced
- 2 tablespoons fresh lime juice
- 4 cups cooked jasmine rice
- 2 tablespoons chopped fresh cilantro leaves

1. In a large pot, heat the oil over medium-high heat until it shimmers. Add the onion and cook for 5 minutes, or until it begins to soften. Add the garlic, ginger, and curry paste and cook for another minute or two, until fragrant.

2. Stir in the coconut milk, stock, peanut butter, green beans, and sweet potato. Bring the mixture to a boil, then reduce the heat to medium. Simmer, stirring occasionally, for 15 to 20 minutes, until the sweet potatoes are fork-tender.

3. Remove the pan from the heat and stir in the lime juice.

4. Divide the rice evenly among 4 bowls. Top with the curry. Garnish with the cilantro to serve.

> **Substitution Tip:** Green curry paste gets its color from green chiles, basil, cilantro, and lime leaves. It tends to be milder in flavor than red curry paste, but red curry paste can be used if you'd like a little more spice. Always check the ingredients list, as curry pastes sometimes contain ingredients derived from fish or shrimp.

**PER SERVING:** CALORIES: 557; FAT: 30G; SATURATED FAT: 20G; CHOLESTEROL: 0G; PROTEIN: 12G; FIBER: 10G; SODIUM: 77MG

# CAULIFLOWER PICCATA

SOY-FREE

**SERVES 4 | PREP TIME:** 15 MINUTES **| COOK TIME:** 30 MINUTES

This is one of those dishes that's ritzy enough for dinner parties, but there's no reason you can't treat yourself to a little piccata on a weeknight. Serve it over pasta, mashed potatoes, or rice.

1 medium head cauliflower, stem and leaves removed

½ cup plain unsweetened Almond Milk (page 214) or store-bought nondairy milk

1 tablespoon cornstarch

2 teaspoons Dijon mustard

1 cup whole wheat or all-purpose flour

1 tablespoon nutritional yeast

½ teaspoon garlic powder

½ teaspoon onion powder

½ teaspoon salt

¼ teaspoon freshly ground black pepper

1 teaspoon neutral-flavored vegetable oil

2 medium shallots, thinly sliced (about ½ cup)

4 garlic cloves, thinly sliced

¾ cup dry white wine (see Tip)

½ cup vegetable stock

3 tablespoons fresh lemon juice

2 tablespoons capers, drained

2 tablespoons chopped fresh parsley leaves

1. Preheat the oven to 400°F. Line a baking sheet with parchment paper.

2. Place the cauliflower on a cutting board, stem-side down, and, using a sharp knife, slice it the way you would a loaf of bread, ½ to ¾ inch thick.

3. Set up a workstation with 2 medium bowls and place the prepared baking sheet at the end. In the first bowl, stir together the almond milk, cornstarch, and mustard. In the second bowl, stir together the flour, nutritional yeast, garlic powder, onion powder, salt, and pepper.

4. Dip the cauliflower into the almond milk mixture and then dredge it in the flour mixture to coat. Arrange the pieces in a single layer on the prepared baking sheet.

5. Bake the cauliflower for 15 minutes, flip the pieces, and bake for another 10 to 15 minutes, until crisp and golden brown.

6. Meanwhile, in a medium skillet, heat the oil over medium-high heat until it shimmers. Add the shallots and cook for 5 minutes, or until they begin to soften. Add the garlic and cook for another minute or two, until fragrant.

7. Add the wine, stock, lemon juice, and capers to the pan and reduce the heat to medium. Cook the sauce for about 5 minutes, until the liquid has reduced slightly.

8. Divide the cauliflower evenly among 4 plates. Top with the sauce. Garnish with the parsley to serve.

PER SERVING: CALORIES: 246; FAT: 3G; SATURATED FAT: 1G; CHOLESTEROL: 0G; PROTEIN: 9G; FIBER: 5G; SODIUM: 560MG

# LEMON PEPPER BROCCOLI

NUT-FREE, SOY-FREE, 30-MINUTE MEAL, ONE-PAN/ONE-POT

**SERVES 4 | PREP TIME:** 5 MINUTES | **COOK TIME:** 20 MINUTES

Lemon and pepper are a match made in heaven. Or at least a match made in a really nice kitchen. I find that most recipes involving the two wimp out on both ingredients, but I've loaded on the flavor with lots of lemon juice and black pepper. You may find yourself puckering at the first bite, but soon the pepper will kick in, causing you to work up a mild sweat. Serve as is or with cooked pasta or brown rice.

**2 teaspoons neutral-flavored vegetable oil**

**½ cup diced yellow onion (about ½ onion)**

**5 cups chopped broccoli (cut into bite-size florets)**

**1 (15-ounce) can chickpeas, drained and rinsed**

**⅔ cup vegetable stock**

**3 tablespoons fresh lemon juice**

**1½ teaspoons freshly ground black pepper**

**½ teaspoon cornstarch**

**½ teaspoon dried rosemary**

**½ teaspoon dried thyme**

**½ teaspoon garlic powder**

**½ teaspoon salt**

**1 lemon, cut into wedges**

1. In a large skillet, heat the oil over medium-high heat until it shimmers. Add the onion and cook for 5 minutes, until it begins to soften. Add the broccoli and chickpeas and cook, stirring frequently, for about 10 minutes, until the broccoli has turned bright green and softened slightly.

2. In a small bowl, whisk together the stock, lemon juice, pepper, cornstarch, rosemary, thyme, garlic powder, and salt. Pour the sauce mixture into the pan and cook, stirring frequently, for 2 to 3 minutes, until the sauce thickens.

3. Serve with the lemon wedges alongside.

**Substitution Tip:** If broccoli isn't your thing, you can use cauliflower, summer squash, mushrooms, or carrots—or a mix of all these. If desired, 2 sliced Chic'un Patties (page 234), 2 cups chopped store-bought seitan, or 2 cups Baked Tofu, Three Ways (page 230) can be used in place of the chickpeas.

**PER SERVING:** CALORIES: 153; FAT: 4G; SATURATED FAT: 0G; CHOLESTEROL: 0G; PROTEIN: 8G; FIBER: 7G; SODIUM: 392MG

# PORTABELLA SCHNITZEL

SOY-FREE, KID-FRIENDLY

**SERVES 4 | PREP TIME:** 15 MINUTES | **COOK TIME:** 30 MINUTES

Years ago, one of my favorite vegan restaurants in New York City had a vegan schnitzel on the menu. It was a delicious meal of thin slices of seitan that had been breaded and fried. Sadly, the eatery closed, but my love for their schnitzel is still strong. I've done my best to re-create it at home, using hearty portabellas in place of the seitan. Serve the schnitzel as is or with steamed vegetables and roasted potatoes.

½ cup plain unsweetened Almond Milk (page 214) or store-bought nondairy milk

½ cup chickpea flour

¾ cup panko bread crumbs

½ teaspoon dried basil

½ teaspoon dried thyme

½ teaspoon dried rosemary

½ teaspoon sweet paprika

½ teaspoon salt

¼ teaspoon garlic powder

¼ teaspoon onion powder

¼ teaspoon freshly ground black pepper

4 large portabella mushrooms

2 teaspoons neutral-flavored vegetable oil

1 small red onion, thinly sliced (about 1 cup)

4 cups loosely packed shredded green cabbage (about ½ head)

2 tablespoons fresh lemon juice

2 tablespoons chopped fresh parsley leaves

1 lemon, cut into wedges

1. Preheat the oven to 350°F. Line a baking sheet with parchment paper.

2. Set up a workstation with 2 medium bowls and place the prepared baking sheet at the end. In the first bowl, combine the almond milk and chickpea flour. In the second bowl, combine the bread crumbs, basil, thyme, rosemary, paprika, salt, garlic powder, onion powder, and pepper.

3. Dip each mushroom into the almond milk mixture and then into the bread crumb mixture, coating them well. Arrange the mushrooms in a single layer on the prepared baking sheet.

4. Bake for 15 minutes, flip the mushrooms, and bake for another 10 to 15 minutes, until golden brown.

5. Meanwhile, in a large skillet, heat the oil over medium-high heat until it shimmers. Add the onion and cook, stirring occasionally, for 5 minutes, until it begins to soften. Add the cabbage and cook, stirring frequently, for 5 to 10 minutes, until it's crisp-tender. Remove the pan from the heat and stir in the lemon juice.

6. Divide the cabbage mixture evenly among 4 plates. Top with a breaded mushroom and garnish with the parsley. Serve with the lemon wedges alongside.

PER SERVING: CALORIES: 186; FAT: 5G; SATURATED FAT: 2G; CHOLESTEROL: 0G; PROTEIN: 9G; FIBER: 6G; SODIUM: 438MG

# ZUCCHINI BOATS

NUT-FREE, GLUTEN-FREE, SOY-FREE, KID-FRIENDLY

**SERVES 4 | PREP TIME:** 15 MINUTES | **COOK TIME:** 40 MINUTES

These little "boats" wouldn't get you very far on the open sea, but they are a delicious mode of transportation when you're headed to Tasty Dinner Land. This is a great end-of-summer dish, when home gardens and farmers' markets are bursting with zucchini and summer squash, but it can be enjoyed any time of year. You can serve these boats on their own as a light dinner or alongside pasta for a hearty supper.

4 medium zucchini

2 teaspoons neutral-flavored vegetable oil

½ cup diced yellow onion (about ½ onion)

2 cups finely chopped cremini or white button mushrooms (about 8 ounces)

2 garlic cloves, minced

½ teaspoon dried oregano

½ teaspoon dried basil

¼ teaspoon red pepper flakes

2 cups Marinara (page 226) or store-bought marinara sauce

1. Preheat the oven to 400°F.

2. Cut the zucchini in half lengthwise. Using a spoon or melon baller, carefully scoop the flesh from the center of each zucchini half, leaving a ¼-inch-thick shell. Finely chop the zucchini flesh; set the zucchini halves aside.

3. In a large skillet, heat the oil over medium-high heat until it shimmers. Add the onion and cook for about 5 minutes, until it begins to soften. Add the zucchini flesh, mushrooms, garlic, oregano, basil, and red pepper flakes, and cook for another 10 minutes or so, until the vegetables have softened and browned.

4. Spread half the marinara sauce over the bottom of a 9-by-13-inch baking dish. Spoon the vegetable mixture into each zucchini half. Carefully place the stuffed zucchini boats in the baking dish over the marinara and top with the remaining marinara.

5. Cover the dish with aluminum foil and bake for 25 minutes. Remove the foil and bake for 5 minutes more, until the zucchini is tender and the edges begin to brown. Serve.

**Substitution Tip:** For a heartier stuffing, replace the mushrooms with a 14-ounce can of brown lentils (or 1¾ cups cooked lentils). If desired, 2 cups crumbled vegan sausage can be used, too.

**PER SERVING:** CALORIES: 101; FAT: 3G; SATURATED FAT: 0G; CHOLESTEROL: 0G; PROTEIN: 5G; FIBER: 5G; SODIUM: 123MG

# RATATOUILLE

NUT-FREE, GLUTEN-FREE, SOY-FREE, KID-FRIENDLY, ONE-PAN/ONE-POT

**SERVES 4** | **PREP TIME:** 15 MINUTES, PLUS DRAINING TIME | **COOK TIME:** 30 MINUTES

Okay, who else used to think ratatouille had something to do with rodents? Well, I didn't actually think it was mouse stew, but I knew it was French, and French cuisine isn't known for being very vegan-friendly. It turns out that this dish is very vegan-friendly, though, as it's nothing but vegetables and herbs. You can give your dish a little extra *oomph* by throwing in a can of white beans.

1 large eggplant, diced

2 teaspoons salt, divided

3 tablespoons olive oil

1 medium yellow onion, diced

4 garlic cloves, minced

2 bell peppers, seeded and diced

2 medium zucchini, diced

2 medium summer squash, diced

3 medium tomatoes, diced

1 teaspoon dried basil

1 teaspoon dried oregano

1 teaspoon dried thyme

½ teaspoon dried rosemary

¼ teaspoon freshly ground black pepper

1. Place the eggplant in a colander and toss it with 1½ teaspoons of the salt. Let it sit for about 20 minutes. Squeeze out any excess water with your hands.

2. In a large pot, heat the oil over medium-high heat until it shimmers. Add the onion and cook for 5 minutes, or until it begins to soften. Add the garlic and bell peppers and cook for another 5 minutes, until the peppers begin to soften.

3. Add the eggplant, zucchini, squash, tomatoes, basil, oregano, thyme, rosemary, black pepper, and remaining ½ teaspoon salt to the pot. Cook, stirring occasionally, until the mixture comes to a simmer, about 5 minutes.

4. Reduce the heat to medium, cover the pot with the lid ajar, and cook, stirring occasionally, for 15 minutes to let the flavors come together. Serve.

**Technique Tip:** I like my veggies on the chunky side, so I simmer them for 15 minutes. If you prefer softer, stewlike vegetables, you can simmer them for up to 1 hour 30 minutes.

**PER SERVING:** CALORIES: 208; FAT: 11G; SATURATED FAT: 2G; CHOLESTEROL: 0G; PROTEIN: 6G; FIBER: 9G; SODIUM: 312MG

# STUFFED EGGPLANT

NUT-FREE, GLUTEN-FREE, SOY-FREE, KID-FRIENDLY

**SERVES 4 | PREP TIME:** 15 MINUTES | **COOK TIME:** 30 MINUTES

When an eggplant is sliced in half and the flesh scooped out, the halves resemble edible bowls, so why not load them up with a savory filling of lentils and peppers? Plus, stuffed eggplant looks pretty impressive on the dinner table.

2 large eggplant

4 teaspoons neutral-flavored
   vegetable oil, divided

1 teaspoon salt, divided

½ teaspoon freshly ground
   black pepper, divided

1 medium yellow onion,
   diced (about 1 cup)

2 garlic cloves, minced

1 red bell pepper, seeded
   and diced

1 (14-ounce) can diced
   tomatoes, drained

1 (15-ounce) can brown
   lentils, drained
   and rinsed

2 tablespoons
   balsamic vinegar

1 teaspoon dried oregano

1 teaspoon dried parsley

½ teaspoon dried thyme

1. Preheat the oven to 400°F. Line a baking sheet with parchment paper.

2. Cut the eggplant in half lengthwise. Using a spoon or melon baller, carefully scoop out the flesh of the egg-plant, leaving a ½-inch-thick shell; set the eggplant halves aside. Using a sharp knife, chop the flesh into small pieces, about ¼ inch thick.

3. Brush the insides of the eggplant halves with 2 teaspoons of the oil. Sprinkle with ½ teaspoon of the salt and ¼ teaspoon of the black pepper. Place the eggplant halves on the prepared baking sheet, cut-side down, and bake for 15 minutes, or until tender. Remove from the oven and reduce the oven temperature to 350°F.

4. Meanwhile, in a large skillet, heat the remaining 2 teaspoons oil over medium-high heat until it shimmers. Add the onion and cook for 5 minutes. Add the garlic and bell pepper and cook for another 5 minutes. Add the diced tomatoes, lentils, vinegar, oregano, parsley, and thyme to the pan. Cook for another 5 minutes, or until the vegetables are soft.

5. Flip the eggplant halves cut-side up and fill them with the vegetable mixture. Cover with aluminum foil and bake for 15 minutes. Serve.

**Technique Tip:** If it's tough to spoon out the eggplant flesh, you can use a paring knife to score a line around the edge of the eggplant for the spoon to follow.

**PER SERVING:** CALORIES: 241; FAT: 5G; SATURATED FAT: 1G; CHOLESTEROL: 0G; PROTEIN: 11G; FIBER: 17G; SODIUM: 562MG

# ZUCCHINI MANICOTTI

NUT-FREE, GLUTEN-FREE, KID-FRIENDLY, ONE-PAN/ONE-POT

**SERVES 4 | PREP TIME:** 20 MINUTES | **COOK TIME:** 30 MINUTES

Zucchini is one of those sneaky vegetables that likes to disguise itself as other foods. Its specialty is pasta, and it does a really great job of impersonating spaghetti. It's not too bad at mimicking manicotti shells either, as thinly sliced zucchini topped with ricotta can be easily rolled up and baked with tomato sauce. Top with shredded nondairy mozzarella, if you like.

2 cups Marinara (page 226) or store-bought marinara sauce

1 (8-ounce) package frozen spinach, thawed, drained, squeezed dry, and chopped

2 cups Tofu Ricotta (page 229) or store-bought nondairy ricotta

4 large zucchini, cut into ¼-inch-thick slices

1. Preheat the oven to 400°F. Spread half the marinara sauce over the bottom of a 9-by-13-inch baking dish.

2. Fold the spinach into the ricotta, then stir until well incorporated.

3. Lay two zucchini strips next to each other lengthwise, with about ½ inch of overlap. Spoon about 2 tablespoons of the ricotta about 1 inch from one of the short ends. Carefully roll up the zucchini and place the roll seam-side down in the baking dish over the marinara. Repeat with the rest of the zucchini and ricotta.

4. Cover the baking dish with aluminum foil and bake for 20 to 30 minutes, until the sauce is bubbling and the zucchini is tender. Serve.

**Technique Tip:** The thinner the zucchini slices, the better, so they'll be easier to roll up. A mandoline is handy for creating thin slices. A vegetable peeler can be used, too.

**Troubleshooting Tip:** If your spinach is too watery, it can cause the ricotta filling to be runny, so squeeze out as much liquid as possible. You can do this by wrapping the thawed spinach in a clean kitchen towel or a piece of cheesecloth, then twisting and squeezing it by hand, or by placing it in a tofu press, if you have one.

PER SERVING: CALORIES: 176; FAT: 6G; SATURATED FAT: 1G; CHOLESTEROL: 0G; PROTEIN: 16G; FIBER: 7G; SODIUM: 658MG

# GARLIC HERB ROASTED CAULIFLOWER

NUT-FREE, GLUTEN-FREE, SOY-FREE, KID-FRIENDLY, ONE-PAN/ONE-POT

**SERVES 4 | PREP TIME:** 5 MINUTES | **COOK TIME:** 1 HOUR

I know it might seem intimidating, but if you've never roasted a whole cauliflower, it's time to change that. It's one of those dishes that looks impressive but actually takes minimal effort on your part. Just brush on some seasonings and pop the cauliflower in the oven. When it's done, slice the head into wedges or carve it like a roast. It's sure to elicit *oohs* and *ahhs* from your fellow diners.

4 tablespoons
  neutral-flavored vegetable
  oil, divided

2 tablespoons fresh
  lemon juice

1 large head cauliflower,
  stem and leaves removed

½ teaspoon salt

¼ teaspoon freshly ground
  black pepper

3 garlic cloves, minced

1 tablespoon
  nutritional yeast

2 tablespoons chopped
  fresh parsley leaves

2 tablespoons chopped
  fresh thyme

1 tablespoon chopped fresh
  rosemary leaves

1. Position an oven rack in the middle of the oven. Preheat the oven to 400°F. Line an 8-inch square baking dish with parchment paper.

2. In a small bowl, combine 2 tablespoons of the vegetable oil and the lemon juice. Place the cauliflower in the prepared baking dish and brush it with the oil mixture. Sprinkle with the salt and pepper. Roast for 45 minutes.

3. Meanwhile, in a small bowl, whisk together the remaining 2 tablespoons oil, the garlic, nutritional yeast, parsley, thyme, and rosemary.

4. Remove the pan from the oven and brush the cauliflower with the herb mixture. Return the pan to the oven and bake for 15 minutes more, or until the cauliflower is tender with a few brown edges. Serve.

**Troubleshooting Tip:** Make sure the bottom of your cauliflower is flat to keep it from wobbling around in the baking dish. You may need to cut off some of the florets to create a flat surface.

**Variation Tip:** Pretty much any type of seasoning can be used in place of the garlic and herbs. Try maple-mustard cauliflower by mixing together 3 tablespoons pure maple syrup and 3 tablespoons Dijon mustard. You can also use ¼ cup Chimichurri (page 223) or pesto (see page 225).

**PER SERVING:** CALORIES: 162; FAT: 15G; SATURATED FAT: 1G; CHOLESTEROL: 0G; PROTEIN: 5G; FIBER: 5G; SODIUM: 489MG

# BUFFALO CAULIFLOWER PIZZA

**SERVES 4 | PREP TIME:** 15 MINUTES | **COOK TIME:** 35 MINUTES

It's possible that Buffalo cauliflower has jumped the shark at this point. I'm one of those loyal fans who sticks with my favorites *waaaay* after their prime, so I still enjoy it. I mean, why punish cauliflower for being the perfect delivery system for spicy sauce? And whereas Buffalo cauliflower is great on its own, it's even better when it's the star topping on a pizza. Add 1 cup shredded nondairy mozzarella if you're feeling cheesy.

Vegetable oil, for the pizza pan

⅓ cup hot sauce

3 tablespoons olive oil

1 teaspoon garlic powder

½ teaspoon salt

5 cups chopped cauliflower (about 1 medium head)

1 (15-inch) prepared pizza crust

1 cup Creamy White Sauce (page 227) or store-bought dairy-free Alfredo sauce

4 cups loosely packed arugula, chopped

½ cup Ranch Dressing (page 217) or store-bought dairy-free ranch dressing

1. Preheat the oven to 400°F. Line a baking sheet with parchment paper. Lightly oil a 15-inch pizza pan.

2. In a small bowl, whisk together the hot sauce, olive oil, garlic powder, and salt.

3. Put the cauliflower in a large bowl and pour the hot sauce mixture over it. Toss to coat well.

4. Spread the cauliflower in a single layer over the prepared baking sheet. Bake until fork-tender, about 20 minutes, flipping the pieces once after 10 minutes. Remove the cauliflower from the oven and increase the oven temperature to 450°F.

5. Place the pizza crust on the prepared pizza pan. Spread the white sauce over the crust in an even layer. Top it with the arugula, followed by the cauliflower. Bake for 12 to 15 minutes, until the crust is golden brown.

6. Drizzle the ranch dressing over the finished pizza and cut into slices to serve.

> **Substitution Tip:** If you'd rather have a barbecue cauliflower pizza, omit the olive oil and hot sauce and toss the cauliflower with ½ cup barbecue sauce.

**PER SERVING:** CALORIES: 685; FAT: 48G; SATURATED FAT: 18G; CHOLESTEROL: 0G; PROTEIN: 15G; FIBER: 6G; SODIUM: 987MG

# BROCCOLI BAC'UN PIZZA

KID-FRIENDLY, 30-MINUTE MEAL

**SERVES 4 | PREP TIME:** 10 MINUTES | **COOK TIME:** 20 MINUTES

When I was in college, I worked evenings in a store. After closing, my coworkers and I would head across the street to a diner for some after-work grub. I was a newly minted vegetarian, and my go-to order was a broccoli and cheddar pita. It was simply a toasted pita topped with steamed broccoli and melted cheddar, and I loved it. This pizza is a grown-up version of that late-night meal, and you don't have to wait until closing time to enjoy it.

2 teaspoons neutral-flavored vegetable oil, plus more for the pizza pan

2 garlic cloves, minced

2 scallions, sliced

5 cups chopped broccoli (cut into bite-size florets)

1 (15-inch) prepared pizza crust

1 cup Marinara (page 226) or store-bought tomato sauce

1 batch Tempeh Bac'un (page 233), or 16 ounces store-bought tempeh bacon, cooked according to the package instructions, chopped

2 cups Say Cheese! Sauce (page 228), store-bought nondairy cheese sauce, or shredded nondairy cheddar cheese

1. Preheat the oven to 450°F. Lightly oil a 15-inch pizza pan.

2. In a large skillet, heat the oil over medium-high heat until it shimmers. Add the garlic, scallions, and broccoli and cook for about 5 minutes, until the broccoli turns bright green and softens.

3. Put the pizza crust on the prepared pizza pan. Spread the marinara sauce evenly over the crust. Top with the broccoli and tempeh bac'un. Drizzle on the cheese sauce.

4. Bake for 12 to 15 minutes, until the crust is golden brown and the cheese sauce is bubbling. Cut into wedges to serve.

> **Variation Tip:** I've topped my pizza with broccoli, but tempeh bac'un pairs well with lots of other veggies. Try steamed spinach and caramelized onions, or roasted Brussels sprouts and thinly sliced fresh tomatoes.

**PER SERVING:** CALORIES: 764; FAT: 42G; SATURATED FAT: 7G; CHOLESTEROL: 0G; PROTEIN: 31G; FIBER: 12G; SODIUM: 1,901MG

# KALE AND SQUASH CASSEROLE

SOY-FREE, KID-FRIENDLY

**SERVES 6 | PREP TIME:** 10 MINUTES, PLUS 2 HOURS SOAKING TIME |
**COOK TIME:** 55 MINUTES

The word "casserole" has a vintage vibe to it, conjuring up images of colorful Pyrex bakeware and Grandma's kitchen table. Casseroles seemed to have fallen out of fashion for a while, but they're back, baby! And rightly so. There's nothing cozier than a casserole hot from the oven, especially on chilly autumn evenings. Old meets new in this recipe—a modern dish with a retro flair that even Grandma would approve of.

Vegetable oil, for the baking dish

1½ cups raw cashews, soaked for 2 hours, drained, and rinsed

¾ cup water, plus more as needed

3 tablespoons nutritional yeast

3 tablespoons fresh lemon juice

1½ tablespoons Dijon mustard

3 garlic cloves, minced

½ teaspoon salt

¼ teaspoon freshly ground black pepper

1 medium butternut squash (about 2½ pounds), peeled, seeded, and diced

6 cups loosely packed finely chopped kale leaves (1 large bunch)

½ cup panko bread crumbs

1. Preheat the oven to 400°F. Lightly oil a 9-by-13-inch baking dish.

2. In a blender, combine the cashews, water, nutritional yeast, lemon juice, mustard, garlic, salt, and pepper and blend until smooth and creamy. Add a little more water if the mixture seems too thick.

3. Toss the squash and kale together in the prepared baking dish. Pour the cashew mixture over it and gently stir to combine.

4. Cover the baking dish with aluminum foil and bake for 40 minutes. Remove the foil, sprinkle evenly with the panko, and bake for another 10 to 15 minutes, until the panko is golden brown and the squash is tender. Serve.

**Technique Tip:** To prepare your squash, use a vegetable peeler to remove the skin. Cut the neck of the squash just above the bulb and slice the neck in half lengthwise. Cut each half into sticks, 1 to 1½ inches long, then cut each stick into cubes. Use a spoon to dig out the seeds and stringy bits from the bulb, then cut the bulb into 1- to 1½-inch dice. If you want to skip this altogether, you can buy prechopped squash; you'll need 4 to 5 cups.

PER SERVING: CALORIES: 327; FAT: 17G; SATURATED FAT: 3G; CHOLESTEROL: 0G; PROTEIN: 12G; FIBER: 6G; SODIUM: 560MG

# SPINACH ARTICHOKE GALETTE

NUT-FREE, KID-FRIENDLY

**SERVES 6 | PREP TIME:** 15 MINUTES | **COOK TIME:** 45 MINUTES

"Galette" is a fancy word for a messy pie. They're usually free-form pies made without the pie pan, with the crust partially folded over the filling. They can be made sweet for dessert or savory for supper. I like to think of savory galettes as a cross between a tart and a pizza. I've made this one with spinach and artichokes, turning my favorite dip into dinner.

FOR THE CRUST

**2 cups whole wheat flour**

**½ cup ice-cold water**

**¼ cup olive oil**

**½ teaspoon salt**

FOR THE FILLING

**1 (8-ounce) package frozen spinach, thawed, drained, squeezed dry, and chopped**

**1 (14-ounce) can artichoke hearts, drained and chopped**

**¼ cup sun-dried tomatoes, sliced**

**¼ cup kalamata olives, sliced**

**1 cup Tofu Ricotta (page 229) or store-bought nondairy ricotta**

**1 teaspoon neutral-flavored vegetable oil**

**¼ teaspoon salt**

**2 tablespoons sliced fresh basil leaves**

1. Preheat the oven to 350°F.

2. **Make the crust:** In a large bowl, combine the flour, water, oil, and salt. Put a piece of parchment paper on a flat surface and place the dough on it. Use a rolling pin to roll it out into a round about 15 inches in diameter. Gently transfer the dough, still on the parchment paper, to a baking sheet.

3. **Add the filling:** Top the crust with the spinach, artichoke hearts, sun-dried tomatoes, and olives, leaving a 2-inch border. Dollop the ricotta on top of the vegetables. Gently fold the exposed dough over the filling, pleating it if necessary and leaving the filling at the center uncovered. Brush the dough with the oil and sprinkle with the salt.

4. Bake for 40 to 45 minutes, until the crust is golden brown. Remove the pan from the oven and top the galette with the basil. Set aside to cool for about 10 minutes before slicing and serving.

**Variation Tip:** To make a chard and mushroom galette, replace the spinach and artichoke hearts with 4 cups chopped Swiss chard and 2 cups chopped mushrooms. Sauté the chard and mushrooms in a little vegetable oil for 5 to 10 minutes to soften them before using them to top the galette in step 3.

PER SERVING: CALORIES: 298; FAT: 13G; SATURATED FAT: 2G; CHOLESTEROL: 0G; PROTEIN: 11G; FIBER: 10G; SODIUM: 401MG

# SAVORY ONION TART

**SERVES 6 | PREP TIME:** 15 MINUTES | **COOK TIME:** 1 HOUR 5 MINUTES

I grew up despising onions. I found their pungent bite a little strong for my developing tastes. I've since grown to enjoy them ("love" is too strong a word for my current feelings). If you, too, don't enjoy them, this tart might win you over. Be sure to use sweet onions, such as Vidalia, and give them enough time to caramelize, which will make them even sweeter.

### FOR THE CRUST

Vegetable oil, for the tart pan

2 cups whole wheat flour

½ cup ice-cold water

¼ cup olive oil

½ teaspoon salt

### FOR THE FILLING

2 teaspoons neutral-flavored vegetable oil

4 sweet onions, thinly sliced

2 tablespoons balsamic vinegar

1 teaspoon salt, divided

1 (14-ounce) package extra-firm tofu, drained and pressed (see Tip, page 18)

¼ cup nutritional yeast

¼ cup plain unsweetened Almond Milk (page 214) or store-bought nondairy milk

2 tablespoons fresh lemon juice

1 teaspoon Dijon mustard

1 teaspoon dried thyme

1. **Make the crust:** Preheat the oven to 350°F. Lightly oil a 9-inch tart pan or pie pan.

2. In a large bowl, combine the flour, water, olive oil, and salt. Put a piece of parchment paper on a flat surface and place the dough on it. Use a rolling pin to roll the dough into a round, about 13 inches in diameter. Gently pick up the dough round and place it in the prepared pan. Press it into all the crevices and trim away any excess dough. Place the crust in the refrigerator while you prepare the filling.

3. **Make the filling:** In a large skillet, heat the oil over medium heat until it shimmers. Add the onions, vinegar, and ½ teaspoon of the salt. Cook, stirring occasionally, for about 20 minutes, until the onions are browned and fragrant.

4. Meanwhile, crumble the tofu into a food processor. Add the nutritional yeast, almond milk, lemon juice, mustard, thyme, and remaining ½ teaspoon salt and process until the mixture resembles ricotta cheese.

5. In a large bowl, stir together the cooked onions and the tofu mixture until well incorporated. Spoon the filling into the prepared crust.

6. Bake for 40 to 45 minutes, until the top is golden brown and the filling is firm. Set aside to cool for about 10 minutes before slicing and serving.

PER SERVING: CALORIES: 391; FAT: 16G; SATURATED FAT: 2G; CHOLESTEROL: 0G; PROTEIN: 17G; FIBER: 7G; SODIUM: 821MG

# MUSHROOM WELLINGTON

NUT-FREE, SOY-FREE, KID-FRIENDLY

**SERVES 6 | PREP TIME:** 15 MINUTES | **COOK TIME:** 55 MINUTES

Beef Wellington is a UK favorite, and it's super easy to veganize using hearty portabellas. I like to make this recipe for holidays and special occasions, and sometimes those special occasions include random Thursdays.

2 tablespoons
    neutral-flavored vegetable
    oil, divided

1 yellow onion, diced

2 garlic cloves, minced

6 large portabella
    mushrooms, stems
    trimmed, cut into
    1-inch-thick slices

¼ cup dry red wine

2 tablespoons
    balsamic vinegar

1 teaspoon Dijon mustard

1 tablespoon chopped fresh
    rosemary leaves

1 tablespoon chopped
    fresh thyme

½ teaspoon salt

¼ teaspoon freshly ground
    black pepper

5 cups loosely packed baby
    spinach (about 5 ounces)

1 sheet frozen puff pastry,
    thawed (see Tip)

1. Preheat the oven to 400°F. Line a baking sheet with parchment paper.

2. In a large skillet over medium-high heat, heat 1 tablespoon of the oil until it shimmers. Add the onion and cook for 5 minutes, or until it begins to soften. Add the garlic and mushrooms and cook, stirring often, until the mushrooms begin to soften, about 5 minutes more.

3. Add the wine, vinegar, mustard, rosemary, thyme, salt, and pepper to the pan and cook, stirring occasionally, until all the liquid has been absorbed, about 10 minutes. Add the spinach and cook for another minute or two, until it wilts.

4. Use a rolling pin to roll out the puff pastry to about 9 by 13 inches. Place it on the prepared baking sheet. Spoon the mushroom mixture lengthwise over the center third of the pastry. Fold the sides over the filling and seal the edges by pressing them together. Carefully flip the pastry so the seam is on the bottom. Use a paring knife to gently score the top in a crisscross pattern. Brush the top of the pastry with the remaining tablespoon oil.

5. Bake for 30 to 35 minutes, until golden brown. Set aside to cool for 10 minutes before slicing and serving.

> **Ingredient Tip:** Most brands of puff pastry are vegan, but—as with every kind of packaged food—be sure to read the label before buying it. Thaw the pastry according to the package instructions before making your Wellington.

PER SERVING: CALORIES: 321; FAT: 21G; SATURATED FAT: 8G; CHOLESTEROL: 0G; PROTEIN: 6G; FIBER: 3G; SODIUM: 339MG

Super Easy Tostadas,
page 144

# CHAPTER EIGHT

# SPILL THE BEANS

## LEGUME AND GRAIN MAINS

# SUPER EASY TOSTADAS

GLUTEN-FREE, SOY-FREE, KID-FRIENDLY, 30-MINUTE MEAL, ONE-PAN/ONE-POT

**MAKES 4 TOSTADAS | PREP TIME:** 15 MINUTES | **COOK TIME:** 10 MINUTES

The word *tostada* means "toasted" in Spanish, and these beauties get their name because the tortillas they're made with are toasted beforehand. If you have an old package of tortillas languishing at the back of the fridge, use them here. Much like stale bread being turned into toast, old tortillas do well when transformed into tostadas. I like to pile 'em high with lots of fixin's, so feel free to add some nondairy sour cream, salsa, guacamole, and hot sauce.

4 small (6- to 8-inch) corn tortillas

1 teaspoon neutral-flavored vegetable oil

½ cup chopped red onion (about ½ onion)

2 garlic cloves, minced

1 jalapeño pepper, seeded and chopped

1 batch Refried Beans (page 232) or 1 (14-ounce) can store-bought refried beans (see Tip)

4 cups chopped romaine lettuce

2 tomatoes, diced

1 avocado, pitted, peeled, and diced

1 cup Say Cheese! Sauce (page 228), Creamy Queso Dip (page 32), store-bought nondairy cheese sauce, or shredded nondairy cheddar cheese

¼ cup chopped fresh cilantro leaves

1 lime, cut into wedges

1. Preheat the oven to 350°F.

2. Place the tortillas on a baking sheet. Bake for 10 minutes, or until crisp and golden brown.

3. Meanwhile, in a medium skillet, heat the oil over medium-high heat until it shimmers. Add the onion and cook, stirring frequently for 5 minutes, or until it softens and begins to brown. Add the garlic and jalapeño and cook for a minute or two more, until the garlic is fragrant.

4. Spread about ⅓ cup of the refried beans over each tortilla. Top each with some of the onion mixture, 1 cup of the lettuce, some of the tomato and avocado, and ¼ cup of the cheese sauce. Garnish each with 1 tablespoon of the cilantro and serve with the lime wedges alongside.

**Ingredient Tip:** If you're using canned refried beans, be sure to check the label, as some brands are made with lard or other animal fat.

PER SERVING (1 TOSTADA): CALORIES: 387; FAT: 16G; SATURATED FAT: 3G; CHOLESTEROL: 0G; PROTEIN: 20G; FIBER: 21G; SODIUM: 372MG

# SPICY CHICKPEA STIR-FRY

**SERVES 4 | PREP TIME:** 5 MINUTES | **COOK TIME:** 16 MINUTES

It's been a minute since I talked about my love of spicy stir-fries. This one was inspired by Szechuan chicken. Not everyone can take the heat, so feel free to cut back on the red pepper flakes and dried chile peppers if you like things less fiery. Some people eat the chiles, but I don't. I include them for flavor but draw the line at consuming them. (I once ate one accidentally, and it was so hot that I swear I could see sounds. Don't say you weren't warned.)

½ cup reduced-sodium soy sauce or tamari

2 tablespoons unseasoned rice vinegar

3 garlic cloves, minced

1 tablespoon minced peeled fresh ginger

1 tablespoon agave nectar

2 teaspoons cornstarch

½ to 1 teaspoon red pepper flakes

½ teaspoon freshly ground black pepper

2 teaspoons neutral-flavored vegetable oil

1 red bell pepper, seeded and chopped

1 green bell pepper, seeded and chopped

6 to 10 dried Asian chile peppers

2 (15-ounce) cans chickpeas, drained and rinsed

4 cups cooked brown rice

¼ cup chopped roasted peanuts

2 scallions, sliced

1. In a small bowl, combine the soy sauce, vinegar, garlic, ginger, agave, cornstarch, red pepper flakes, and black pepper.

2. In a large skillet, heat the oil over medium-high heat until it shimmers. Add the bell peppers and cook, stirring frequently, until they have softened, about 10 minutes. Add the dried chiles and chickpeas and cook until the chickpeas are heated through, 2 to 3 minutes more. Pour the sauce into the pan and stir to coat. Cook for another 2 to 3 minutes, until the sauce has thickened.

3. Divide the rice evenly among 4 plates. Top with some of the chickpea mixture. Garnish with the peanuts and scallions to serve.

**Substitution Tip:** Four diced Chic'un Patties (page 234) or store-bought vegan chicken patties, or 16 ounces chopped cooked seitan can be used in this recipe instead of the chickpeas. They'll need to be cooked a little longer than the chickpeas do when added to the pan in step 2; I suggest cooking them for 5 to 10 minutes, until they begin to brown.

PER SERVING: CALORIES: 516; FAT: 12G; SATURATED FAT: 3G; CHOLESTEROL: 0G; PROTEIN: 20G; FIBER: 14G; SODIUM: 1,965MG

# BLACK PEPPER CHIC'UN

NUT-FREE, 30-MINUTE MEAL, ONE-PAN/ONE-POT

**SERVES 4 | PREP TIME:** 5 MINUTES | **COOK TIME:** 20 MINUTES

Winner, winner, chic'un dinner! Dennis (that's my sweetie) loves black pepper so much that he'll automatically give the pepper grinder a few twists over his plate no matter what he's eating. I oblige his pepper passion from time to time by making meals centered around it. He loves this recipe, and yes, he does add more pepper to it. Add some broccoli or mushrooms if you want to make sure you're getting in your daily veggies.

¼ cup vegetable stock

¼ cup reduced-sodium soy sauce or tamari

1 tablespoon unseasoned rice vinegar

1 tablespoon minced peeled fresh ginger

2 teaspoons cornstarch

1½ teaspoons freshly ground black pepper, plus more (optional) for serving

2 teaspoons neutral-flavored vegetable oil

1 cup diced yellow onion (about 1 medium)

4 celery stalks, thinly sliced

3 garlic cloves, minced

4 Chic'un Patties (page 234) or store-bought vegan chicken patties, diced

4 cups cooked brown rice

2 tablespoons toasted sesame seeds

1. In a small bowl, whisk together the stock, soy sauce, vinegar, ginger, cornstarch, and pepper.

2. In a large skillet, heat the oil over medium-high heat until it shimmers. Add the onion and celery and cook, stirring frequently, for 5 minutes, or until they soften. Add the garlic to the pan and cook for another minute or two, until fragrant. Add the chic'un patties to the pan and cook, stirring frequently, for 7 to 10 minutes more, until they brown. Pour the sauce into the pan and stir to coat. Cook for another 2 to 3 minutes, until the sauce has thickened.

3. Divide the rice evenly among 4 plates. Top with some of the chic'un mixture. Garnish with the sesame seeds and more pepper (if using) to serve.

> **Substitution Tip:** If you'd like to make your dish gluten-free, use 4 sliced large portabella mushrooms in place of the chic'un patties, and make sure to use wheat-free tamari instead of the soy sauce.

PER SERVING: CALORIES: 489; FAT: 17G; SATURATED FAT: 4G; CHOLESTEROL: 0G; PROTEIN: 28G; FIBER: 8G; SODIUM: 1,643MG

# TOFU FRIED RICE

NUT-FREE, KID-FRIENDLY, ONE-PAN/ONE-POT

**SERVES 4 | PREP TIME:** 10 MINUTES | **COOK TIME:** 25 MINUTES

I think it's funny to see characters on TV eating lo mein and fried rice straight out of take-out containers. Who actually does that IRL? I prefer to eat my fried rice from a big shallow bowl with a fork. I'm not going to stop you if you want to serve this dish in paper cartons so you feel like the star of a sitcom, but a plate is a much easier vessel for dinner.

4 teaspoons neutral-flavored vegetable oil, divided

1 (14-ounce) package extra-firm tofu, drained, pressed (see Tip, page 18), and diced

2 scallions, sliced

2 garlic cloves, minced

1 tablespoon minced peeled fresh ginger

5 cups chopped broccoli (cut into bite-size florets)

1 carrot, diced

1 cup peas

3 cups cooked brown rice, cooled

2 tablespoons reduced-sodium soy sauce or tamari

2 tablespoons unseasoned rice vinegar

2 tablespoons toasted sesame seeds

1. In a large pan, heat 2 teaspoons of the oil over medium-high heat until it shimmers. Add the tofu, and cook, stirring frequently, until it begins to brown, about 10 minutes. Remove from the pan and set aside on a plate.

2. In the same pan, heat the remaining 2 teaspoons oil over medium-high heat until it shimmers. Add the scallions, garlic, and ginger and cook for 2 to 3 minutes, until they soften.

3. Add the broccoli, carrot, and peas and cook, stirring frequently, for about 10 minutes, until they soften.

4. Add the rice and tofu to the pan, then add the soy sauce and vinegar and stir to coat. Cook, stirring frequently, until the rice is heated through, about 5 minutes more.

5. Divide the rice evenly among 4 plates and top with the sesame seeds to serve.

**Troubleshooting Tip:** Make sure your rice is completely cooled before using it in this recipe. Cooled rice is drier and firmer, and will fry easier. Warm rice contains more moisture and could turn mushy if used to make fried rice.

**PER SERVING:** CALORIES: 374; FAT: 14G; SATURATED FAT: 5G; CHOLESTEROL: 0G; PROTEIN: 18G; FIBER: 7G; SODIUM: 586MG

# PINEAPPLE FRIED QUINOA

**SERVES 4 | PREP TIME:** 10 MINUTES | **COOK TIME:** 20 MINUTES

Who needs separate recipes for vegetables, protein, and grains when you can have one dish that has it all? Throw in a fruit, and it's like a party on your plate. This meal gets bonus points for being quick and easy to make, too. If you want a flashy dinnertime centerpiece, serve your finished quinoa in a hollowed-out pineapple half.

2 teaspoons neutral-flavored vegetable oil

½ cup diced red onion (about ½ onion)

3 garlic cloves

1 tablespoon minced peeled fresh ginger

¼ teaspoon red pepper flakes (optional)

1 red bell pepper, seeded and diced

1½ cups diced pineapple

½ cup unsalted cashews, chopped

1 cup shelled edamame

3 cups cooked quinoa, cooled

3 tablespoons reduced-sodium soy sauce or tamari

1 tablespoon fresh lime juice

2 scallions, sliced

1. In a large pan, heat the oil over medium-high heat until it shimmers. Add the onion and cook, stirring frequently, for 5 minutes, or until it softens. Add the garlic, ginger, and red pepper flakes (if using) and cook for another 2 to 3 minutes, until fragrant.

2. Add the bell pepper and pineapple to the pan. Cook for about 5 minutes, until the pepper softens and the pineapple begins to brown around the edges. Add the cashews and cook for another minute or two.

3. Add the edamame and quinoa to the pan, then add the soy sauce and lime juice and stir. Cook, stirring frequently, until the rice is heated through, about 5 minutes more.

4. Divide the quinoa evenly among 4 plates. Garnish with the scallions to serve.

**Substitution Tip:** Cooked rice can be used in place of the quinoa. If you're allergic to pineapple, try mango in its place.

PER SERVING: CALORIES: 396; FAT: 15G; SATURATED FAT: 4G; CHOLESTEROL: 0G; PROTEIN: 16G; FIBER: 9G; SODIUM: 773MG

# CURRY IN A HURRY

**SERVES 4 | PREP TIME:** 5 MINUTES **| COOK TIME:** 25 MINUTES

The word "curry" has a double meaning. It can be a spice blend or the dish that's made with it. Indian curries are made with ground spices, whereas the Thai variety are usually made with a paste. This recipe is based on a favorite Indian dish known as dal—and the word "dal" has a double meaning, too. It's used to describe beans as well as the thick stew made with them. Serve the curry as is or with cooked rice.

1 teaspoon neutral-flavored vegetable oil

1 cup diced onion (about 1 medium)

3 garlic cloves, minced

1 tablespoon minced peeled fresh ginger

2 teaspoons curry powder (see Tip)

1 teaspoon ground cumin

1 teaspoon ground turmeric

¼ teaspoon freshly ground black pepper

3 cups vegetable stock

1 (14-ounce) can diced tomatoes

1 (15-ounce) can chickpeas, drained and rinsed

½ cup dried red lentils

5 cups loosely packed chopped baby spinach

½ teaspoon salt

1 tablespoon fresh lemon juice

1. In a large pot, heat the oil over medium-high heat until it shimmers. Add the onion and cook for 5 minutes, or until softened. Add the garlic, ginger, curry powder, cumin, turmeric, and pepper and cook for another 2 to 3 minutes, until fragrant.

2. Add the stock, tomatoes, chickpeas, and lentils to the pot. Bring to a boil, then reduce the heat to medium. Cover the pot and cook for 10 to 15 minutes, until the lentils are tender.

3. Stir in the spinach and salt. Cook for 2 to 3 minutes more, until the spinach wilts.

4. Remove the pan from the heat. Stir in the lemon juice. Serve.

**Ingredient Tip:** In traditional Indian cooking, chefs prefer to grind their own spices and mix their own spice blends for curry. We lazy cooks reach for premixed blends labeled "curry powder," and the flavor of your finished dish will depend on the type of curry powder you use. Some are sweet, whereas others are hot. I like a mix of both.

**PER SERVING:** CALORIES: 228; FAT: 4G; SATURATED FAT: 1G; CHOLESTEROL: 0G; PROTEIN: 13G; FIBER: 10G; SODIUM: 561MG

# PEANUT TEMPEH CURRY

ONE-PAN/ONE-POT

**SERVES 4 | PREP TIME:** 10 MINUTES | **COOK TIME:** 30 MINUTES

I think we can all agree that peanut sauce makes everything better. I especially like it with broccoli, as all those little florets like to really hold on to the sauce, in much the same way I do. Serve this dish as is or with cooked rice.

1 (14-ounce) can full-fat coconut milk

1 cup vegetable stock

½ cup creamy natural peanut butter

2 tablespoons reduced-sodium soy sauce or tamari

2 tablespoons fresh lime juice

2 tablespoons red curry paste

4 teaspoons vegetable oil, divided

2 (8-ounce) packages tempeh, cut into 1½-inch cubes (see Tip)

½ cup diced yellow onion (about ½ onion)

3 garlic cloves, minced

1 tablespoon minced peeled fresh ginger

5 cups chopped broccoli (cut into bite-size florets)

¼ cup chopped roasted peanuts

¼ cup chopped fresh cilantro leaves

1. In a small bowl, whisk together the coconut milk, stock, peanut butter, soy sauce, lime juice, and curry paste. Set aside.

2. In a large skillet, heat 2 teaspoons of the oil over medium-high heat until it shimmers. Add the tempeh and cook, flipping the pieces frequently, for about 10 minutes, until they begin to brown. Transfer the cooked tempeh to a plate and set aside.

3. In the same pan, combine the remaining 2 teaspoons oil and the onion. Cook, stirring frequently, for 5 minutes, until the onion softens. Add the garlic and ginger and cook for another 2 to 3 minutes, until fragrant. And the broccoli and cook until it begins to soften and turn bright green, about 5 minutes more.

4. Return the tempeh to the pan and add the peanut sauce. Bring the mixture to a boil, then reduce the heat to medium. Simmer the mixture for 5 to 10 minutes, until the peanut sauce is heated through and the vegetables are tender.

5. Divide the curry evenly among 4 bowls. Top with the peanuts and cilantro to serve.

**Ingredient Tip:** Some people don't like the fermented flavor of tempeh. That fermented taste can be dissipated by simmering the tempeh in vegetable stock or water for about 20 minutes or steaming it for about 15 minutes.

**PER SERVING:** CALORIES: 767; FAT: 62G; SATURATED FAT: 25G; CHOLESTEROL: 0G; PROTEIN: 37G; FIBER: 9G; SODIUM: 640MG

# POLENTA MARINARA

NUT-FREE, SOY-FREE, KID-FRIENDLY

**SERVES 4 | PREP TIME:** 10 MINUTES | **COOK TIME:** 30 MINUTES

Who says marinara is just for pasta? I like to pour it over warm polenta. If you have never tried polenta marinara, you need to hurry up and right this wrong. It's cozy and comforting in a way that spaghetti could only dream of. Top the polenta with beans and 'shrooms, and you have yourself a complete meal.

3½ cups vegetable stock

1½ cups quick-cooking polenta

3 tablespoons nutritional yeast

2 tablespoons plus 2 teaspoons olive oil, divided

½ teaspoon salt

¼ teaspoon freshly ground black pepper

1 cup diced yellow onion (about 1 onion)

3 garlic cloves, minced

2 cups chopped cremini or white button mushrooms (about 8 ounces)

1 (15-ounce) can cannellini beans, drained and rinsed

1 teaspoon dried basil

1 teaspoon dried oregano

4 cups Marinara (page 226) or store-bought marinara sauce, warmed

1. In a large pot, bring the stock to a boil over medium-high heat. Slowly whisk in the polenta. Reduce the heat to medium and cook, stirring frequently, until the mixture is thick and smooth and pulls away from the pot, 5 to 10 minutes. Whisk in the nutritional yeast, 2 tablespoons of the olive oil, the salt, and the pepper. Keep the polenta warm while you prepare the mushrooms.

2. In a large skillet, heat the remaining 2 teaspoons oil over medium-high heat until it shimmers. Add the onion and cook for 5 minutes, or until it begins to brown. Add the garlic and cook for another 2 to 3 minutes, until fragrant. Add the mushrooms, beans, basil, and oregano, and cook for another 10 minutes or so, until the mushrooms soften and begin to brown.

3. Divide the polenta evenly among 4 bowls. Top each with 1 cup of the marinara, then divide the mushroom mixture evenly among the bowls to serve.

**Variation Tip:** If you'd prefer your polenta in solid form, pour it into a parchment paper–lined baking dish and pop it in the refrigerator for an hour or so to set. Slice it into slabs and brush each side with a little oil, then grill or panfry it for about 5 minutes per side; it can also be baked in a preheated 450°F oven for 15 to 20 minutes.

PER SERVING: CALORIES: 465; FAT: 9G; SATURATED FAT: 1G; CHOLESTEROL: 0G; PROTEIN: 17G; FIBER: 8G; SODIUM: 912MG

# CHICKPEA À LA QUEEN

SOY-FREE, ONE-PAN/ONE-POT

**SERVES 4 | PREP TIME:** 10 MINUTES | **COOK TIME:** 25 MINUTES

This recipe is a kinder, more peas-full version of chicken à la king. (See what I did there?) Since I consider myself to be queen of the kitchen, I've swapped monarchs. It *is* a meal fit for royalty, as it consists of luxurious mushrooms and chickpeas served in a decadent creamless cream sauce. *Yaaas, queen!* Chicken à la king is often served over biscuits or toast, but I like to serve this dish over rice or pasta.

2 teaspoons neutral-flavored vegetable oil

1 cup diced yellow onion (about 1 onion)

2 cups chopped cremini or white button mushrooms (about 8 ounces)

1 red bell pepper, seeded and diced

½ cup whole wheat flour

2 cups plain unsweetened Almond Milk (page 214) or store-bought nondairy milk

½ cup dry white wine or sherry

2 (14-ounce) cans chickpeas, drained and rinsed

½ cup peas

½ teaspoon ground sage

½ teaspoon dried thyme

½ teaspoon garlic powder

½ teaspoon onion powder

½ teaspoon sweet paprika

½ teaspoon salt

¼ teaspoon freshly ground black pepper

¼ cup chopped fresh parsley leaves

1. In a large pot, heat the oil over medium-high heat until it shimmers. Add the onion and cook for 5 minutes, or until it begins to soften. Add the mushrooms and bell pepper and cook for 5 minutes more, or until they begin to soften.

2. Sprinkle the vegetables with the flour and stir to coat. Cook for 2 to 3 minutes, until the flour looks paste-like.

3. Reduce the heat to medium. Gradually add the almond milk to the pot, whisking as you go to avoid lumps. Stir in the wine. Cook, stirring continually, until the mixture thickens, 3 to 5 minutes.

4. Stir in the chickpeas, peas, sage, thyme, garlic powder, onion powder, paprika, salt, and black pepper. Cook for another 3 to 5 minutes, until the chickpeas are warmed through. Garnish with the parsley to serve.

**Substitution Tip:** You can use 4 Chic'un Patties (page 234) or store-bought vegan chicken patties, 16 ounces seitan, or 14 ounces extra-firm tofu in this recipe in place of the chickpeas. Cook them in a little oil in a large pan over medium-high heat for about 5 minutes on each side to brown them before adding them to the recipe in step 4.

**PER SERVING:** CALORIES: 370; FAT: 8G; SATURATED FAT: 2G; CHOLESTEROL: 0G; PROTEIN: 17G; FIBER: 13G; SODIUM: 603MG

# SCANDINAVIAN-INSPIRED BEANBALLS

KID-FRIENDLY

**SERVES 4 | PREP TIME:** 15 MINUTES | **COOK TIME:** 30 MINUTES

You know veganism has almost reached the tipping point when you can get meatless meatballs at a certain furniture store while shopping for bookcases and heart-shaped pillows. I'd rather make them myself at home, which is *waaaay* easier than navigating a mazelike store. Serve your beanballs on their own or over pasta, rice, or roasted potatoes.

### FOR THE BEANBALLS

1 cup quick-cooking rolled oats

1 (14-ounce) can lentils, drained and rinsed

2 cups chopped cremini or white button mushrooms (about 8 ounces)

½ cup diced yellow onion

2 garlic cloves, minced

2 tablespoons tomato paste

2 tablespoons flax meal (ground flaxseed)

1 tablespoon reduced-sodium soy sauce or tamari

½ teaspoon salt

¼ teaspoon freshly ground black pepper

### FOR THE GRAVY

¼ cup olive oil

½ cup whole wheat flour

2 cups vegetable stock

½ cup plain unsweetened Almond Milk (page 214) or store-bought nondairy milk

1 tablespoon reduced-sodium soy sauce or tamari

2 teaspoons Dijon mustard

½ teaspoon salt

1. **Make the beanballs:** Preheat the oven to 400°F. Line a baking sheet with parchment paper.

2. In a food processor, process the oats until they resemble a coarse flour. Add the lentils, mushrooms, onion, garlic, tomato paste, flax meal, soy sauce, salt, and pepper. Pulse until well combined.

3. Form the mixture into balls, 1 to 1½ inches in diameter. (You should have 20 to 24 balls total.) Place them on the prepared baking sheet.

4. Bake the balls for 30 minutes, or until golden brown and firm, flipping them once halfway through.

5. **Meanwhile, make the gravy:** Heat a medium pot over medium heat. Add the oil and flour and whisk until they form a paste.

6. Slowly whisk in the stock, stirring as you go to prevent lumps. Whisk in the almond milk, soy sauce, mustard, and salt. Cook, whisking continually, until the mixture thickens, 5 to 10 minutes.

7. Add the meatballs to the gravy and serve.

> **Variation Tip:** If you'd preer beanballs with an Italian flair, add ½ teaspoon each of dried basil, oregano, rosemary, and thyme to the lentil mixture in step 2. Serve your beanballs with Marinara (page 226) or store-bought pasta sauce.

**PER SERVING:** CALORIES: 414; FAT: 18G; SATURATED FAT: 2G; CHOLESTEROL: 0G; PROTEIN: 17G; FIBER: 12G; SODIUM: 1,022MG

# LEMON ASPARAGUS RISOTTO

NUT-FREE, SOY-FREE

**SERVES 4 | PREP TIME:** 10 MINUTES | **COOK TIME:** 35 MINUTES

Risotto seems like a labor-intensive undertaking, but it's actually pretty easy to make. It does require constant stirring, but rather than get bored, I suggest finding your inner Zen and just breathing into it. You might not need all the vegetable stock that's called for here, but I still follow the Girl Scout motto, and find it's best to be prepared.

**4 cups vegetable stock**

**1 pound asparagus, chopped into 1½-inch pieces**

**¼ cup olive oil**

**2 medium shallots, chopped (about ½ cup)**

**1 cup uncooked Arborio rice**

**½ cup dry white wine**

**¼ cup nutritional yeast**

**1 tablespoon grated lemon zest**

**2 tablespoons fresh lemon juice**

**½ teaspoon salt**

**¼ teaspoon freshly ground black pepper**

> **Technique Tip:**
> As the risotto cooks, you may need to adjust the heat under the pan. The stock in the pan with the rice should always remain at a simmer or gentle boil.

1. In a medium pot, bring the stock to a simmer over medium-low heat.

2. Bring a medium pot of water to a boil over medium-high heat and have a large bowl of ice water ready. Add the asparagus to the boiling water and cook for 2 to 3 minutes, until it turns bright green. Using a slotted spoon or skimmer, transfer the asparagus to the ice water and let cool for 2 to 3 minutes. Drain and set aside on a plate.

3. In a large pan, heat the oil over medium heat. Add the shallots and cook for 5 minutes, or until they begin to soften.

4. Add the rice and cook, stirring continually, until the rice is completely coated in oil and the garlic is fragrant, 2 to 3 minutes.

5. Reduce the heat to medium. Add the wine to the pan and cook, stirring often, until the wine has been absorbed by the rice.

6. Ladle ¾ cup of the warm stock into the pan with the rice. Cook, stirring frequently, until all the stock has been absorbed by the rice. Continue to add stock to the pan in ¾-cup increments, stirring frequently and allowing the stock to be totally absorbed by the rice before adding more. The rice is done when it's translucent around the edges and creamy in consistency. This should take around 20 minutes.

7. Stir in the asparagus, nutritional yeast, lemon zest, lemon juice, salt, and pepper. Serve.

**PER SERVING:** CALORIES: 374; FAT: 14G; SATURATED FAT: 2G; CHOLESTEROL: 0G; PROTEIN: 9G; FIBER: 4G; SODIUM: 663MG

# RED BEANS AND RICE

NUT-FREE, SOY-FREE

**SERVES 4 | PREP TIME:** 10 MINUTES | **COOK TIME:** 45 MINUTES

I've had people tell me that they'd love to go vegan, but they're afraid they'll tire of rice and beans quickly. Where did this idea that all we vegans eat is rice and beans come from? Here's a whole cookbook to prove otherwise, with just this one little rice-and-beans recipe. And since it's loaded with flavorful veggies and lots of herbs and spices, I can pretty much guarantee you won't tire of it anytime soon.

2½ cup vegetable stock or water

1¼ cups uncooked brown rice

2 teaspoons neutral-flavored vegetable oil

1 red onion, diced

2 garlic cloves, minced

1 green bell pepper, seeded and diced

3 celery stalks, chopped

2 (14-ounce) cans kidney beans, drained and rinsed

1 teaspoon dried oregano

1 teaspoon dried thyme

½ teaspoon garlic powder

½ teaspoon ground cumin

½ teaspoon sweet paprika

½ teaspoon salt

¼ teaspoon freshly ground black pepper

¼ teaspoon cayenne pepper

2 scallions, sliced

1. In a medium pot, combine the stock and rice. Bring to a boil over medium-high heat, then reduce the heat to medium-low. Cover the pot and cook for 40 to 45 minutes, until all the liquid has been absorbed and the rice is tender. Remove the pan from the heat and set aside, covered, for 10 minutes.

2. Meanwhile, in a large pot, heat the oil over medium-high heat until it shimmers. Add the onion and cook for 5 minutes, or until it begins to soften. Add the garlic, bell pepper, and celery and cook, stirring occasionally, for 5 to 10 minutes more, until they soften. Stir in the beans, oregano, thyme, garlic powder, cumin, paprika, salt, black pepper, and cayenne and cook for 5 minutes more, or until the beans are heated through.

3. Divide the rice evenly among 4 plates. Top with the beans. Garnish with the scallions to serve.

**Time-Saving Tip:** Brown rice is more nutritious than the white variety, but white does have its merits, one of those being that it cooks much faster. White rice can be used here, if you want to speed things up; it takes between 15 and 20 minutes to cook.

PER SERVING: CALORIES: 411; FAT: 5G; SATURATED FAT: 2G; CHOLESTEROL: 0G; PROTEIN: 14G; FIBER: 4G; SODIUM: 518MG

# JUMPIN' JACK BLACK-EYED PEAS

NUT-FREE, SOY-FREE, 30-MINUTE MEAL, ONE-PAN/ONE-POT

**SERVES 4 | PREP TIME:** 10 MINUTES | **COOK TIME:** 20 MINUTES

This recipe is inspired by the Southern dish hoppin' John. It's traditionally served on New Year's Day to bring luck and prosperity for the year ahead, as some people believe black-eyed peas are symbolic of coins. Why wait till the beginning of the new year, though? I think we could all use a little extra luck from day to day, don't you agree? Serve this dish as is or over cooked rice or quinoa.

2 teaspoons neutral-flavored vegetable oil

1 yellow onion, diced

2 garlic cloves, minced

1 green bell pepper, seeded and diced

3 celery stalks, chopped

½ cup vegetable stock

½ teaspoon liquid smoke

10 ounces collard greens or kale, leaves stemmed and sliced into strips

1 (14-ounce) can diced tomatoes

1 (15-ounce) can black-eyed peas, drained and rinsed

½ teaspoon dried oregano

½ teaspoon dried thyme

½ teaspoon salt

¼ teaspoon smoked paprika

¼ teaspoon freshly ground black pepper

¼ teaspoon cayenne pepper

2 scallions, sliced

1. In a large pan, heat the oil over medium-high heat until it shimmers. Add the onion and cook for 5 minutes, or until it begins to soften. Add the garlic, bell pepper, and celery and cook, stirring occasionally, for 5 minutes more, or until they begin to soften.

2. Add the stock, liquid smoke, and collard greens to the pan. Cook, stirring frequently, until the collards have wilted and most of the liquid has been absorbed, about 5 minutes.

3. Add the tomatoes, black eyed peas, oregano, thyme, salt, paprika, black pepper, and cayenne to the pan. Cook, stirring frequently, for another 5 minutes, or until the tomatoes and beans are heated through.

4. Serve garnished with the scallions.

> **Variation Tip:** Omnivore hoppin' John is often made with ham hocks or bacon. You can add 1 cup chopped cooked Tempeh Bac'un (page 233) or store-bought vegan bacon or sausage to your dish in step 3, if you'd like.

**PER SERVING:** CALORIES: 168; FAT: 3G; SATURATED FAT: 2G; CHOLESTEROL: 0G; PROTEIN: 10G; FIBER: 12G; SODIUM: 373MG

# LENTIL LOAF

NUT-FREE, SOY-FREE, KID-FRIENDLY

**SERVES 6 | PREP TIME:** 10 MINUTES | **COOK TIME:** 1 HOUR

There was a time when I would make a lentil loaf for pretty much any special occasion. It's Thanksgiving? *Boom*—lentil loaf! Today's your birthday? Celebrate with a lentil loaf! We made it to Friday? TGI lentil loaf! I slowed down as vegan roasts and premade meatless loaves started to come on the market. Sometimes I find myself yearning for the simplicity of a cozy homemade lentil loaf, though—no special occasion necessary.

2 teaspoons neutral-flavored vegetable oil, plus more for the loaf pan

1 small yellow onion, diced

2 garlic cloves, minced

1 carrot, chopped

2 cups finely chopped cremini or white button mushrooms (about 8 ounces)

½ cup quick-cooking rolled oats

2 (15-ounce) cans brown lentils, drained and rinsed

2 cups cooked rice

2 tablespoons flax meal (ground flaxseed)

2 tablespoons tomato paste

1 teaspoon dried thyme

1 teaspoon dried sage

½ teaspoon salt

¼ teaspoon freshly ground black pepper

¼ cup ketchup

1 tablespoon pure maple syrup

1 tablespoon balsamic vinegar

1. Preheat the oven to 350°F. Lightly oil a 9-by-5-inch loaf pan.

2. In a large skillet, heat the oil over medium-high heat until it shimmers. Add the onion and cook for 5 minutes, or until it begins to soften. Add the garlic, carrots, and mushrooms and cook, stirring occasionally, for 10 minutes more, or until they soften.

3. In a food processor, pulse the oats until they resemble a coarse flour. Add the cooked vegetables, lentils, rice, flax meal, tomato paste, thyme, sage, salt, and pepper and pulse a few times just to incorporate everything (be careful not to process the mixture into a paste). Transfer the mixture to the prepared loaf pan.

4. Cover the loaf pan with aluminum foil and bake for 30 minutes.

5. Meanwhile, in a small bowl, stir together the ketchup, maple syrup, and vinegar.

6. Remove the foil from the pan and brush the ketchup mixture over the loaf. Return the loaf to the oven and bake for 15 minutes more. Remove the pan from the oven and set aside to cool slightly before slicing and serving.

PER SERVING: CALORIES: 285; FAT: 4G; SATURATED FAT: 2G; CHOLESTEROL: 0G; PROTEIN: 14G; FIBER: 15G; SODIUM: 304MG

# WHITE BEAN SHAKSHUKA

NUT-FREE, GLUTEN-FREE, KID-FRIENDLY, ONE-PAN/ONE-POT

**SERVES 4 | PREP TIME:** 10 MINUTES | **COOK TIME:** 30 MINUTES

Shakshuka is a dish that originated in North Africa and consists of eggs poached in a sauce of tomatoes, peppers, and onion, and it's easily veganized using tofu. I've also added some beans here, because that's how I roll. Shakshuka is often served for breakfast, but in some countries it's a dinner dish. You can think of it as "brinner," if you like. Serve the shakshuka as is or with cooked rice or roasted potatoes.

1 (14-ounce) package
  extra-firm tofu, drained
  and pressed (see Tip,
  page 18)

5 teaspoons neutral-flavored
  vegetable oil, divided

½ cup diced yellow onion
  (about ½ onion)

1 red bell pepper, seeded
  and diced

2 garlic cloves, minced

1 (28-ounce) can
  crushed tomatoes

1 (14-ounce) can navy
  beans, drained
  and rinsed

2 cups loosely packed
  baby spinach

1 teaspoon ground cumin

1 teaspoon smoked paprika

1 teaspoon dried oregano

½ teaspoon
  ground coriander

½ teaspoon salt

¼ teaspoon freshly ground
  black pepper

¼ cup chopped fresh
  parsley leaves

1. Cut your tofu into 8 slabs about ½ inch thick. Cut each slab into two triangles.

2. In a large skillet, heat 2 teaspoons of the oil over medium-high heat until it shimmers. Add the tofu and cook, undisturbed, for 5 minutes, or until browned slightly on the bottom. Flip the pieces, add another teaspoon of the oil to the pan, and cook for another 5 minutes. Transfer the cooked tofu to a plate and set aside.

3. In the same pan, heat the remaining 2 teaspoons oil over medium-high heat until it shimmers. Add the onion and cook for 5 minutes, or until it begins to soften. Add the bell pepper and garlic and cook, stirring occasionally, for 5 minutes more, or until they begin soften.

4. Stir in the tomatoes, beans, spinach, cumin, paprika, oregano, coriander, salt, and black pepper. Return the tofu to the pan and bring the mixture to a simmer. Cook for about 10 minutes, until the tomatoes have thickened slightly. Top with the parsley.

**Variation Tip:** For a green shakshuka, use a green bell pepper instead of the red one and add it to the pan along with 6 cups chopped Swiss chard or kale in step 3. Sauté until the pepper is soft and the greens are wilted. In step 4, omit the crushed tomatoes.

**PER SERVING:** CALORIES: 301; FAT: 14G; SATURATED FAT: 5G; CHOLESTEROL: 0G; PROTEIN: 18G; FIBER: 13G; SODIUM: 487MG

# TACO CASSEROLE

SOY-FREE, KID-FRIENDLY

**SERVES 6 | PREP TIME:** 15 MINUTES **| COOK TIME:** 40 MINUTES

Tacos and lasagna have both been favorites of mine since childhood. Tacos are super fun to eat, and lasagna is super comforting. Why not combine their superpowers into one heroically epic meal? Dinner doesn't get any better than this.

FOR THE TOMATO SAUCE

**2 (14-ounce) cans fire-roasted diced tomatoes**

**½ cup vegetable stock**

**1 tablespoon chili powder**

**2 teaspoons garlic powder**

**2 teaspoons onion powder**

**1 teaspoon ground cumin**

**1 teaspoon dried oregano**

**½ teaspoon salt**

FOR THE CASSEROLE

**2 teaspoons neutral-flavored vegetable oil**

**1 red onion, diced**

**2 garlic cloves, minced**

**1 bell pepper, seeded and diced**

**1 (15-ounce) can pinto beans, drained and rinsed**

**1 cup fresh or thawed frozen corn kernels**

1. Preheat the oven to 400°F.

2. **Make the tomato sauce:** In a blender, combine the tomatoes, stock, chili powder, garlic powder, onion powder, cumin, oregano, and salt. Blend until smooth.

3. **Make the casserole:** In a large pan, heat the oil over medium-high heat until it shimmers. Add the onion and cook for 5 minutes, or until it begins to soften. Add the garlic and bell pepper and cook, stirring occasionally, for 5 minutes more, or until they begin to soften. Stir in the pinto beans, corn, chili powder, onion powder, garlic powder, cumin, salt, and black pepper. Remove from the heat.

4. Spoon about three-quarters of the tomato sauce over the bottom of a 9-by-13-inch baking dish. Layer 4 of the tortillas over the sauce. Spread about ¾ cup of the refried beans over the tortillas. Top with half the pinto bean mixture and another ¾ cup of the tomato sauce. Top with 4 more tortillas, the rest of the refried beans, and the rest of the pinto bean mixture. Spread another ¾ cup of the tomato sauce over the bean layer. Layer the remaining 4 tortillas on top, followed by the rest of the tomato sauce and finally the cheese sauce.

1 teaspoon chili powder

½ teaspoon onion powder

½ teaspoon garlic powder

½ teaspoon ground cumin

½ teaspoon salt

¼ teaspoon freshly ground black pepper

12 small (6- to 8-inch) corn tortillas

1½ cups Refried Beans (page 232) or store-bought refried beans

1 cup Say Cheese! Sauce (page 228), Creamy Queso Dip (page 32), or shredded nondairy cheddar cheese

½ cup chopped fresh cilantro leaves

3 scallions, sliced

5. Cover the dish with aluminum foil. Bake for 30 minutes, or until bubbling and heated through.

6. Remove the pan from the oven and set aside to cool for about 5 minutes before slicing. Top with the cilantro and scallions to serve.

**Troubleshooting Tip:** You may need to cut your tortillas in half when layering them in your baking dish to get the best fit.

PER SERVING: CALORIES: 428; FAT: 9G; SATURATED FAT: 3G; CHOLESTEROL: 0G; PROTEIN: 20G; FIBER: 16G; SODIUM: 1,301MG

# WHITE BEAN COTTAGE PIE

**SERVES 6 | PREP TIME:** 15 MINUTES | **COOK TIME:** 45 MINUTES

What we know as shepherd's pie used to be called "cottage pie," because it was consumed mainly by the working class who lived in tiny cottages. It was an economical dish, made using leftovers topped with a crust of inexpensive potatoes. In other words, it was peasant food. I don't know about you, but I'll take it over a hoity-toity meal any day. Mashed potatoes, beans, and veggies? Yes, please!

## FOR THE CRUST

- 2 pounds Yukon Gold potatoes, diced
- ¼ cup plain unsweetened Almond Milk (page 214) or store-bought nondairy milk
- 2 tablespoons olive oil
- 2 tablespoons nutritional yeast
- 1 teaspoon salt
- ½ teaspoon freshly ground black pepper

## FOR THE FILLING

- 2 teaspoons neutral-flavored vegetable oil
- 1 small yellow onion, diced
- 2 garlic cloves, minced
- 1 carrot, chopped
- 2 cups chopped cremini or white button mushrooms (about 8 ounces)
- 2 cups chopped green beans (1-inch pieces)
- 1 teaspoon dried thyme
- 1 teaspoon dried rosemary

1. Preheat the oven to 400°F.

2. **Make the crust:** Place the potatoes in a large pot and add enough water to cover them by 2 inches. Bring to a boil over medium-high heat, then reduce the heat to medium-low. Simmer the potatoes for about 15 minutes, until fork-tender.

3. **Meanwhile, make the filling:** In a large skillet, heat the oil over medium-high heat until it shimmers. Add the onion and cook for 5 minutes, or until it begins to soften. Add the garlic, carrot, mushrooms, green beans, thyme, and rosemary and cook, stirring occasionally, for 5 minutes more, or until the vegetables begin to soften.

4. Sprinkle the vegetables with the flour, then add the stock and soy sauce to the pan and stir to combine. Cook, stirring frequently, until the mixture thickens, about 5 minutes more. Stir in the great northern beans and the peas. Transfer the mixture to a 9-by-13-inch baking dish.

5. When the potatoes are done cooking, drain them and return them to the pot. Using a potato masher, mash them. Add the almond milk, oil, nutritional yeast, salt, and pepper and mash until the potatoes reach the desired consistency. Spread the mashed potatoes over the vegetables in the baking dish.

¼ cup whole wheat flour

1 cup vegetable stock

2 tablespoons
reduced-sodium soy
sauce or tamari

2 (14-ounce) cans great
northern beans, drained
and rinsed

1 cup peas

6. Bake for 30 minutes, or until the potatoes are golden brown. Remove the pan from the oven and set aside to cool for about 5 minutes before serving.

**Technique Tip:** I like to keep the peels on my potatoes for two reasons: It's easier, and the skins do have nutritional value. I like my mashed potatoes on the chunky side, so I don't mash them much. If you prefer creamier potatoes, you can peel them and mash away until they're smooth.

PER SERVING: CALORIES: 387; FAT: 7G; SATURATED FAT: 2G; CHOLESTEROL: 0G; PROTEIN: 16G; FIBER: 14G; SODIUM: 929MG

# CHEESY QUINOA CASSEROLE

SOY-FREE, KID-FRIENDLY, ONE-PAN/ONE-POT

**SERVES 6 | PREP TIME:** 10 MINUTES, PLUS 2 HOURS SOAKING TIME | **COOK TIME:** 50 MINUTES

Let's face it—comfort food cravings are often accompanied by seemingly endless hours in the kitchen spent chopping, measuring, mixing, and stirring. Although I admit that this recipe does include all those activities, they take mere minutes. This casserole couldn't be easier to make, as it requires just a little prep work before you mix everything together. Pop it in the oven, prop your feet up, and relax while dinner cooks itself.

3 cups vegetable stock

1 cup raw cashews, soaked for 2 hours, drained, and rinsed

½ cup nutritional yeast

2 teaspoons Dijon mustard

1 teaspoon onion powder

1 teaspoon garlic powder

1 teaspoon salt

1 cup uncooked quinoa, rinsed

5 cups chopped broccoli (cut into bite-size florets)

1 (14-ounce) can chickpeas, drained and rinsed

1. Preheat the oven to 400°F.

2. In a blender, combine the stock, cashews, nutritional yeast, mustard, onion powder, garlic powder, and salt. Blend until smooth and creamy.

3. Put the quinoa, broccoli, and chickpeas in a 9-by-13-inch baking dish. Pour the cashew mixture over them. Stir to combine everything well.

4. Cover the baking dish with aluminum foil. Bake for 45 to 50 minutes, until the quinoa is cooked and the liquid has thickened. Remove the pan from the oven and set aside to cool for about 5 minutes before serving.

**Variation Tip:** For a taste of the Southwest, add 2 teaspoons chili powder and 1 teaspoon ground cumin to the sauce. Replace the chickpeas with black beans and add a can of fire-roasted tomatoes to the dish in step 3.

**PER SERVING:** CALORIES: 295; FAT: 13G; SATURATED FAT: 2G; CHOLESTEROL: 0G; PROTEIN: 14G; FIBER: 6G; SODIUM: 791MG

# Go with the Grain

Grains are often thought of as a side dish, but as you can see from this chapter, they're totally main-dish worthy. Rice and quinoa are probably the most popular grains (and they're the ones I cook with the most), but don't be afraid to try millet, amaranth, rye, spelt, Kamut, freekeh, teff, sorghum, and wheat berries.

Before cooking, give your grains a good rinse. Place them in a fine-mesh sieve, check them for debris, and rinse them with cold water. Heartier grains, such as rice and barley, can be soaked before cooking to help soften them and improve their digestibility, but it's not mandatory.

To cook your grains, add them to a pot with water and bring to a boil over medium-high heat. As soon as the water begins to boil, reduce the heat to medium-low and cover the pot with a lid. Simmer the grains until they are tender and the water has been absorbed. Turn the heat off and set the pot aside, covered, for 5 to 10 minutes, then uncover the pot and fluff the grains with a fork.

I sometimes like to cook my grains in vegetable stock rather than water to give them a little boost of added flavor. You can also add salt, bay leaves, garlic cloves, onion wedges, and spices to the cooking liquid.

If you have a gluten sensitivity, you should avoid barley, farro, spelt, Kamut, freekeh, wheat, and rye. While oats are naturally gluten-free, they are sometimes processed on equipment shared with wheat, causing cross-contamination, so look for oats specifically labeled "gluten-free."

| TYPE OF GRAIN (1 CUP DRY) | WATER | COOKING TIME | YIELD |
|---|---|---|---|
| BARLEY, HULLED | 3 cups | 50 to 60 minutes | 3½ cups |
| BARLEY, PEARLED | 2 cups | 25 to 30 minutes | 4 cups |
| BROWN RICE | 2½ cups | 35 to 45 minutes | 3 cups |
| FARRO, PEARLED | 2½ cups | 15 to 20 minutes | 3 cups |
| FARRO, SEMI-PEARLED | 2½ cups | 20 to 30 minutes | 3 cups |
| FARRO, WHOLE | 2½ cups | 40 minutes | 3 cups |
| OATS, ROLLED | 2 cups | 5 to 10 minutes | 2 cups |
| OATS, STEEL-CUT | 3 cups | 20 to 30 minutes | 3 cups |
| QUINOA | 2 cups | 12 to 15 minutes | 3 cups |
| WHITE RICE | 2 cups | 15 to 20 minutes | 3 cups |
| WILD RICE | 3 cups | 45 to 50 minutes | 3½ cups |

Red Curry Noodles, page 185

# CHAPTER NINE

# USE YOUR NOODLE

## PASTA AND NOODLE MAINS

# PASTA ARRABBIATA

NUT-FREE, SOY-FREE, 30-MINUTE MEAL

**SERVES 4** | **PREP TIME:** 5 MINUTES | **COOK TIME:** 10 MINUTES

In Italian, the word *arrabbiata* literally translates to "angry." Don't worry—this pasta isn't irate, and you definitely won't get into an argument with your dinner. The sauce gets its name from its spicy nature. The amount of red pepper flakes you use depends on your tolerance for heat. I like to pour them on, and I also like to serve my arrabbiata with a generous sprinkling of cheesy nutritional yeast.

**8 ounces dried penne, rigatoni, or fusilli pasta**

**½ teaspoon salt**

**2 tablespoons olive oil**

**3 garlic cloves, minced**

**1 tablespoon tomato paste**

**1 (14-ounce can) diced tomatoes, with their juices**

**½ to 1 teaspoon red pepper flakes**

**2 tablespoons thinly sliced fresh basil leaves**

1. Cook the pasta according to the package instructions, seasoning the water with the salt. Drain the pasta and return it to the pot.

2. Meanwhile, in a medium skillet, heat the oil over medium heat until it shimmers. Add the garlic and cook for a minute or two, until fragrant. Add the tomato paste and cook, stirring often, for another 2 to 3 minutes. Add the tomatoes and red pepper flakes. Increase the heat to medium-high and bring the mixture to a boil. Cook, stirring often, until the sauce has reduced slightly, about 5 minutes.

3. Add the sauce and basil to the pot with the pasta and toss to coat the pasta. Serve.

**Technique Tip:** If you're using wheat-based pasta, there's no need to rinse it. The starches on the cooked pasta will help the sauce stick. If you're using gluten-free pasta, you should rinse it, because gluten-free pasta tends to absorb more sauce.

**PER SERVING:** CALORIES: 293; FAT: 8G; SATURATED FAT: 1G; CHOLESTEROL: 0G; PROTEIN: 8G; FIBER: 4G; SODIUM: 411MG

# SPAG BOL

NUT-FREE, SOY-FREE, KID-FRIENDLY, 30-MINUTE MEAL

**SERVES 4 | PREP TIME:** 5 MINUTES | **COOK TIME:** 12 MINUTES

"Spag bol" is what the Brits like to call spaghetti Bolognese. In the past, I've made hearty vegan Bolognese sauce using veggie burger crumbles, finely chopped veggies, and even walnuts, but I've found lentils to be my favorite. Split red lentils need only about 10 minutes to cook, so I just throw them in the water with the pasta, making this recipe so easy that it almost feels like cheating.

8 ounces dried spaghetti

⅔ cup dried split red lentils

4 cups chopped stemmed kale leaves

3 cups Marinara (page 226) or store-bought marinara sauce, warmed

1. Bring a large pot of water to a boil over medium-high heat. Add the pasta and lentils. Cook for about 8 minutes, then add the kale and cook until the pasta is al dente and the lentils are soft, 2 to 4 minutes more.

2. Drain the pasta mixture and return it to the pot. Stir in the marinara sauce to coat. Serve.

**Technique Tip:** The amount of time it takes to cook your pasta is going to depend on the package instructions. In general, it takes 10 to 12 minutes for spaghetti to cook, but it will vary depending on the type you use. Don't salt your pasta water, as salt toughens beans and lentils, causing them to require a longer cooking time. You can add salt to the dish later, if you feel it needs a little flavor.

**PER SERVING:** CALORIES: 377; FAT: 2G; SATURATED FAT: 0G; CHOLESTEROL: 0G; PROTEIN: 18G; FIBER: 9G; SODIUM: 332MG

# PENNE À LA VODKA

SOY-FREE

**SERVES 4 | PREP TIME:** 10 MINUTES, PLUS 2 HOURS SOAKING TIME |
**COOK TIME:** 15 MINUTES

My mom was a teetotaler. We went to an Italian restaurant for dinner once, and she pooh-poohed my order of penne à la vodka. I did my best to assure her that my meal would not get me tipsy, and I even offered her a bite, to no avail. I hope you will believe me when I tell you that you will not become inebriated from eating this dish.

8 ounces dried penne pasta

1 teaspoon salt, divided

1 teaspoon neutral-flavored
  vegetable oil

2 garlic cloves, minced

1 tablespoon tomato paste

1 (28-ounce) can
  crushed tomatoes

¼ cup freshly ground
  black pepper

½ cup vodka

½ cup water

½ cup raw cashews, soaked
  for 2 hours, drained,
  and rinsed

¼ cup chopped fresh
  parsley leaves

1. Cook the pasta according to the package instructions, seasoning the water with ½ teaspoon of the salt. Drain the pasta and return it to the pot.

2. Meanwhile, in a large skillet, heat the oil over medium heat until it shimmers. Add the garlic and cook for a minute or two, until fragrant. Add the tomato paste and cook, stirring often, for another 2 to 3 minutes. Add the crushed tomatoes, remaining ½ teaspoon of salt, the pepper, and vodka to the pan. Simmer, stirring often, for about 10 minutes, until the alcohol has cooked off.

3. Transfer the tomato mixture to a blender. Add the water and cashews and blend until smooth and creamy.

4. Pour the sauce over the pasta and stir to coat the pasta well. Garnish with the parsley. Serve.

**Substitution Tip:** White wine can be used instead of the vodka. If, like my mom, you eschew alcohol altogether, you can use vegetable stock in its place.

PER SERVING: CALORIES: 427; FAT: 11G; SATURATED FAT: 3G; CHOLESTEROL: 0G; PROTEIN: 13G; FIBER: 7G; SODIUM: 820MG

# PASTA PUTTANESCA

**SERVES 4 | PREP TIME:** 10 MINUTES | **COOK TIME:** 12 MINUTES

Puttanesca has a rather colorful history. The word *puttanesca* roughly translates to "lady of the night," and legend has it that this dish earned its name because it could be quickly cooked and eaten between clients. I don't know how true that is, but I do know that it's super easy to make, so it's a great dinner option for busy weekday evenings.

2 tablespoons olive oil

4 garlic cloves, minced

1 (28-ounce) can crushed tomatoes

½ cup pitted kalamata olives, sliced (see Tip)

½ cup pitted green olives, sliced (see Tip)

¼ cup capers, drained

2 teaspoons chopped fresh oregano

½ teaspoon red pepper flakes

8 ounces dried spaghetti or linguine

½ teaspoon salt

1. In a large pan, heat the oil over medium heat until it shimmers. Add the garlic and cook for a minute or two, until fragrant. Add the tomatoes, olives, capers, oregano, and red pepper flakes. Bring to a boil, then reduce the heat to medium-low and simmer for 10 minutes, or until the sauce has reduced slightly.

2. Meanwhile, cook the pasta according to the package instructions, seasoning the water with the salt. Drain the pasta and return it to the pot. Add the sauce and gently toss to combine. Serve.

**Ingredient Tip:** When buying olives, I recommend getting the jarred type, rather than canned, because they're tastier. Or, better yet, hit up your grocery store's olive bar, if it has one. Look for olives that have already been pitted, to save yourself time.

PER SERVING: CALORIES: 328; FAT: 10G; SATURATED FAT: 1G; CHOLESTEROL: 0G; PROTEIN: 9G; FIBER: 6G; SODIUM: 665MG

# PESTO PASTA

SOY-FREE, KID-FRIENDLY, 30-MINUTE MEAL

**SERVES 4 | PREP TIME:** 10 MINUTES | **COOK TIME:** 17 MINUTES

I could probably eat pasta with pesto every night of the week and not get sick of it. I make pesto in bulk and store it in cup-sized containers in the freezer so I have it on hand when a craving strikes. Mushrooms, broccoli, and sun-dried tomatoes are my favorite pesto pasta additions, but you can go crazy with this recipe and use any type of veggie your taste buds desire.

8 ounces dried penne, shells, or farfalle (bow-tie) pasta

1 teaspoon salt, divided

2 teaspoons neutral-flavored vegetable oil

½ cup diced yellow onion (about ½ onion)

2 garlic cloves, minced

2 cups finely chopped cremini or white button mushrooms (about 8 ounces)

4 cups chopped broccoli (cut into bite-size florets)

¼ teaspoon freshly ground black pepper

1 cup Popeye Pesto (page 225) or store-bought dairy-free pesto

¼ cup sun-dried tomatoes, sliced

1. Cook the pasta according to the package instructions, seasoning the water with ½ teaspoon of the salt. Drain the pasta and return it to the pot.

2. Meanwhile, in a large skillet, heat the oil over medium-high heat until it shimmers. Add the onion and cook for 5 minutes, or until softened. Add the garlic and cook for another minute or two, until fragrant. Add the mushrooms, broccoli, pepper, and remaining ½ teaspoon salt and cook, stirring often, until the vegetables soften, 7 to 10 minutes.

3. Add the pesto to the cooked pasta and toss to combine. Add the cooked vegetables and sun-dried tomatoes, and toss again to combine. Serve.

**Variation Tip:** For pasta primavera, use 2 cups Creamy White Sauce (page 227) instead of the pesto.

PER SERVING: CALORIES: 619; FAT: 38G; SATURATED FAT: 8G; CHOLESTEROL: 0G; PROTEIN: 18G; FIBER: 6G; SODIUM: 984MG

# CHIC'UN TETRAZZINI

SOY-FREE, KID-FRIENDLY

**SERVES 4 | PREP TIME:** 10 MINUTES | **COOK TIME:** 28 MINUTES

I don't have anything against marinara, but dreamy, creamy pasta sauces are my weakness. They can elevate pasta night from humdrum to sensational. Dairy products are simply not needed. The sauce in this recipe is made with flour and nondairy milk, but it's so velvety smooth that no one will know. I won't judge you if you lick your plate.

8 ounces dried spaghetti or linguine

1 teaspoon salt, divided

3 teaspoons neutral-flavored vegetable oil, divided

2 Chic'un Patties (page 234) or 8 ounces store-bought seitan, diced

½ cup diced yellow onion (about ½ onion)

2 garlic cloves, minced

2 cups finely chopped cremini or white button mushrooms (about 8 ounces)

½ cup whole wheat flour

2 cups plain unsweetened Almond Milk (page 214) or store-bought nondairy milk

¼ cup nutritional yeast

2 tablespoons fresh lemon juice

½ teaspoon garlic powder

½ teaspoon onion powder

¼ teaspoon freshly ground black pepper

1 cup fresh or frozen peas

1. Cook the pasta according to the package instructions, seasoning the water with ½ teaspoon of the salt. Drain the pasta and return it to the pot.

2. Meanwhile, in a large pot, heat 2½ teaspoons of the oil over medium-high heat until it shimmers. Add the chic'un and cook, stirring frequently, for 5 minutes, or until it begins to brown. Remove from the pan and set aside on a plate.

3. Add the remaining ½ teaspoon oil and the onion to the pot and cook for 5 minutes, or until softened. Add the garlic and cook for another minute or two, until fragrant. Add the mushrooms and cook, stirring often, until they begin to soften, about 5 minutes.

4. Sprinkle the vegetables with the flour and stir to coat. Cook for 2 to 3 minutes, until the flour looks pastelike.

5. Reduce the heat to medium. Gradually add the almond milk to the pot, whisking as you go to avoid lumps. Stir in the nutritional yeast, lemon juice, garlic powder, onion powder, pepper, and remaining ½ teaspoon salt. Cook, stirring continually, until the mixture thickens, 3 to 5 minutes.

6. Return the chic'un to the pot, add the peas, and cook, stirring often, until warmed through, 3 to 5 minutes.

7. Add the sauce to the cooked pasta and gently toss to coat. Serve.

PER SERVING: CALORIES: 534; FAT: 13G; SATURATED FAT: 5G; CHOLESTEROL: 0G; PROTEIN: 30G; FIBER: 7G; SODIUM: 633MG

# CHILI MAC

SOY-FREE, KID-FRIENDLY, 30-MINUTE MEAL

**SERVES 6 | PREP TIME:** 10 MINUTES | **COOK TIME:** 22 MINUTES

I usually make chili mac when I have leftovers of both chili and mac and cheese in the fridge. But sometimes I have a hankering for it when I don't have either on hand, so I was forced to create a recipe to make it from scratch.

**12 ounces dried elbow macaroni**

**1 teaspoon salt, divided**

**2 teaspoons neutral-flavored vegetable oil**

**½ cup diced red onion**

**2 garlic cloves, minced**

**1 red bell pepper, seeded and diced**

**1 green bell pepper, seeded and diced**

**½ cup all-purpose flour**

**3 cups plain unsweetened nondairy milk**

**½ cup nutritional yeast**

**2 teaspoons chili powder**

**1 teaspoon ground cumin**

**1 teaspoon onion powder**

**1 teaspoon garlic powder**

**¼ teaspoon red pepper flakes**

**¼ teaspoon freshly ground black pepper**

**1 (15-ounce) can pinto beans, drained and rinsed**

**1 (15-ounce) can black beans, drained and rinsed**

**1 (14-ounce) can fire-roasted tomatoes, drained**

**2 scallions, sliced**

1. Cook the pasta according to the package instructions, seasoning the water with ½ teaspoon of the salt. Drain the pasta and return it to the pot.

2. Meanwhile, in a large pot, heat the oil over medium-high heat until it shimmers. Add the onion and cook, stirring frequently for about 5 minutes, until the onion begins to soften. Add the garlic and cook for another minute or two, until fragrant. Add the bell peppers and cook for another 5 minutes, or until they begin to soften.

3. Add the flour to the pot and stir to coat the vegetables. Cook for about 2 minutes, until the flour forms a paste.

4. Gradually whisk in the almond milk, then whisk in the nutritional yeast, chili powder, cumin, onion powder, garlic powder, red pepper flakes, black pepper, and remaining ½ teaspoon salt. Bring the mixture to a boil, then reduce the heat to maintain a simmer.

5. Add the beans and tomatoes and cook, stirring frequently, for about 10 minutes, until the sauce is thick and creamy.

6. Remove the pan from the heat and stir in the cooked pasta. Top with the scallions. Serve.

> **Substitution Tip:** Store-bought veggie burger crumbles can be used in place of (or in addition to) the beans.

PER SERVING: CALORIES: 466; FAT: 5G; SATURATED FAT: 2G; CHOLESTEROL: 0G; PROTEIN: 22G; FIBER: 10G; SODIUM: 808MG

# BAKED MAC 'N' CHEESY

SOY-FREE, KID-FRIENDLY, 30-MINUTE MEAL

**SERVES 6 | PREP TIME:** 10 MINUTES | **COOK TIME:** 20 MINUTES

When I get a new cookbook, I usually turn right to the mac and cheese recipe and make that first. And I encourage you to do the same with this book. In fact, I thought about putting a note in the beginning urging you to jump right ahead to this page. Because, really, there's nothing better than a plate of pasta drenched in hot, bubbling cheese sauce, is there?

**12 ounces dried elbow macaroni**

**½ teaspoon salt**

**4 cups Say Cheese! Sauce (page 228) or store-bought nondairy cheese sauce**

**1 cup panko bread crumbs**

**¼ cup olive oil**

**1 tablespoon nutritional yeast**

**½ teaspoon sweet paprika**

1. Preheat the oven to 350°F.

2. Cook the pasta according to the package instructions, seasoning the water with the salt. Drain the pasta and return it to the pot.

3. Add the cheese sauce to the pot and gently stir to combine. Transfer the mixture to a 9-by-13-inch baking dish.

4. In a small bowl, combine the bread crumbs, oil, and nutritional yeast. Spread the bread crumb mixture evenly over the pasta. Sprinkle with the paprika.

5. Bake for 20 minutes, or until the bread crumbs are golden and the cheese sauce is bubbling. Serve.

**Troubleshooting Tip:** It's important to cook your pasta until it's al dente (meaning firm to the bite) or slightly undercooked. The pasta will continue cooking in the oven, so if it's overcooked, it will turn mushy.

**Variation Tip:** Don't have the patience to wait for your dinner to be baked? Un-casserole it! Cook the pasta until it's done, rather than al dente, and simply toss it together with warmed cheese sauce. Skip the bread crumbs, unless you want the crunchy topping.

**PER SERVING:** CALORIES: 446; FAT: 14G; SATURATED FAT: 3G; CHOLESTEROL: 0G; PROTEIN: 16G; FIBER: 6G; SODIUM: 1,001MG

# STUFFED PASTA SHELLS

NUT-FREE, KID-FRIENDLY

**SERVES 4 | PREP TIME:** 15 MINUTES | **COOK TIME:** 35 MINUTES

I don't know anyone who doesn't like stuffed shells. Who can resist the lure of pasta filled will cheesy ricotta? The beauty of this dish is that it is super easy to make, so it's a great dinner for busy weeknights, but it looks impressive on the plate, so it can be served on date night or at dinner parties. Top your shells with a sprinkling of dairy-free mozzarella, if you have some on hand.

16 dried jumbo pasta shells

½ teaspoon salt

1 (12-ounce) package frozen kale, thawed, drained, and squeezed dry

2 cups Tofu Ricotta (page 229) or store-bought nondairy ricotta

3 cups Marinara (page 226) or store-bought marinara sauce

¼ cup chopped fresh basil leaves

1. Preheat the oven to 350°F.

2. Cook the pasta according to the package instructions, seasoning the water with the salt. Drain the pasta and return it to the pot.

3. Meanwhile, in a medium bowl, fold the kale into the ricotta and stir well.

4. Spread half the marinara sauce on the bottom of a 9-by-13-inch baking dish.

5. Place a large spoonful of the ricotta mixture in each shell and place the shells in the baking dish. Top with the remaining marinara.

6. Bake for 25 minutes. Top with the basil. Serve.

> **Technique Tip:** Having trouble spooning the ricotta into the shells? You can put the filling in a pastry bag (or a large plastic bag with the tip of one corner cut off), then pipe it into the shells.

**PER SERVING:** CALORIES: 354; FAT: 6G; SATURATED FAT: 1G; CHOLESTEROL: 0G; PROTEIN: 20G; FIBER: 7G; SODIUM: 337MG

# SPAGHETTI PIE

NUT-FREE, KID-FRIENDLY

**SERVES 6 | PREP TIME:** 20 MINUTES | **COOK TIME:** 40 MINUTES

Does that boring plate of spaghetti marinara have you down? May I suggest turning that frown into a pie? Spaghetti pie, that is! This dish is much more fun than your average bowl of pasta, and it's a great way to use up leftovers that might otherwise sit in the back of the fridge. Add some extra veggies to the mushroom layer, if you like, or add chopped Italian sausage or a ground veggie burger. For a spicier taco variation, check out the Variation Tip.

**2 teaspoons neutral-flavored vegetable oil, plus more for the pie plate**

**1 cup silken tofu**

**3 tablespoons nutritional yeast**

**1 teaspoon garlic powder**

**1 teaspoon onion powder**

**8 ounces dried spaghetti**

**½ teaspoon salt**

**2 garlic cloves, minced**

**2 cups chopped mushrooms (about 8 ounces)**

**2 cups loosely packed baby spinach, chopped**

**1 cup Tofu Ricotta (page 229) or store-bought nondairy ricotta**

**2 cups Marinara (page 226) or store-bought marinara sauce**

1. Preheat the oven to 350°F. Lightly oil a 9-inch pie plate.

2. In a blender, combine the tofu, nutritional yeast, garlic powder, and onion powder. Blend until smooth and creamy; if the mixture is too thick, add water 1 teaspoon at a time. Set aside.

3. Bring a large pot of water to a boil over medium-high heat. Add the spaghetti and salt. Cook for 8 to 9 minutes, until the pasta is al dente. Drain the pasta and return it to the pot.

4. Meanwhile, in a large skillet, heat the oil over medium-high heat until it shimmers. Add the garlic and cook for a minute or two, until fragrant. Add the mushrooms and cook until they begin to soften, 5 to 7 minutes. Add the spinach and cook for another minute or two, until it begins to wilt.

5. Add the tofu mixture to the cooked spaghetti and toss to coat. Place the spaghetti in the prepared pie plate and press it down to form an even layer. Spread the ricotta over the pasta in an even layer, then spread the vegetables in an even layer over the ricotta. Top with the marinara sauce. Cover the pan with aluminum foil. Bake for 25 to 30 minutes. Serve.

PER SERVING: CALORIES: 250; FAT: 6G; SATURATED FAT: 2G; CHOLESTEROL: 0G; PROTEIN: 14G; FIBER: 4G; SODIUM: 400MG

## The Big Cheese

Dairy cheese—with all its salty, fatty tastiness—can be difficult to say no to. If I had a dollar for every time someone told me that they "want to go vegan but could never give up cheese," I'd be sitting pretty right now. I assure you that there are *tons* of nondairy cheeses on the market, and they're all quite tasty. You can find melty mozzarellas, sandwich slices, and smooth spreads in most grocery stores. If you're looking to "zhuzh up" your pasta with a little cheesy flavor, just sprinkle (or shower) it with nutritional yeast, affectionately known in vegan circles as "nooch." And if you're feeling so inclined, you can try making your own nondairy cheese sauce at home with the recipe on page 228.

# LASAGNA PRIMAVERA

KID-FRIENDLY, ONE-PAN/ONE-POT

**SERVES 8 | PREP TIME:** 20 MINUTES | **COOK TIME:** 50 MINUTES

Lasagna is the quintessential meal. It has it all: noodles, veggies, sauce, and creamy (nondairy) cheese, all baked together in a cozy casserole dish. It may take a little more time to make than your average pasta dinner, but the payoff is worth the effort. The beauty of lasagna is that there are always leftovers, which tend to taste even better the next day. Am I right, or am I right?

12 to 15 dried
   lasagna noodles

1 teaspoon salt, divided

2 teaspoons neutral-flavored
   vegetable oil

½ cup diced yellow onion
   (about ½ onion)

2 garlic cloves, minced

2 cups chopped cremini or
   white button mushrooms
   (about 8 ounces)

1 zucchini, chopped

½ teaspoon dried basil

½ teaspoon dried oregano

¼ teaspoon freshly ground
   black pepper

4 cups chopped stemmed
   kale leaves

5 cups Creamy White Sauce
   (page 227) or
   store-bought dairy-free
   Alfredo sauce

2 cups Tofu Ricotta
   (page 229) or store-bought
   nondairy ricotta

**Time-Saving Tip:**
Use no-boil lasagna
noodles and skip step 2
to save a little time.

1. Preheat the oven to 400°F.

2. Cook the pasta according to the package instructions, seasoning the water with ½ teaspoon of the salt. Drain the pasta and return it to the pot.

3. Meanwhile, in a large pan, heat the oil over medium-high heat until it shimmers. Add the onion and cook for 5 minutes, or until softened. Add the garlic and cook for another minute or two, until fragrant. Add the mushrooms, zucchini, basil, oregano, pepper, and remaining ½ teaspoon salt and cook, stirring often, until the vegetables begin to soften, about 5 minutes. Add the kale and cook until it wilts and turns bright green, about 3 minutes more.

4. To assemble the lasagna, spread 1 cup of the sauce over the bottom of a 9-by-13-inch baking dish. Arrange one-third of the noodles over the sauce. Spread half the ricotta over the noodles. Top with half the mushroom-kale mixture and that with 1 cup of the sauce. Arrange another one-third of the noodles over the sauce, then top with the remaining ricotta and mushroom-kale mixture. Spoon another 1 cup of the sauce over the top. Layer on the rest of the noodles and finish with the rest of the sauce.

5. Cover tightly with aluminum foil. Bake for 40 minutes, or until the sauce is bubbling and the lasagna is warmed through. Serve.

**PER SERVING:** CALORIES: 425; FAT: 16G; SATURATED FAT: 4G; CHOLESTEROL: 0G; PROTEIN: 16G; FIBER: 3G; SODIUM: 1,150MG

# PEANUT NOODLES

**SERVES 4 | PREP TIME:** 10 MINUTES | **COOK TIME:** 5 MINUTES

I've said it before and I'll say it again: Spicy Peanut Sauce (page 221) makes everything taste better. And noodles are no exception. Not that noodles had a bad reputation before they were paired with a nutty sauce. On the contrary, the sauce is there to complement the noodles, elevating them from good to great, from super to superb. This dish can be eaten warm or chilled, straight from the fridge, and it's a great make-ahead meal for sweltering summer days.

**8 ounces uncooked rice noodles**

**1 teaspoon toasted sesame oil**

**1 cup Spicy Peanut Sauce (page 221) or store-bought peanut sauce**

**2 medium English cucumbers, thinly sliced**

**¾ cup shelled edamame**

**¼ cup roasted peanuts, chopped**

**¼ cup chopped fresh cilantro leaves**

**2 scallions, sliced**

1. Cook the noodles according to the package instructions, about 5 minutes. Drain and rinse with cold water.

2. Put the noodles in a medium bowl. Add the sesame oil and toss to coat (this prevents the noodles from sticking together). Add the peanut sauce and gently toss again to coat. Fold in the cucumbers and edamame, then half the peanuts, cilantro, and scallions.

3. Divide the noodles evenly among 4 plates. Top with the remaining peanuts, cilantro, and scallions to serve.

**Variation Tip:** If you'd like to add more veggies to your noodles, try julienned carrot, shredded cabbage, or thinly sliced red bell pepper.

PER SERVING: CALORIES: 515; FAT: 19G; SATURATED FAT: 3G; CHOLESTEROL: 0G; PROTEIN: 15G; FIBER: 6G; SODIUM: 222MG

# GINGER SCALLION NOODLES

NUT-FREE, 30-MINUTE MEAL

**SERVES 4** | **PREP TIME:** 10 MINUTES | **COOK TIME:** 10 MINUTES

The name tells you all you need to know about this recipe: It's noodles with lots of ginger and scallions. The dish is super simple yet super flavorful, and it comes together almost as quickly as calling your favorite restaurant to order takeout. Throw in some cubed baked tofu (see page 230) or shelled edamame, if you'd like to add a little protein.

**9 ounces uncooked ramen noodles (see Tip)**

**¼ cup vegetable stock**

**¼ cup reduced-sodium soy sauce or tamari**

**2 tablespoons unseasoned rice vinegar**

**2 teaspoons toasted sesame oil**

**1 teaspoon cornstarch**

**1 tablespoon neutral-flavored vegetable oil**

**2 cups sliced scallions (1 large bunch)**

**⅓ cup minced peeled fresh ginger**

**4 garlic cloves, minced**

1. Cook the noodles according to the package instructions, about 5 minutes. Drain and set aside.

2. In a small bowl, whisk together the stock, soy sauce, vinegar, sesame oil, and cornstarch. Set the sauce aside.

3. In a large skillet, heat the vegetable oil over medium heat until it shimmers. Add the scallions, ginger, and garlic and cook, stirring continually, for 2 to 3 minutes, until they soften and turn fragrant. Add the noodles and sauce to the pan. Toss to coat. Cook for another minute or two, until the noodles are well coated and the sauce has thickened slightly. Serve.

**Ingredient Tip:** If you can't find plain ramen noodles, buy three 3-ounce packages of flavored ramen and simply discard the seasoning packets.

**Technique Tip:** When you're mixing vegetables and sauce with noodles using a large spoon or spatula, the vegetables can sometimes fall to the bottom of the pan. I've found that tongs work best for incorporating everything together.

**PER SERVING:** CALORIES: 318; FAT: 6G; SATURATED FAT: 3G; CHOLESTEROL: 0G; PROTEIN: 10G; FIBER: 4G; SODIUM: 1,932MG

# OODLES OF TAHINI NOODLES

NUT-FREE, 30-MINUTE MEAL, ONE-PAN/ONE-POT

**SERVES 4 | PREP TIME:** 15 MINUTES **| COOK TIME:** 5 MINUTES

If you've never used tahini as a sauce for your noodles, it's time to fix that! With their creamy texture and crunchy veggies, these tahini noodles are an obsession of mine, and I predict that after a few bites, you'll be obsessed, too. I say this recipe serves 4, but I could easily polish it off all by my lonesome in one sitting. Much like the Peanut Noodles on page 181, this dish can be enjoyed warm or chilled.

½ cup tahini

½ cup water

1 tablespoon reduced-sodium soy sauce or tamari

1 tablespoon fresh lime juice

1 teaspoon grated peeled fresh ginger

1 garlic clove, minced

¼ teaspoon red pepper flakes

9 ounces uncooked udon noodles

1 carrot, grated or julienned

2 cups loosely packed baby spinach, chopped

2 scallions, sliced

1 avocado, pitted, peeled, and sliced

2 tablespoons toasted sesame seeds

1. In a small bowl, whisk together the tahini, water, soy sauce, lime juice, ginger, garlic, and red pepper flakes.

2. Cook the noodles according to the package instructions, about 5 minutes. Drain and rinse with cold water.

3. Put the noodles in a large bowl and pour the tahini sauce over them. Gently toss to coat the noodles well. Fold in the carrot, spinach, and scallions. Top with the avocado and sesame seeds to serve.

**Substitution Tip:** Any type of noodle can be used in place of the udon noodles. Try rice noodles, soba noodles, or even whole wheat spaghetti.

PER SERVING: CALORIES: 537; FAT: 26G; SATURATED FAT: 4G; CHOLESTEROL: 0G; PROTEIN: 16G; FIBER: 12G; SODIUM: 1,609MG

# VEGETABLE LO MEIN

NUT-FREE, KID-FRIENDLY, 30-MINUTE MEAL

**SERVES 4 | PREP TIME:** 10 MINUTES | **COOK TIME:** 17 MINUTES

Lo mein is a Chinese food favorite, but I always feel like the local take-out places skimp on the veggies. When I make it at home, I can load it up with whatever I like, and I like lots of mushrooms, bell pepper, and snow peas. If you like something else—say broccoli or bok choy, perhaps—go ahead and add it. You can throw in a sliced Chic'un Patty (page 234) or some cubed baked tofu (see page 230) if you'd like to give your meal a protein boost.

**10 ounces uncooked lo mein noodles (see Tip)**

**⅓ cup vegetable stock**

**⅓ cup reduced-sodium soy sauce or tamari**

**4 teaspoons toasted sesame oil, divided**

**2 teaspoons cornstarch**

**2 garlic cloves, minced**

**1 tablespoon minced peeled fresh ginger**

**1 red bell pepper, seeded and thinly sliced**

**1 carrot, grated or julienned**

**½ cup thinly sliced shiitake mushrooms**

**½ cup snow peas, sliced**

**1 cup thinly sliced baby bok choy**

**2 scallions, sliced**

1. Cook the noodles according to the package instructions, about 5 minutes. Drain and set aside.

2. Meanwhile, in a small bowl, whisk together the stock, soy sauce, 2 teaspoons of the sesame oil, and the cornstarch. Set the sauce aside.

3. In a large skillet or wok, heat the remaining 2 teaspoons oil over medium-high heat until it shimmers. Add the garlic and ginger and cook for a minute or two, until fragrant. Add the bell pepper, carrot, mushrooms, and snow peas and cook, stirring frequently, until they soften, about 10 minutes.

4. Add the bok choy, the cooked noodles, and half the sauce to the pan. Toss to combine the noodles and the veggies. Add the rest of the sauce and toss to coat well. Top with the sliced scallions. Serve.

**Ingredient Tip:** Some lo mein noodles contain eggs, so make sure you read the label. If you can't find eggless lo mein, use ramen, soba, or rice noodles instead.

PER SERVING: CALORIES: 339; FAT: 5G; SATURATED FAT: 1G; CHOLESTEROL: 0G; PROTEIN: 15G; FIBER: 3G; SODIUM: 1,903MG

# RED CURRY NOODLES

**SERVES 4 | PREP TIME:** 10 MINUTES | **COOK TIME:** 17 MINUTES

This recipe is a little bit slurpy and a little bit saucy, with a whole lotta delicious flavor. It has all the components of a good Thai curry—curry paste, coconut milk, lime juice, peanuts, and cilantro—with none of the fear that fish sauce may find its way into your meal. It's a cold-weather favorite for me, but I wouldn't say no to a bowl of it in the warmer months.

8 ounces uncooked rice vermicelli noodles

1 (14-ounce) can full-fat coconut milk

3 tablespoons red curry paste

2 tablespoons reduced-sodium soy sauce or tamari

1 tablespoon fresh lime juice

2 teaspoons neutral-flavored vegetable oil

2 garlic cloves, minced

1 tablespoon minced peeled fresh ginger

1 carrot, thinly sliced

4 cups chopped broccoli (cut into bite-size florets)

4 cups loosely packed baby spinach, chopped

1 cup diced Sriracha Baked Tofu (page 230), or 8 ounces store-bought baked tofu, diced

¼ cup chopped roasted peanuts

¼ cup chopped fresh cilantro leaves

1. Cook the noodles according to the package instructions, about 5 minutes. Drain the noodles and return them to the pot.

2. Meanwhile, in a medium bowl, whisk together the coconut milk, curry paste, soy sauce, and lime juice. Set the curry sauce aside.

3. In a large pan, heat the oil over medium-high heat until it shimmers. Add the garlic and ginger and cook for a minute or two, until fragrant. Add the carrot and broccoli and cook until they begin to soften, about 5 minutes.

4. Add the spinach, baked tofu, and curry sauce to the pan. Cook until the sauce is heated through and the spinach has wilted, about 5 minutes.

5. Add the tofu-vegetable mixture and the sauce to the pan with the noodles. Use tongs to toss everything together well.

6. Serve topped with the peanuts and cilantro.

**Variation Tip:** You don't have to stick with the veggies I use here. Go wild! Try diced red bell pepper, chopped bok choy, sliced mushrooms, baby corn, or whatever you happen to have in the fridge.

PER SERVING: CALORIES: 618; FAT: 34G; SATURATED FAT: 22G; CHOLESTEROL: 0G; PROTEIN: 22G; FIBER: 9G; SODIUM: 686MG

# TERIYAKI CHICKPEA NOODLES

NUT-FREE, KID-FRIENDLY

**SERVES 4 | PREP TIME:** 15 MINUTES **| COOK TIME:** 20 MINUTES

Teriyaki always reminds me of my childhood. Whenever my Poppop would come for a visit, we'd go out to dinner, and I'd order teriyaki chicken and a Shirley Temple. Dining out always seemed like a special occasion, and I felt very grown-up and sophisticated. I created this recipe as a cruelty-free nod to that meal. This dish makes me feel classy any time I want, even if I'm just eating noodles in my pajamas at home.

9 ounces uncooked soba noodles

2 teaspoons neutral-flavored vegetable oil

5 cups chopped broccoli (cut into bite-size florets)

2 cups shiitake mushrooms, sliced

1 red bell pepper, seeded and thinly sliced

½ cup reduced-sodium soy sauce or tamari

¼ cup vegetable stock

2 tablespoons unseasoned rice vinegar

2 tablespoons agave nectar or pure maple syrup

1 tablespoon cornstarch

2 teaspoons grated peeled fresh ginger

2 garlic cloves, minced

1 (14-ounce) can chickpeas, drained and rinsed

2 scallions, sliced

2 tablespoons toasted sesame seeds

1. Cook the noodles according to the package instructions, about 5 minutes. Drain the noodles and return them to the pot.

2. Meanwhile, in a large pan, heat the oil over medium-high heat until it shimmers. Add the broccoli, mushrooms, and bell pepper. Cook, stirring frequently, until they soften, 7 to 10 minutes.

3. Meanwhile, in a small bowl, whisk together the soy sauce, stock, vinegar, agave, cornstarch, ginger, and garlic.

4. Add the chickpeas to the pan with the vegetables, then pour in the sauce. Stir well. Cook, stirring frequently, until the sauce begins to thicken, about 5 minutes more.

5. Add the vegetables and sauce to the pot with the noodles. Use tongs to toss everything together well.

6. Serve topped with the scallions and sesame seeds.

**Substitution Tip:** Any type of noodle can be used in place of the soba noodles. If desired, panfry 4 diced Chic'un Patties (page 234) or 16 ounces sliced seitan for 5 to 10 minutes, then use in place of the chickpeas.

**PER SERVING:** CALORIES: 453; FAT: 7G; SATURATED FAT: 2G; CHOLESTEROL: 0G; PROTEIN: 22G; FIBER: 9G; SODIUM: 2,413MG

# DRUNKEN NOODLES

NUT-FREE, 30-MINUTE MEAL

**SERVES 4 | PREP TIME:** 10 MINUTES | **COOK TIME:** 20 MINUTES

There's no booze in these noodles, so I'm not sure where the name came from. Some say they pair perfectly with ice-cold beer, and legend has it that they can help nurse a hangover. I can't speak to either of those theories, but I can urge you to make these noodles now, rather than the morning after a night on the town. When buying rice noodles for this dish, look for the thick variety, between ½ and 1 inch wide.

3 teaspoons vegetable
oil, divided

1 (14-ounce) package
extra-firm tofu, drained,
pressed (see Tip,
page 18), and cut into
1-inch cubes

8 ounces uncooked wide
rice noodles

1 teaspoon toasted
sesame oil

⅓ cup vegetable stock

⅓ cup reduced-sodium soy
sauce or tamari

3 tablespoons fresh
lime juice

2 teaspoons sugar

2 teaspoons sambal oelek
(Indonesian chile paste)

2 scallions, sliced

2 garlic cloves, minced

1 green chile pepper,
seeded and sliced

1 red bell pepper, seeded
and cut into thin strips

2 plum tomatoes, cut
into wedges

¼ cup fresh basil
leaves, sliced

1. In a large pan, heat 2 teaspoons of the vegetable oil over medium-high heat until it shimmers. Add the tofu and cook, stirring often, until it begins to brown, about 10 minutes. Transfer the tofu to a plate and set aside (reserve the pan).

2. Meanwhile, cook the noodles according to the package instructions, about 5 minutes. Drain the noodles and return them to the pot. Toss the noodles with the sesame oil (this prevents the noodles from sticking together).

3. In a small bowl, whisk together the stock, soy sauce, lime juice, sugar, and sambal oelek. Set the sauce aside.

4. In the same pan you used for the tofu, heat the remaining 1 teaspoon vegetable oil until it shimmers. Add the scallions, garlic, and green chile. Cook for a minute or two, until fragrant. Add the bell pepper and cook, stirring frequently, until it begins to soften, about 5 minutes. Add the tofu, tomatoes, and cooked noodles and stir to combine.

5. Add the sauce to the pan and stir to coat everything well. Cook for another minute or two to let the noodles absorb the sauce slightly. Remove the pan from the heat and stir in the basil. Serve.

**PER SERVING:** CALORIES: 386; FAT: 11G; SATURATED FAT: 1G; CHOLESTEROL: 0G; PROTEIN: 17G; FIBER: 3G; SODIUM: 1,443MG

No-Bake Chocolate Cherry Cheesecake, page 208

# CHAPTER TEN

# TREAT YOURSELF

## DESSERTS AND SWEETS

# COWGIRL COOKIES

SOY-FREE, KID-FRIENDLY

**MAKES 36 COOKIES | PREP TIME:** 15 MINUTES **| COOK TIME:** 14 MINUTES

When it comes to cookies, there's a great divide between the oatmeal and chocolate chip camps. One cookie's soft and chewy, the other's sweet and chocolaty. They're both classics, so there's really no need for the sugar-based discord. Made with rolled oats, chocolate chips, pecans, and coconut, these cookies lasso up Team Oatmeal and Team Chocolate Chip and bring them together in sweet confectionery harmony.

1½ cups all-purpose flour

1½ cups quick-cooking rolled oats

1 teaspoon baking powder

1 teaspoon baking soda

½ teaspoon salt

¾ cup granulated sugar

¾ cup packed brown sugar

⅔ cup neutral-flavored vegetable oil

¾ cup plain unsweetened Almond Milk (page 214) or store-bought nondairy milk

1 tablespoon flax meal (ground flaxseed)

1 teaspoon pure vanilla extract

1 cup unsweetened shredded coconut

1 cup dairy-free chocolate chips (see Tip)

1 cup chopped pecans

1. Preheat the oven to 350°F. Line two baking sheets with parchment paper.

2. In a medium bowl, stir together the flour, oats, baking powder, baking soda, and salt.

3. In a large bowl, stir together the granulated sugar, brown sugar, oil, almond milk, flax meal, and vanilla. Add the flour mixture and stir until just combined.

4. Gently fold in the coconut, chocolate chips, and pecans.

5. Scoop the dough by the tablespoonful onto the prepared baking sheets, spacing the cookies about 2 inches apart.

6. Bake for 11 to 14 minutes, until the edges of the cookies are golden brown. Remove from the oven and let the cookies cool on the pans for 2 minutes, then transfer them to a wire rack to cool completely before serving. Store the cookies in an airtight container in the refrigerator for up to 5 days.

**Ingredient Tip:** When buying chocolate chips, check the ingredients for milk, milkfat, and milk solids. Cocoa butter, despite the name, comes from cacao beans, so it's safe for vegans.

**PER SERVING (1 COOKIE):** CALORIES: 167; FAT: 10G; SATURATED FAT: 2G; CHOLESTEROL: 0G; PROTEIN: 2G; FIBER: 2G; SODIUM: 73MG

# NO-BAKE PEANUT BUTTER OATMEAL COOKIES

**MAKES 36 COOKIES | PREP TIME:** 15 MINUTES, PLUS CHILLING TIME

Have you ever wandered into the kitchen for something sweet to snack on, only to find that the cookie jar is empty? In those moments, pulling out lots of ingredients and baking seem like a chore. Well, whipping up a batch of these little beauties is anything but a hassle! They're made with just a few ingredients, they require minimal effort, and you don't even have to turn the oven on. Just mix everything together, form the batter into cookies, and pop them in the fridge. And voilà—your cookies are ready!

1¼ cups creamy natural peanut butter

1 cup pure maple syrup

1 teaspoon pure vanilla extract

½ teaspoon ground cinnamon

½ teaspoon salt

3 cups quick-cooking rolled oats

1. Line two baking sheets with parchment paper or wax paper.

2. In a large pot, combine the peanut butter and maple syrup. Heat over medium-low heat, stirring, until soft. Add the vanilla, cinnamon, and salt and stir well.

3. Remove the pan from the heat and stir in the oats.

4. Using a tablespoon or small scoop, form the dough into balls about 1½ inches in diameter. Place them on the prepared baking sheets and gently flatten them with the back of a spoon.

5. Put the baking sheets in the refrigerator to chill and set for 30 minutes to 1 hour before serving.

6. Store the cookies in an airtight container in the refrigerator for up to 5 days.

> **Variation Tip:** Try adding ¾ cup raisins, dried cherries, or dairy-free chocolate chips to your cookies for a little variety.

**PER SERVING (1 COOKIE):** CALORIES: 111; FAT: 5G; SATURATED FAT: 1G; CHOLESTEROL: 0G; PROTEIN: 4G; FIBER: 2G; SODIUM: 65MG

# LEMON TAHINI COOKIES

NUT-FREE, SOY-FREE, KID-FRIENDLY

**MAKES 36 COOKIES | PREP TIME:** 15 MINUTES | **COOK TIME:** 14 MINUTES

When we think of sweet flavor pairings, peanut butter and chocolate or oatmeal and raisins often come to mind, but lemon and tahini are a combo that deserves a mention, too. Tart lemon complements the earthy bitterness of tahini nicely. I think of these as "tea cookies," and I like to nibble on them while sipping herbal tea on a relaxing Sunday morning.

**2 cups all-purpose flour**

**1 teaspoon baking soda**

**½ teaspoon baking powder**

**½ teaspoon ground cinnamon**

**½ cup pure maple syrup**

**½ cup tahini**

**1 tablespoon grated lemon zest**

**½ cup fresh lemon juice**

**1 teaspoon pure vanilla extract**

**¼ cup raw black sesame seeds**

**¼ cup raw white sesame seeds**

1. Preheat the oven to 350°F. Line two baking sheets with parchment paper.

2. In a large bowl, stir together the flour, baking soda, baking powder, and cinnamon.

3. In a medium bowl, stir together the maple syrup, tahini, lemon zest, lemon juice, and vanilla. Add the wet ingredients to the dry ingredients and mix until a dough forms.

4. In a shallow dish, stir together the black and white sesame seeds.

5. Using your hands, roll the dough into 1-inch balls and then roll them in the sesame seeds to coat. Place the balls on the prepared baking sheets, leaving about 2 inches between each cookie, then flatten them slightly with the palm of your hand.

6. Bake for 11 to 14 minutes, until the edges of the cookies are golden brown. Remove from the oven and let the cookies cool on the pans for 2 minutes, then transfer them to a wire rack to cool completely before serving.

**Technique Tip:** You'll get about 1 tablespoon grated zest from 1 medium lemon. To zest a lemon, make sure it's clean and dry. Use a lemon zester or Microplane grater to gently grate just the bright yellow layer of the peel. If you don't have either, you can use the small holes of a box grater.

**PER SERVING (1 COOKIE):** CALORIES: 71; FAT: 3G; SATURATED FAT: 0G; CHOLESTEROL: 0G; PROTEIN: 2G; FIBER: 1G; SODIUM: 41MG

# DOUBLE-DECKER CHOCOLATE ALMOND FUDGE

GLUTEN-FREE, SOY-FREE, KID-FRIENDLY

**MAKES 32 BARS | PREP TIME:** 20 MINUTES, PLUS CHILLING TIME

It's confession time: I'm a chocoholic. I just can't resist a square of dark, lush chocolate. If I had to pick just one type of dessert for the rest of my life, it would be rich, chocolaty fudge. This fudge, actually. Here, chocolate is paired with sweet almond butter for an extra-decadent treat. I've added avocado for an extra touch of creaminess. Make sure your avocado is very ripe—if it's unripe, it will add a bitter taste.

## FOR THE BOTTOM LAYER

1¾ cups dairy-free chocolate chips

⅓ cup smooth natural almond butter

¼ cup pure maple syrup

½ avocado, mashed

½ teaspoon pure vanilla extract

¼ teaspoon salt

## FOR THE TOP LAYER

1½ cups smooth natural almond butter

⅓ cup pure maple syrup

¼ cup coconut oil, melted

½ avocado, mashed

2 teaspoons pure vanilla extract

¼ teaspoon salt

## FOR THE GARNISH

¼ cup dairy-free chocolate chips

¼ cup chopped toasted almonds

½ teaspoon flaky sea salt

1. Line an 8-inch square baking pan with parchment paper, leaving a few inches of overhang on two sides.

2. **Make the bottom layer:** Fill a medium pot with a few inches of water. Bring the water to a simmer over medium heat. Place another pot or a heatproof bowl on top (the bottom of the pot or bowl should not touch the water). Place the chocolate chips and almond butter in the top pot or bowl and heat, stirring, until the mixture is melted and smooth (do not allow the chocolate to burn).

3. Transfer the chocolate mixture to a food processor (set the pot or bowl aside). Add the maple syrup, avocado, vanilla, and salt and process until smooth and creamy. Using a spatula, spread the mixture evenly over the bottom of the prepared pan. Clean the food processor bowl.

4. **Make the top layer:** In the food processor, combine the almond butter, maple syrup, oil, avocado, vanilla, and salt and process until smooth and creamy. Using a spatula, carefully spread the mixture evenly over the bottom layer in the pan.

5. **Make the garnish:** Return the water in the pot to a simmer over medium heat and set the second pot or bowl on top. Place the chocolate chips in the pot or bowl and stir until melted and smooth.

6. Scatter the almonds over the top layer of the fudge, gently pressing them down. Drizzle with the melted chocolate. Sprinkle with the flaky salt.

7. Refrigerate the fudge for 2 hours, or until firm. Using the overhanging parchment as handles, remove the fudge from the pan and set it on a cutting board. Using a sharp knife, cut the fudge into 1-by-2-inch bars to serve. Store the fudge in an airtight container in the refrigerator for up to 1 week.

**Troubleshooting Tip:** To avoid burning the chocolate as it melts, I recommend removing the top pot or bowl from over the water just before all the chips are melted. Continue stirring the chocolate until smooth. The heat from the warm chocolate will melt any remaining chunks.

**Time-Saving Tip:** To save time, the chocolate chips can be melted in the microwave. Place them in a microwave-safe glass or ceramic bowl and microwave in 20-second increments, stirring after each, until the chocolate is melted and smooth.

PER SERVING (1 BAR): CALORIES: 197; FAT: 15G; SATURATED FAT: 5G; CHOLESTEROL: 0G; PROTEIN: 4G; FIBER: 3G; SODIUM: 108MG

# CHEWY CHOCOLATE CHIP BLONDIES

SOY-FREE, KID-FRIENDLY

**MAKES 16 BLONDIES | PREP TIME:** 10 MINUTES | **COOK TIME:** 30 MINUTES

We vegans can be known for adding ingredients to foods where they don't normally belong, like avocado in fudge (see page 194), spinach in smoothies (see page 12), or chickpeas in blondies. Yes, yes, I know, beans don't really belong in baked goods, but have faith in me and give it a try anyway. Chickpeas add a moist, chewy bite that you won't get from flour.

Vegetable oil, for the baking pan

1 tablespoon flax meal (ground flaxseed)

3 tablespoons water

½ cup quick-cooking rolled oats

1 (15-ounce) can chickpeas, drained and rinsed

½ cup creamy natural peanut butter

⅓ cup pure maple syrup

2 tablespoons brown sugar

2 teaspoons ground cinnamon

2 teaspoons pure vanilla extract

1 teaspoon baking powder

½ teaspoon baking soda

½ teaspoon salt

½ cup dairy-free chocolate chips

1. Preheat the oven to 350°F. Line an 8-inch square baking pan with parchment paper, leaving a few inches of overhang on two sides. Lightly oil the parchment.

2. In a small bowl, combine the flax meal and water. Set aside for a few minutes, until the mixture gels.

3. In a food processor, process the oats until they resemble coarse flour. Add the chickpeas, peanut butter, maple syrup, brown sugar, cinnamon, vanilla, baking powder, baking soda, salt, and flax meal mixture and process until a smooth dough forms. Using a spatula, fold in the chocolate chips.

4. Transfer the dough to the prepared baking pan and use the spatula to smooth it into an even layer.

5. Bake for 20 to 30 minutes, until a toothpick inserted into the center comes out clean.

6. Remove from the oven and let the blondies cool completely in the pan. Using the overhanging parchment as handles, lift the cooled blondies from the pan and set on a cutting board. Slice into 16 squares and serve.

**Substitution Tip:** Any type of nut butter or sunflower seed butter can be used in place of the peanut butter.

**Variation Tip:** For espresso blondies, skip the cinnamon and add 1 tablespoon instant espresso powder to the mix.

**PER SERVING (1 BLONDIE):** CALORIES: 138; FAT: 7G; SATURATED FAT: 2G; CHOLESTEROL: 0G; PROTEIN: 4G; FIBER: 3G; SODIUM: 173MG

# RASPBERRY ALMOND SHORTBREAD BARS

SOY-FREE, KID-FRIENDLY

**MAKES 16 BARS | PREP TIME:** 15 MINUTES **| COOK TIME:** 35 MINUTES

In my house, we often debate about the best type of dessert. My vote is always with anything chocolaty, whereas Dennis prefers fruit-based confections. He could probably subsist on nothing but shortbread, too, so I created these bars for him. With their crumbly base and warm raspberry filling, I have to ration them out to prevent him from eating them all at once—and so I can partake in them, too. Even this chocoholic gives them a thumbs-up!

### FOR THE FILLING

**2 cups fresh or thawed frozen raspberries**

**2 tablespoons pure maple syrup**

**2 tablespoons chia seeds**

### FOR THE BASE AND TOPPING

**2 cups all-purpose flour**

**⅔ cup sugar**

**1 teaspoon pure almond extract**

**½ teaspoon salt**

**¾ cup refined coconut oil, at room temperature**

**¼ cup very cold plain unsweetened Almond Milk (page 214) or store-bought nondairy milk**

**½ cup chopped or slivered almonds**

### FOR THE GLAZE

**½ cup confectioners' sugar (see Tip)**

**1 tablespoon plain unsweetened Almond Milk (page 214) or store-bought nondairy milk, plus more as needed**

1. Preheat the oven to 350°F. Line an 8-inch square baking pan with parchment paper, leaving a few inches of overhang on two sides.

2. **Make the filling:** In a small pot, cook the raspberries over medium heat until they begin to break down, about 5 minutes. Remove the pot from the heat and stir in the maple syrup and chia seeds. Set aside to cool for 5 minutes (the jam will thicken as it cools).

3. **Make the base and topping:** In a medium bowl, combine the flour, sugar, almond extract, and salt. Add the oil and almond milk and stir until just combined (the mixture will be a little crumbly). Set aside ½ cup of the dough. Press the remaining dough into an even layer over the prepared baking pan.

4. Spread the raspberry filling over the dough.

5. In a small bowl, combine the reserved ½ cup dough and the almonds. Crumble the mixture and sprinkle it evenly over the filling.

6. Bake for 30 minutes, or until the topping is golden brown and the jam is bubbling.

7. **Meanwhile, make the glaze:** In a small bowl, combine the confectioners' sugar and almond milk and stir until smooth; if the glaze is too thick to drizzle, add more almond milk ¼ teaspoon at a time.

8. Remove the shortbread bars from the oven and let cool completely in the pan. Using the overhanging parchment as handles, lift the bars from the pan and set on a cutting board. Drizzle the bars with the glaze, then slice into 16 squares. Serve. Store in an airtight container in the refrigerator for up to 1 week.

**Ingredient Tip:** Some brands of confectioners' sugar contain bone char, an animal-derived ingredient used to whiten the sugar. Be sure to check the label on your bag of sugar, or contact the manufacturer to find out if their product contains bone char.

**Time-Saving Tip:** If desired, 1 cup store-bought raspberry jam can be used instead of making your own.

**Troubleshooting Tip:** Make sure your coconut oil is softened slightly but not melted. Melted oil will result in a shortbread base that isn't as crumbly.

**PER SERVING (1 BAR):** CALORIES: 234; FAT: 13G; SATURATED FAT: 9G; CHOLESTEROL: 0G; PROTEIN: 3G; FIBER: 3G; SODIUM: 76MG

# OOEY-GOOEY MAGIC COOKIE BARS

SOY-FREE, KID-FRIENDLY

**MAKES 16 BARS | PREP TIME:** 10 MINUTES | **COOK TIME:** 45 MINUTES

It's difficult to convey the magical qualities of these cookie bars with words. You have to try one for yourself to understand. Something otherworldly happens when pecans, coconut, and chocolate chips collide with sweetened coconut milk. Their lure is irresistible. These bars are so sublime, they can be used to settle arguments, apologize for wrongdoings, and heal great divides. Believe me when I say, "If you bake it, they will come."

1 (14-ounce) can full-fat coconut milk

⅓ cup coconut sugar

1½ cups quick-cooking rolled oats

1½ cups almond flour

½ cup pure maple syrup

¼ cup unrefined coconut oil, at room temperature

½ teaspoon pure vanilla extract

¾ cup unsweetened shredded coconut

¾ cup chopped pecans

¾ cup dairy-free chocolate chips

**Substitution Tip:**
Any type of nut can be used in place of the pecans. Dairy-free white chocolate chips or peanut butter chips can be used in place of the chocolate chips. Dried fruit can be used in place of the shredded coconut.

1. Preheat the oven to 350°F. Line an 8-inch square baking pan with parchment paper, leaving a few inches of overhang on two sides.

2. In a medium saucepan, combine the coconut milk and coconut sugar. Bring to a boil over medium-high heat, whisking to prevent burning, then reduce the heat to medium-low. Simmer, stirring frequently, for 12 to 15 minutes, until the mixture has thickened slightly. Remove the pan from the heat and set aside.

3. In a food processor, process the oats until they resemble coarse flour. Add the almond flour, maple syrup, coconut oil, and vanilla and pulse until a dough forms. Press the dough into an even layer over the prepared baking pan.

4. Sprinkle the coconut, pecans, and chocolate chips evenly over the dough. Pour the sweetened coconut milk over the top.

5. Bake for 30 minutes, or until the edges are golden brown and the filling is bubbling (the bars will firm up as they cool). Remove from the oven and let the bars cool completely in the pan. Using the overhanging parchment as handles, lift the bars from the pan and set on a cutting board. Slice into 16 squares to serve.

**PER SERVING (1 BAR):** CALORIES: 307; FAT: 22G; SATURATED FAT: 11G; CHOLESTEROL: 0G; PROTEIN: 5G; FIBER: 4G; SODIUM: 7MG

# CHOCOLATE TAHINI BROWNIES

SOY-FREE, KID-FRIENDLY

**MAKES 16 BROWNIES | PREP TIME:** 10 MINUTES **| COOK TIME:** 35 MINUTES

Growing up, "homemade" baked goods always came from a boxed mix, so I always thought that it was *waaaay* too complicated to bake from scratch. Years later, I was given a dessert cookbook, and the first thing I made was a peanut butter brownie recipe. To my delight, they were easy to make, and they tasted much better than their boxed counterparts. This recipe is a throwback to those brownies that opened my eyes to baking without a box.

Vegetable oil, for the baking pan

½ cup aquafaba (the liquid from a can of chickpeas)

¾ cup all-purpose flour

¾ cup unsweetened cocoa powder

⅓ cup packed brown sugar

⅓ cup granulated sugar

½ teaspoon ground cinnamon

½ teaspoon baking powder

½ teaspoon baking soda

¼ teaspoon salt

¾ cup plain unsweetened Almond Milk (page 214) or store-bought nondairy milk

⅓ cup plus 3 tablespoons tahini, divided

2 teaspoons pure vanilla extract

1 tablespoon agave nectar

1. Preheat the oven to 350°F. Line an 8-inch square baking pan with parchment paper, leaving a few inches of overhang on two sides. Lightly oil the parchment.

2. In a medium bowl, whisk the aquafaba until foamy.

3. In a large bowl, combine the flour, cocoa powder, brown sugar, granulated sugar, cinnamon, baking powder, baking soda, and salt.

4. Add the aquafaba, almond milk, ⅓ cup of the tahini, and the vanilla to the dry ingredients and stir until just combined (be careful not to overmix; the batter will be thick). Scrape the batter into the prepared baking pan.

5. In a small bowl, stir together the remaining 3 tablespoons tahini and the agave. Drizzle the mixture over the batter in the pan. Using a toothpick or skewer, create a zigzag or swirled pattern in the batter.

6. Bake for 25 to 30 minutes, until a toothpick inserted into the center comes out clean. Remove from the oven and let the brownies cool completely in the pan. Using the overhanging parchment as handles, lift the brownies from the pan and set them on a cutting board. Slice into 16 squares. Serve.

**Substitution Tip:** Peanut butter, almond butter, or sunflower seed butter can be used in place of the tahini.

**PER SERVING (1 BROWNIE):** CALORIES: 128; FAT: 6G; SATURATED FAT: 1G; CHOLESTEROL: 0G; PROTEIN: 3G; FIBER: 2G; SODIUM: 94MG

# RICE PUDDING

NUT-FREE, GLUTEN-FREE, SOY-FREE, KID-FRIENDLY, ONE-PAN/ONE-POT

**SERVES 4 | PREP TIME:** 5 MINUTES | **COOK TIME:** 20 MINUTES

When I was little, I was afraid of rice pudding. Afraid of a pudding? Yup. You see, it was lumpy, and pudding is supposed to be smooth. It was made with rice, which is supposed to be part of dinner. And it was warm, and I was used to chilled pudding. It was too strange for my young palate. But things have changed, and I've grown to appreciate this warm, cozy pudding, which is akin to a hug in a bowl.

1 (14-ounce) can full-fat
coconut milk

1 cup water

¾ cup uncooked short-grain
white rice

⅓ cup pure maple syrup

½ cup raisins

1 teaspoon
ground cinnamon

½ teaspoon ground nutmeg

1 teaspoon pure
vanilla extract

½ teaspoon salt

1. In a medium pot, combine the coconut milk, water, rice, maple syrup, raisins, cinnamon, and nutmeg. Bring to a boil over medium-high heat, then reduce the heat to medium. Cook, stirring frequently, for about 20 minutes, until the pudding thickens to the desired consistency.

2. Remove the pot from the heat. Stir in the vanilla and salt. Serve the pudding warm or chilled.

**Substitution Tip:** Short-grain brown rice can be used instead of the white rice, but keep in mind that it will take about 50 minutes to cook instead of 20 minutes.

**Time-Saving Tip:** To cut back on the cooking time, 2 cups cooked rice can be used in place of cooking ¾ cup from scratch. Add the cooked rice to the pot with all the ingredients in step 1 and simmer, stirring occasionally, for 15 to 20 minutes, until the pudding thickens to the desired consistency.

PER SERVING: CALORIES: 457; FAT: 21G; SATURATED FAT: 19G; CHOLESTEROL: 0G; PROTEIN: 5G; FIBER: 2G; SODIUM: 309MG

# CHEESECAKE-STUFFED BAKED APPLES

KID-FRIENDLY

**SERVES 6 | PREP TIME:** 10 MINUTES | **COOK TIME:** 45 MINUTES

Every year, we mark the beginning of autumn with a road trip to New York State for a day of apple picking. We load up the trunk of my Mini Cooper with freshly picked apples and head home, dreaming of the apple-based delicacies we'll make. Sure, we could just eat the apples plain, but coring them and filling them with a cheesecake stuffing is far more fun (and more scrumptious, too). You can use your leftover apple innards in an Apple Berry Crumble (page 204).

1 (12-ounce) package silken tofu, drained

⅓ cup sugar

2 tablespoons smooth natural almond butter

2 tablespoons fresh lemon juice

1 tablespoon cornstarch

½ teaspoon pure vanilla extract

1 teaspoon ground cinnamon, divided

¼ teaspoon ground nutmeg, divided

¼ cup quick-cooking rolled oats

¼ cup chopped walnuts

¼ cup pure maple syrup

6 medium baking apples (see Tip)

¾ cup unsweetened apple juice

1. Preheat the oven to 375°F.

2. In a blender, combine the tofu, sugar, almond butter, lemon juice, cornstarch, vanilla, ½ teaspoon of the cinnamon, and ⅛ teaspoon of the nutmeg. Blend until smooth and creamy.

3. In a small bowl, combine the oats, walnuts, maple syrup, remaining ½ teaspoon cinnamon, and remaining ⅛ teaspoon nutmeg.

4. Using a paring knife, cut ¼ inch off the top of each apple. Use a melon baller or spoon to hollow them out, leaving about ½ inch of flesh around the edges.

5. Fill the apples with the tofu mixture, leaving about ½ inch unfilled at the top of each. Top with the oat mixture.

6. Pour the apple juice into a 9-by-13-inch baking dish. Stand the stuffed apples upright in the baking dish. Bake for 35 to 45 minutes, until the apples are soft but not mushy (a small knife should be able to slide into the apple easily). Serve.

**Ingredient Tip:** The best apples for baking are Granny Smith, Honeycrisp, Jonagold, Golden Delicious, Braeburn, Pink Lady, and Cortland.

**PER SERVING:** CALORIES: 314; FAT: 9G; SATURATED FAT: 1G; CHOLESTEROL: 0G; PROTEIN: 7G; FIBER: 6G; SODIUM: 22MG

# APPLE BERRY CRUMBLE

SOY-FREE, KID-FRIENDLY

**SERVES 8 | PREP TIME:** 15 MINUTES | **COOK TIME:** 40 MINUTES

Fun fact: Fruit crisps and fruit crumbles aren't the same thing, though I've learned that many people tend to confuse the two. They're similar, but the difference is in the topping. Crisps usually have an oat-based topping, which crisps up (as the name suggests) when you bake it. The topping on a crumble is a flour-based streusel, which is crumbly. Sometimes oats are added to crumble toppings, too, hence the confusion. Hopefully this PSA has helped to clear up things.

**5 baking apples (such as Honeycrisp, Jonagold, or Braeburn), peeled, cored, and diced (about 10 cups)**

**2 cups mixed berries, sliced if large (see Tip)**

**½ cup pure maple syrup**

**1 tablespoon fresh lemon juice**

**2½ teaspoons ground cinnamon, divided**

**¼ teaspoon ground nutmeg**

**¼ teaspoon ground ginger**

**1 cup whole wheat flour**

**½ cup sugar**

**¼ teaspoon salt**

**½ cup refined coconut oil, solid**

**½ cup chopped hazelnuts**

1. Preheat the oven to 350°F.

2. In a large bowl, toss together the apples, berries, maple syrup, lemon juice, 2 teaspoons of the cinnamon, the nutmeg, and the ginger. Spread the mixture over the bottom of a 9-by-13-inch baking dish.

3. In a large bowl, stir together the flour, sugar, and salt. Add the coconut oil and, using a pastry cutter or your hands, break it up and work it into the flour mixture until you have small pieces the size of peas (some of it might seem sandlike; that's okay). Stir in the hazelnuts and remaining ½ teaspoon cinnamon.

4. Sprinkle the topping over the fruit (it's okay if it's uneven).

5. Bake for 40 minutes, or until the top is golden and the fruit is bubbling. Serve warm.

**Ingredient Tip:** Fresh or frozen berries can be used. If you're using frozen berries, there's no need to thaw them first.

**Troubleshooting Tip:** Your coconut oil should be solid, or it won't crumble when you add it to the flour mixture. If it's soft, place it in the refrigerator for a few minutes to solidify before making your topping.

**PER SERVING:** CALORIES: 404; FAT: 20G; SATURATED FAT: 12G; CHOLESTEROL: 0G; PROTEIN: 4G; FIBER: 7G; SODIUM: 77MG

# LEMON LOAF

SOY-FREE, KID-FRIENDLY

**SERVES 8 | PREP TIME:** 15 MINUTES | **COOK TIME:** 1 HOUR

"Lemon loaf" tends to conjure up images of teapots, cups and saucers, and ladies in fancy dresses gossiping in the garden. No fancy dress is required for a slice (or two or three) of this tangy little cake, but I do recommend enjoying your cake with a nice hot cuppa.

## FOR THE LOAF

Vegetable oil, for the baking pan

2 cups all-purpose flour

1 cup granulated sugar

2 teaspoons baking powder

1 teaspoon salt

⅔ cup extra-virgin olive oil

½ cup plain unsweetened Almond Milk (page 214) or store-bought nondairy milk

2 tablespoons grated lemon zest

¼ cup fresh lemon juice

1 teaspoon pure vanilla extract

## FOR THE GLAZE

1 cup confectioners' sugar

1 teaspoon grated lemon zest

2 tablespoons fresh lemon juice

1. **Make the loaf:** Preheat the oven to 350°F. Line a 9-by-5-inch baking pan with parchment paper, leaving a few inches of overhang on the two long sides. Lightly oil the parchment.

2. In a large bowl, whisk together the flour, granulated sugar, baking powder, and salt.

3. In a medium bowl, whisk together the olive oil, almond milk, lemon zest, lemon juice, and vanilla.

4. Pour the wet ingredients into the dry ingredients and gently stir to combine (be careful not to overmix).

5. Scrape the batter into the prepared baking pan. Bake for 50 to 60 minutes, until a toothpick inserted into the center comes out clean.

6. **Meanwhile, make the glaze:** In a small bowl, whisk together the confectioners' sugar, lemon zest, and lemon juice.

7. Remove the pan from the oven and let the cake cool completely in the pan. Using the overhanging parchment as handles, lift the cake out of the pan. Peel away the parchment, then place the cake on a serving dish.

8. Drizzle the glaze over the cake, allowing it to drip down the sides. Let the glaze set before serving.

> **Variation Tip:** For an orange-cranberry loaf, replace the lemon zest and juice with orange zest and juice, and fold 1 cup cranberries into the batter before baking.

PER SERVING: CALORIES: **432**; FAT: 19G; SATURATED FAT: 3G; CHOLESTEROL: 0G; PROTEIN: 4G; FIBER: 1G; SODIUM: 301MG

# BLUE VELVET CUPCAKES

**MAKES 12 CUPCAKES | PREP TIME:** 20 MINUTES | **COOK TIME:** 25 MINUTES

Most "velvet" cupcakes are red, but I've made these blue as an homage to director David Lynch, and just because I like the color blue. Most red food colorings are made from carmine (which is made from crushed bugs), so they're not technically vegan. Blue is a cooler, kinder color. Add a few drops of blue food coloring to the frosting, too, for extra color. You can use natural (non-bug) red food coloring if you're not feeling blue, or you can skip the food coloring altogether if you're opposed to it.

### FOR THE CUPCAKES

- 1 cup plain unsweetened Almond Milk (page 214) or store-bought almond or soy milk
- 2 tablespoons apple cider vinegar
- ⅓ cup neutral-flavored vegetable oil
- 2 tablespoons blue food coloring
- 1 teaspoon pure vanilla extract
- ¼ teaspoon pure almond extract
- 1½ cups all-purpose flour
- 1 cup granulated sugar
- ¼ cup unsweetened cocoa powder
- 1 teaspoon baking soda
- 1 teaspoon baking powder
- ½ teaspoon salt

1. Preheat the oven to 350°F. Line a 12-cup muffin tin with liners.

2. **Make the cupcakes:** In a small bowl, combine the almond milk and vinegar. Set aside for 5 to 10 minutes, until it looks curdled.

3. Add the oil, food coloring, vanilla, and almond extract to the bowl with the almond milk mixture and stir to combine.

4. In a large bowl, combine the flour, granulated sugar, cocoa powder, baking soda, baking powder, and salt. Add the wet ingredients and mix until well combined.

5. Divide the batter among the prepared muffin cups, filling them three-quarters full.

6. Bake for 20 to 25 minutes, until a toothpick inserted into the center of a cupcake comes out clean. Remove from the oven and let cool completely before frosting.

FOR THE FROSTING

½ cup vegan butter, at room temperature

½ teaspoon pure vanilla extract

2½ cups confectioners' sugar, sifted

1 to 2 tablespoons plain unsweetened Almond Milk (page 214) or store-bought nondairy milk, plus more as needed

7. **Make the frosting:** In a large bowl, combine the vegan butter and vanilla. Using a handheld mixer, beat until creamy, about 2 minutes. Add half the confectioners' sugar and mix until it's well incorporated. Add the remaining confectioners' sugar and 1 tablespoon of the almond milk. Beat the frosting until it's smooth, creamy, and fluffy; if it seems too dry, add more almond milk 1 tablespoon at a time.

8. Spread the frosting over the cooled cupcakes. Serve. Store in an airtight container in the refrigerator for up to 1 week.

**Troubleshooting Tip:** Because of the proteins they contain, soy milk and almond milk are the only types of nondairy milk that will curdle when mixed with apple cider vinegar. If you use another kind of nondairy milk, you may not get the same results.

**PER SERVING (1 CUPCAKE):** CALORIES: 339; FAT: 14G; SATURATED FAT: 6G; CHOLESTEROL: 0G; PROTEIN: 3G; FIBER: 1G; SODIUM: 217MG

# NO-BAKE CHOCOLATE CHERRY CHEESECAKE

GLUTEN-FREE, SOY-FREE, KID-FRIENDLY

**SERVES 12 | PREP TIME:** 25 MINUTES, PLUS 2 HOURS SOAKING TIME AND CHILLING TIME

When I had an office job, I liked to bake treats to share with my coworkers. Once in my pre-vegan days, I baked a dairy-filled chocolate cheesecake for an officemate's birthday, and it was so delectable, I received a marriage proposal from another colleague. (I did not take him up on the offer.) After going vegan, I wasn't sure I'd be able to capture that same level of lusciousness without dairy, but I've managed to do so thanks to the magic of blended cashews.

Vegetable oil, for the pan

1½ cups walnuts

6 Medjool dates, pitted

¼ cup unsweetened cocoa powder

1 (10-ounce) bag frozen cherries, thawed

¼ cup sugar

1 tablespoon cornstarch

1½ cups dairy-free chocolate chips

1½ cups raw cashews, soaked for at least 2 hours, drained, and rinsed

½ cup pure maple syrup

¼ cup fresh lemon juice

⅓ cup refined coconut oil, melted

1 teaspoon pure vanilla extract

1. Lightly oil an 8- or 9-inch springform pan.

2. In a food processor, combine the walnuts, dates, and cocoa powder and process until the mixture resembles crumbs. Press the mixture over the bottom of the prepared pan. Set aside.

3. In a small saucepan, combine the cherries, sugar, and cornstarch. Bring the mixture to a boil over medium-high heat. Reduce the heat to medium and simmer, stirring frequently, for about 5 minutes, until the liquid thickens. Remove from the heat and let cool for about 10 minutes.

4. Meanwhile, fill a medium pot with a few inches of water. Bring the water to a simmer over medium heat. Place another pot or a heatproof bowl on top (the bottom of the pot or bowl should not touch the water). Place the chocolate chips in the top pot or bowl and stir until melted and smooth (do not allow the chocolate to burn). Set aside ¼ cup of the melted chocolate and transfer the rest to a blender.

5. Add the cashews, maple syrup, lemon juice, coconut oil, and vanilla to the blender. Blend until smooth and creamy.

6.  Pour the cashew mixture into the pan over the walnut-date base. Top with the cooled cherry mixture. Drizzle the reserved ¼ cup melted chocolate over the cherries.

7.  Cover the pan with aluminum foil or plastic wrap. Refrigerate for at least 2 hours and up to overnight before slicing and serving.

8.  Store in an airtight container in the refrigerator for up to 5 days or in the freezer for up to 6 months.

**Variation Tip:** For a vanilla cheesecake, omit the chocolate chips and increase the vanilla extract to 2 teaspoons. Any type of berry can be used in place of the cherries.

**PER SERVING:** CALORIES: 389; FAT: 24G; SATURATED FAT: 8G; CHOLESTEROL: 0G; PROTEIN: 7G; FIBER: 3G; SODIUM: 26MG

# GIGGLE PIE

**SERVES 8 | PREP TIME:** 20 MINUTES, PLUS 2 HOURS SOAKING TIME AND CHILLING TIME

This pie is like a turbocharged version of a certain snickering candy bar. The combination of chocolate, peanut butter, and caramel makes me giggle with glee. I'll admit that I'm not much of a pie baker, because I don't like rolling out dough, but this no-bake recipe is easy. You just mix the ingredients for the crust and then press the mixture into the pie pan—no rolling pin required.

FOR THE CRUST

**Vegetable oil, for the pan**

**¾ cup quick-cooking rolled oats**

**¾ cup roasted peanuts**

**6 Medjool dates, pitted (see Tip)**

**¼ cup unsweetened cocoa powder**

**½ teaspoon salt**

FOR THE CARAMEL LAYER

**16 Medjool dates, pitted, soaked for 2 hours, and drained**

**½ cup plain unsweetened Almond Milk (page 214) or store-bought nondairy milk, plus more as needed**

**1 teaspoon pure vanilla extract**

1. **Make the crust:** Lightly oil an 8- or 9-inch springform pan.

2. In a food processor, pulse the oats until they resemble coarse flour. Add the peanuts, dates, cocoa powder, and salt and process until the mixture resembles crumbs. Press the mixture over the bottom of the prepared pan.

3. **Make the caramel layer:** In a blender or food processor, combine the dates, almond milk, and vanilla and process until smooth and creamy; if the mixture is too thick, add more almond milk 1 tablespoon at a time. Spread the caramel in an even layer over the crust.

4. **Make the peanut butter filling:** In a blender, combine the tofu, peanut butter, maple syrup, and salt. Blend until smooth and creamy. Pour the filling over the caramel layer.

5. **Make the topping:** Fill a medium pot with a few inches of water. Bring the water to a simmer over medium heat. Place another pot or a heatproof bowl on top (the bottom of the pot or bowl should not touch the water). Place the chocolate chips and almond milk in the top pot or bowl and stir until the chocolate is melted and smooth.

6. Sprinkle the top of the filling with the peanuts. Drizzle with the melted chocolate.

**1 (12-ounce) package silken tofu, drained**

**1 cup creamy natural peanut butter**

**½ cup pure maple syrup**

**Pinch salt**

FOR THE TOPPING

**½ cup dairy-free chocolate chips**

**2 tablespoons plain unsweetened Almond Milk (page 214) or store-bought nondairy milk**

**½ cup chopped roasted peanuts**

7.  Cover the pan with aluminum foil or plastic wrap and refrigerate for an hour or two before slicing and serving.

8.  Store in an airtight container in the refrigerator for up to 5 days or in the freezer for up to 6 months.

> **Ingredient Tip:** Medjool dates are softer and more caramel-like than other varieties. Make sure you soak them before making the caramel sauce so they'll blend well. Soaking the dates for the crust is optional. If they're soft, they don't need to be soaked, but if they're firm, they can be soaked for 20 minutes or so.

PER SERVING: CALORIES: 707; FAT: 35G; SATURATED FAT: 8G; CHOLESTEROL: 0G; PROTEIN: 21G; FIBER: 11G; SODIUM: 172MG

## Aquafaba: Baking with Bean Juice

If you're dumping the liquid from that can of chickpeas, you're literally flushing a magical egg replacer down the drain. Because of its starch content, aquafaba (which translates to "bean water") has binding properties, and it can be used in place of eggs in many recipes. You can't make an omelet out of it, but you can whip it up to use in meringues, mousse, and even mayo. It can replace eggs in baked goods, too.

Aquafaba works best when it's cold, so chill it in the refrigerator before using it. You can also freeze it if you don't plan on using it right away. To use it in baked goods, just lightly whip it with a whisk until foamy. Note that 3 tablespoons aquafaba equals 1 egg; 2 tablespoons aquafaba equals 1 egg white.

Other egg replacements for baking include flax meal (ground flaxseed), chia seeds, and commercial egg replacers.

Carrot-Ginger Dressing, page 216

# CHAPTER ELEVEN

# DO IT YOURSELF

## HOMEMADE SAUCES AND STAPLES

# ALMOND MILK

GLUTEN-FREE, SOY-FREE, KID-FRIENDLY

**MAKES 4 CUPS | PREP TIME:** 10 MINUTES, PLUS 8 HOURS SOAKING TIME

Sure, it's easy to find almond milk in just about any store these days, but fresh home-made nut milk tastes so much better than anything that comes from a carton. Milking all those almonds may sound intimidating, but I'm here to tell ya that it's actually really simple. If you're in the mood for a vanilla beverage, add vanilla extract. If you like your drink a little on the sweet side, stir in some maple syrup.

1 cup raw almonds, soaked for at least 8 hours, drained, and rinsed

4 cups water

¼ teaspoon salt

1 teaspoon pure vanilla extract (optional)

2 tablespoons pure maple syrup (optional)

1. In a blender, combine the almonds, water, salt, vanilla (if using), and maple syrup (if using). Blend until the nuts have broken down and the liquid is opaque white (this might take several minutes).

2. Place a nut-milk bag over a large pitcher or jar. Pour the almond mixture into it, close the bag's draw-string, and squeeze the pulp in the bag to extract as much of the almond milk as possible (discard the pulp).

3. Store the almond milk in an airtight container in the refrigerator for up to 4 days.

**Technique Tip:** If you don't have a nut-milk bag, you can use a fine-mesh sieve lined with two layers of cheese-cloth. Gather the ends of the cheesecloth and twist them closed before squeezing out the nut milk.

**Substitution Tip:** Cashews, macadamia nuts, or walnuts can be used instead of the almonds.

**PER SERVING (1 CUP):** CALORIES: 30; FAT: 3G; SATURATED FAT: 0G; CHOLESTEROL: 0G; PROTEIN: 1G; FIBER: 0G; SODIUM: 125MG

# SPICY TAHINI DRESSING

**MAKES ABOUT 1 CUP | PREP TIME:** 5 MINUTES

Vegans are often asked about desert-island scenarios and what they'd eat if they found themselves stuck on one. The one thing I'd want with me would be a jar of tahini (okay, many, many buckets of tahini), because it can make just about anything more palatable. Not to sound clichéd, but I wouldn't mind eating nothing but twigs and leaves if they were drenched in this spicy tahini-based dressing. You can control the heat of the dressing by reducing or increasing the amount of red pepper flakes.

½ cup tahini (see Tip)

¼ cup fresh lemon juice

2 tablespoons water, plus more as needed

1 teaspoon Dijon mustard

1 garlic clove, minced

1 teaspoon red pepper flakes

½ teaspoon salt

1. In a medium bowl, combine the tahini, lemon juice, water, mustard, garlic, red pepper flakes, and salt. Whisk until smooth and creamy (the dressing can also be mixed together in a blender). If the dressing seems too thick, add more water 1 teaspoon at a time.

2. Store the dressing in an airtight container in the refrigerator for up to 1 week.

**Ingredient Tip:** Tahini is a paste made from ground sesame seeds, and it's often used in Middle Eastern cooking. It's kind of bitter straight out of the jar, but a little lemon juice and water transform it into a luscious dressing. It can usually be found in the same area of the grocery store as peanut butter.

**PER SERVING (2 TABLESPOONS):** CALORIES: 92; FAT: 8G; SATURATED FAT: 1G; CHOLESTEROL: 0G; PROTEIN: 3G; FIBER: 2G; SODIUM: 170MG

# CARROT-GINGER DRESSING

**MAKES ABOUT 1½ CUPS | PREP TIME:** 10 MINUTES

This recipe was inspired by the carrot-ginger dressing that used to accompany veggie sushi at a local take-out place. After I got hooked, the restaurant stopped including it with their rolls, so I was forced to re-create it at home. It's my sauce of choice on bowl meals and salads. I prefer dunking my avocado rolls in this dressing, rather than straight-up soy sauce, which can be too salty.

2 medium carrots, chopped (about 1 cup)

¼ cup tahini

¼ cup water, plus more as needed (see Tip)

¼ cup unseasoned rice vinegar

2 tablespoons grated peeled fresh ginger

2 tablespoons reduced-sodium soy sauce or tamari

2 tablespoons pure maple syrup

1 teaspoon toasted sesame oil

1. In a blender, combine the carrots, tahini, water, vinegar, ginger, soy sauce, maple syrup, and sesame oil. Blend until smooth and creamy; if the dressing seems too thick, add more water 1 teaspoon at a time.

2. Store the dressing in an airtight container in the refrigerator for up to 1 week.

**Ingredient Tip:** The thickness of tahini can vary from brand to brand or even bottle to bottle. The amount of water needed for this dressing will depend on the tahini. The dressing may thicken as it sits in the refrigerator, so you may need to mix in a little water when you're ready to serve it.

**PER SERVING (2 TABLESPOONS):** CALORIES: 50; FAT: 3G; SATURATED FAT: 0G; CHOLESTEROL: 0G; PROTEIN: 1G; FIBER: 1G; SODIUM: 181MG

# RANCH DRESSING

**MAKES ABOUT 1 CUP | PREP TIME:** 20 MINUTES, PLUS 2 HOURS SOAKING TIME

Is there anything that doesn't taste a little yummier with a drizzle of ranch? Go ahead and think about it—I'll wait. Ranch is usually made with buttermilk, which I've mimicked here by clabbering (or curdling) soy milk with apple cider vinegar. Once the soy milk's combined with a few other ingredients, it magically transforms into a drool-worthy dressing you'll want to pour over almost everything. (P.S.: The answer to that question is chocolate cake—chocolate cake tastes awful with ranch dressing.)

¼ cup unsweetened soy milk

1 tablespoon apple cider vinegar

½ cup raw cashews, soaked for at least 2 hours, drained, and rinsed

1 tablespoon fresh lemon juice

1 garlic clove, minced

½ teaspoon onion powder

½ teaspoon salt

1 teaspoon or more water (optional)

1 tablespoon chopped fresh parsley leaves

1 tablespoon chopped fresh chives

2 teaspoons chopped fresh dill

1. In a small bowl, combine the soy milk and vinegar. Set aside for about 10 minutes (it will look curdled, which is what you want).

2. In a blender, combine the soy milk mixture, cashews, lemon juice, garlic, onion powder, and salt. Blend until smooth and creamy; if the dressing seems too thick, add water 1 teaspoon at a time. Add the parsley, chives, and dill and pulse to combine.

3. Store the dressing in an airtight container in the refrigerator for up to 1 week.

**Time-Saving Tip:** If you're in a rush for your ranch, you can soften the cashews faster by soaking them in boiling water for 20 minutes. Soaking nuts in boiling water destroys some of their nutrients, but your dressing will still be just as tasty.

**Substitution Tip:** Plain unsweetened almond milk, homemade (see page 214) or store-bought, can be used instead of the soy milk. Other types of nondairy milk won't curdle the way soy and almond will.

**PER SERVING (2 TABLESPOONS):** CALORIES: 60; FAT: 4G; SATURATED FAT: 1G; CHOLESTEROL: 0G; PROTEIN: 2G; FIBER: 1G; SODIUM: 151MG

# GREEN GODDESS DRESSING

NUT-FREE, GLUTEN-FREE, SOY-FREE

**MAKES ABOUT 1½ CUPS | PREP TIME:** 10 MINUTES

Empress of salads, queen of the veggies—green goddess dressing is pure tangy, creamy deliciousness. With the addition of capers, it borrows Caesar salad's salty, briny flavor; and its fresh herbs are reminiscent of ranch dressing. I find green goddess rather addictive, and I use it on salads, in sandwiches, and as a dip for cut veggies. Don't say I didn't warn you when you find yourself craving it throughout the day.

¾ cup water, plus more as needed

½ cup tahini

½ cup loosely packed chopped fresh parsley leaves

¼ cup loosely packed chopped fresh basil

1 small avocado, pitted, peeled, and diced

2 tablespoons fresh lemon juice

1 tablespoon Dijon mustard

2 teaspoons apple cider vinegar

2 garlic cloves, minced

1 teaspoon capers, drained

½ teaspoon salt

2 tablespoons chopped fresh chives

1. In a blender, combine the water, tahini, parsley, basil, avocado, lemon juice, mustard, vinegar, garlic, capers, salt, and chives. Blend until smooth and creamy; if the dressing seems too thick, add more water 1 teaspoon at a time.

2. Store the dressing in an airtight container in the refrigerator for up to 1 week.

**Substitution Tip:** Traditionally, green goddess dressing is made with tarragon, which tastes a little too much like licorice for my liking. If you don't mind its flavor, you can swap out the basil for fresh tarragon.

**PER SERVING (2 TABLESPOONS):** CALORIES: 93; FAT: 8G; SATURATED FAT: 1G; CHOLESTEROL: 0G; PROTEIN: 2G; FIBER: 3G; SODIUM: 142MG

# CHIPOTLE-LIME DRESSING

NUT-FREE, GLUTEN-FREE

**MAKES ABOUT 1 CUP | PREP TIME:** 10 MINUTES

A little bit hot, a little bit tangy, this dressing is a kick in the taste buds. Its bold flavor will punch up salads, tacos, burritos, and even sandwiches. With all this punching and kicking, it sounds a little violent, but that's just the spicy nature of this dressing. (No vegetables were harmed in the making of this recipe.)

1 cup silken tofu

3 tablespoons fresh lime juice

1 canned chipotle pepper in adobo, plus 1 teaspoon adobo sauce from the can (see Tip)

1 garlic clove, minced

½ teaspoon onion powder

½ teaspoon salt

¼ teaspoon smoked paprika

¼ teaspoon freshly ground black pepper

2 tablespoons chopped fresh cilantro leaves

1. In a blender, combine the tofu, lime juice, chipotle and adobo sauce, garlic, onion powder, salt, paprika, and black pepper. Blend until smooth and creamy. Add the cilantro and pulse to combine.

2. Store the dressing in an airtight container in the refrigerator for up to 1 week.

**Ingredient Tip:** Chipotles are smoked jalapeños, and they come packed in cans along with adobo sauce. They can usually be found near the taco-making supplies in the grocery store.

**PER SERVING (2 TABLESPOONS):** CALORIES: 24; FAT: 1G; SATURATED FAT: 0G; CHOLESTEROL: 0G; PROTEIN: 2G; FIBER: 0G; SODIUM: 260MG

# BALSAMIC DIJON VINAIGRETTE

NUT-FREE, GLUTEN-FREE, SOY-FREE

**MAKES ABOUT 1 CUP | PREP TIME:** 10 MINUTES

"Balsamic Dijon Vinaigrette" sounds a little luxurious, doesn't it? It's much fancier than "vinegar and mustard dressing," which is what this actually is. While I prefer creamy dressings, I think it's always handy to have a vinaigrette recipe at the ready. In addition to tossing it with leafy greens for a salad, I like to use it as a marinade for tofu and tempeh.

¾ cup olive oil

¼ cup balsamic vinegar
(see Tip)

1 tablespoon Dijon mustard

1 garlic clove, minced

½ teaspoon salt

¼ teaspoon freshly ground
black pepper

In a glass jar with a lid, combine the oil, vinegar, mustard, garlic, salt, and pepper. Place the lid on the jar and shake vigorously until the dressing is thoroughly combined. Store the vinaigrette in an airtight container in the refrigerator for up to 1 week.

**Ingredient Tip:** You can change the flavor profile of your dressing by using different types of balsamic vinegar. I love to use fruity vinegars; fig is my favorite.

**PER SERVING (2 TABLESPOONS):** CALORIES: 188; FAT: 20G; SATURATED FAT: 3G; CHOLESTEROL: 0G; PROTEIN: 0G; FIBER: 0G; SODIUM: 169MG

# SPICY PEANUT SAUCE

MAKES ABOUT 1 CUP | PREP TIME: 10 MINUTES

I love spicy peanut sauce so much that I will look for excuses to make it. I find myself plotting stir-fries and noodle dishes to feed my addiction. If I could, I would probably just guzzle this sauce straight from the bottle, but that would be a little weird, wouldn't it? So, I urge you to make this sauce and start planning your meals around it. You can thank me later.

½ cup full-fat coconut milk, plus more as needed (see Tip)

⅓ cup creamy natural peanut butter

1 tablespoon reduced-sodium soy sauce or tamari

2 teaspoons fresh lime juice

1 garlic clove, minced

1 teaspoon minced peeled fresh ginger

½ teaspoon red pepper flakes

1. In a blender, combine the coconut milk, peanut butter, soy sauce, lime juice, garlic, ginger, and red pepper flakes. Blend until smooth and creamy; if the sauce seems too thick, add more coconut milk 1 teaspoon at a time.

2. Store the sauce in an airtight container in the refrigerator for up to 1 week.

**Ingredient Tip:** When shopping for coconut milk, look for the type in the can. You don't want the coconut milk beverage sold in shelf-stable containers. The canned type is pure milk from a coconut, whereas the type in a carton contains fillers and stabilizers, which will interfere with the taste and texture of your sauce.

PER SERVING (¼ CUP): CALORIES: 187; FAT: 17G; SATURATED FAT: 6G; CHOLESTEROL: 0G; PROTEIN: 5G; FIBER: 2G; SODIUM: 257 MG

# CASHEW AIOLI

GLUTEN-FREE, SOY-FREE

**MAKES ABOUT 1 CUP | PREP TIME:** 5 MINUTES, PLUS 2 HOURS SOAKING TIME

Vampires are sure to leave you alone when you protect yourself with this garlicky concoction. Aioli is just a classy way to say "mayo with garlic." I do love to slather my sandwiches with this dreamy dressing, but I also like to dunk cut veggies into it and toss it into salads. You can add a dash of cayenne if you like your aioli with a spicy kick.

½ cup raw cashews, soaked for at least 2 hours, drained and rinsed

¼ cup water, plus more as needed

2 tablespoons fresh lemon juice

2 garlic cloves, minced (see Tip)

¼ teaspoon onion powder

¼ teaspoon garlic powder

¼ teaspoon salt

1. In a blender, combine the cashews, water, lemon juice, garlic, onion powder, garlic powder, and salt. Blend until smooth and creamy; if the aioli is too thick, add more water 1 teaspoon at a time.

2. Store the aioli in an airtight container in the refrigerator for up to 1 week.

**Ingredient Tip:** If you're feeling fancy, you can use roasted garlic rather than raw. Because roasted garlic is more mellow, you can use more than 2 cloves, if you like; I use 4 or 5, depending on their size. To roast the garlic, preheat the oven to 400°F. Place the garlic cloves (whole, not minced) on a sheet of aluminum foil, drizzle them with about ¼ teaspoon vegetable oil, and sprinkle with ¼ teaspoon each of salt and black pepper. Wrap the garlic in the foil and roast for about 40 minutes, then let cool before popping the soft cloves out of their papery skins.

**PER SERVING (2 TABLESPOONS):** CALORIES: 54; FAT: 2G; SATURATED FAT: 1G; CHOLESTEROL: 0G; PROTEIN: 4G; FIBER: 0G; SODIUM: 74MG

# CHIMICHURRI

NUT-FREE, GLUTEN-FREE, SOY-FREE

**MAKES ABOUT 2 CUPS | PREP TIME:** 15 MINUTES

Chimichurri is pesto's spicy South American cousin. Whereas pesto is usually served with veg-friendly pasta, chimichurri is traditionally served with grilled or roasted meat. We vegans can still enjoy it, though. I love to pair chimichurri with seitan or mushrooms, and I sometimes top my tacos with it instead of hot sauce. If you want to turn up the heat, add a dash of red pepper flakes to the mix.

**2 cups finely chopped fresh flat-leaf parsley (large stems removed before chopping)**

**¼ cup red wine vinegar**

**4 garlic cloves, minced**

**1 red chile pepper, minced**

**2 tablespoons minced fresh oregano leaves**

**½ teaspoon salt**

**¼ teaspoon freshly ground black pepper**

**½ cup extra-virgin olive oil**

1. In a medium bowl, combine the parsley, vinegar, garlic, chile pepper, oregano, salt, and black pepper. Slowly whisk in the oil.

2. Store the chimichurri in an airtight container in the refrigerator for up to 1 week. Bring it to room temperature before serving.

**Time-Saving Tip:** To cut back on chopping time, you can prepare your chimichurri in a food processor. Place the parsley, vinegar, garlic, chile pepper, oregano, salt, and black pepper in the food processor and process until the ingredients are finely chopped and mixed together. With the processor running, drizzle in the olive oil.

**PER SERVING (¼ CUP):** CALORIES: 131; FAT: 14G; SATURATED FAT: 2G; CHOLESTEROL: 0G; PROTEIN: 1G; FIBER: 1G; SODIUM: 155MG

# POPEYE PESTO

GLUTEN-FREE, SOY-FREE

**MAKES ABOUT 2 CUPS | PREP TIME:** 10 MINUTES

I'm a green sauce kinda gal. Pesto is my sauce of choice when it comes to pasta, and I've even been known to put it on my pizzas and sandwiches. It's traditionally made with basil, but I like to use spinach and peas to mix up things. A dash of nooch and a dab of miso stand in for the cheese found in nonvegan pesto.

2 cups tightly packed baby spinach

2 cups tightly packed fresh basil

1 cup peas

¼ cup pine nuts

3 garlic cloves

2 tablespoons fresh lemon juice

2 tablespoons nutritional yeast

1 teaspoon mellow white miso paste

½ teaspoon salt

¼ cup extra-virgin olive oil

1. In a food processor, combine the spinach, basil, peas, pine nuts, garlic, lemon juice, nutritional yeast, miso, and salt and process until well chopped.

2. With the processor running, drizzle in the oil and process until well combined.

3. Store the pesto in an airtight container in the refrigerator for up to 1 week or in the freezer for up to 2 months. Bring it to room temperature before serving.

**Substitution Tip:** You can use just about any leafy green veggie in place of the spinach in this recipe. I like to make it with arugula or baby kale. If you'd like to make your pesto nut-free, try hulled pumpkin seeds or sunflower seeds in place of the pine nuts.

**PER SERVING (¼ CUP):** CALORIES: 118; FAT: 10G; SATURATED FAT: 6G; CHOLESTEROL: 0G; PROTEIN: 3G; FIBER: 2G; SODIUM: 313MG

# MARINARA

NUT-FREE, GLUTEN-FREE, SOY-FREE, KID-FRIENDLY

**MAKES ABOUT 8 CUPS | PREP TIME:** 5 MINUTES | **COOK TIME:** 35 MINUTES

Look, I know it's super easy to reach for a jar of premade sauce when you're making pasta for dinner. In fact, I was a jarred sauce person up until just a few years ago. But homemade sauce tastes *waaaay* better, and it comes together with very minimal effort. You just throw stuff in a pot and let it cook while you prepare the rest of your meal. If you have extra time, you can let the sauce simmer for up to an hour for more flavor.

2 tablespoons olive oil

1 cup diced yellow onion

4 garlic cloves, minced

2 tablespoons tomato paste

2 (28-ounce) cans
    crushed tomatoes

¼ cup chopped fresh
    basil leaves

1 teaspoon chopped
    fresh oregano

Salt

Freshly ground black pepper

1. In a large pot, heat the oil over medium-high heat until it shimmers. Add the onion and cook until it begins to soften and brown, 5 to 10 minutes. Add the garlic and cook for another minute or two, until fragrant. Stir in the tomato paste and cook for another 2 to 3 minutes, until it darkens slightly.

2. Stir in the crushed tomatoes, basil, and oregano. Reduce the heat to low, cover the pot, and simmer the sauce, stirring occasionally, for about 20 minutes, until the sauce reaches the desired consistency. Season with salt and pepper.

3. Store the marinara in an airtight container in the refrigerator for up to 5 days or in the freezer for up to 6 months.

**Variation Tip:** You can vary the flavor of your marinara with different herbs and spices. I like to add a pinch of red pepper flakes and a few glugs of red wine to mine.

PER SERVING (1 CUP): CALORIES: 75; FAT: 4G; SATURATED FAT: 1G; CHOLESTEROL: 0G; PROTEIN: 2G; FIBER: 4G; SODIUM: 251MG

# CREAMY WHITE SAUCE

SOY-FREE, KID-FRIENDLY

**MAKES ABOUT 3 CUPS | PREP TIME:** 10 MINUTES, PLUS 2 HOURS SOAKING TIME

If you've made it this far into the book, you know that I'm a fan of creamy sauces and dressings. Since dairy is out of the picture, we vegans have to get creative with our cream sauces. They can be created by blending liquids with such ingredients as tofu, cauliflower, or even potatoes. Here I've used cannellini beans. This sauce can be used as a pasta sauce or as a base for creamy soups.

1 (15-ounce) can cannellini beans (see Tip)

1 cup vegetable stock or water, plus more water as needed

¾ cup raw cashews, soaked for at least 2 hours, drained, and rinsed

¼ cup nutritional yeast

2 garlic cloves, minced

1 teaspoon garlic powder

1 teaspoon onion powder

½ teaspoon salt

¼ cup fresh lemon juice

1. In a blender, combine the beans, stock, cashews, nutritional yeast, minced garlic, garlic powder, onion powder, and salt. Blend until smooth and creamy, if the sauce seems too thick, add more water 1 tablespoon at a time.

2. Transfer the sauce to a medium pot. Cook over medium heat, stirring frequently, until the sauce is warm and bubbling. Remove the pan from the heat and stir in the lemon juice.

3. Store the sauce in an airtight container in the refrigerator for up to 5 days.

**Ingredient Tip:** Cannellini beans are sometimes called white kidney beans. Any type of white bean will work in this recipe. If you don't have cannellinis on hand, you can use navy, great northern, or Yankee beans.

**PER SERVING (½ CUP):** CALORIES: 180; FAT: 9G; SATURATED FAT: 1G; CHOLESTEROL: 0G; PROTEIN: 9G; FIBER: 2G; SODIUM: 642MG

# SAY CHEESE! SAUCE

SOY-FREE, KID-FRIENDLY

**MAKES ABOUT 4 CUPS | PREP TIME:** 10 MINUTES **| COOK TIME:** 25 MINUTES

I know that a cheeseless life might sound bleak, so I created this recipe to prove to you that as a vegan, you can have your cheese and eat it, too. Vegetables blend up smooth and creamy, whereas nooch gives the sauce a cheesy flavor. You're going to find yourself pouring it all over everything from pasta and potatoes to tacos and sandwiches.

1 carrot, chopped

1 small russet potato, chopped (about 1 cup; see Tip)

2 cups chopped cauliflower

½ cup raw cashews

1 garlic clove

½ cup nutritional yeast

1 tablespoon fresh lemon juice

1 teaspoon Dijon mustard

1 teaspoon onion powder

½ teaspoon salt

1. In a large pot, combine the carrots, potato, cauliflower, cashews, and garlic. Add enough water to cover them by 2 inches. Bring the water to a boil over medium-high heat, then reduce the heat to medium. Simmer until the vegetables are fork-tender, about 15 minutes.

2. Drain the vegetables, reserving the cooking water, and let cool slightly. Transfer the vegetables to a blender and add 2 cups of the reserved cooking water, the nutritional yeast, lemon juice, mustard, onion powder, and salt. Blend until smooth and creamy; if the sauce is too thick, add more of the reserved cooking water 1 tablespoon at a time.

3. Pour the sauce into the pot you used for the vegetables. Cook over medium heat, stirring frequently, until the sauce is hot and bubbling. Store the sauce in an airtight container in therefrigerator for up to 5 days.

**Ingredient Tip:** Although just about any type of potato (including sweet potatoes) will work in this recipe, I find that starchy russets work best. They blend well and are creamier than other varieties.

**Variation Tip:** For a smoky cheese sauce, add 1 teaspoon smoked paprika. For an herbed cheese sauce, add ½ cup chopped fresh herbs such as dill, parsley, and chives when blending your sauce in step 2. For a spicy cheese sauce, add 1 chopped jalapeño to the blender in step 2.

**PER SERVING (½ CUP):** CALORIES: 114; FAT: 4G; SATURATED FAT: 1G; CHOLESTEROL: 0G; PROTEIN: 7G; FIBER: 3G; SODIUM: 701MG

# TOFU RICOTTA

NUT-FREE, GLUTEN-FREE, KID-FRIENDLY

**MAKES ABOUT 2 CUPS | PREP TIME:** 5 MINUTES

Confession: It wasn't until I was well into my 20s that I learned ricotta cheese was essential to lasagna. I grew up eating noodles sandwiched with tomato sauce and mozzarella. I did enjoy it at the time, but now that I've discovered this creamy cheese, I'll never go back. This super-easy dairy-free ricotta is made with tofu and nutritional yeast. Your pasta will thank you for it.

1 (14-ounce) package firm tofu, drained

¼ cup nutritional yeast

2 tablespoons fresh lemon juice

1½ teaspoons mellow white miso paste

2 garlic cloves, minced

½ teaspoon salt

¼ teaspoon freshly ground black pepper

In a food processor, combine the tofu, nutritional yeast, lemon juice, miso paste, garlic, salt, and pepper and process until the mixture is thick and well incorporated, 2 to 3 minutes. Store the ricotta in an airtight container in the refrigerator for up to 5 days.

**Technique Tip:** If you don't have a food processor, combine all the ingredients in a bowl and mash with a potato masher until the mixture is fluffy and resembles ricotta cheese.

PER SERVING (½ CUP): CALORIES: 185; FAT: 9G; SATURATED FAT: 1G; CHOLESTEROL: 0G; PROTEIN: 20G; FIBER: 4G; SODIUM: 918MG

# BAKED TOFU, THREE WAYS

NUT-FREE, KID-FRIENDLY

**SERVES 4 | PREP TIME:** 10 MINUTES, PLUS MARINATING TIME | **COOK TIME:** 30 MINUTES

Tofu sometimes gets a bad rap for being bland and flavorless. But it's kind of like a food sponge, soaking up the flavor of the ingredients around it, so sauces and seasonings are key. Baking tofu after marinating it gives it a chewy, toothsome texture that will win over even picky carnivores. Baked tofu can be used in salads, bowls, and sandwiches, and it also makes a great snack when paired with a dip.

**FOR THE TERIYAKI MARINADE**

**3 tablespoons reduced-sodium soy sauce or tamari**

**1 tablespoon unseasoned rice vinegar**

**1 tablespoon pure maple syrup**

**½ teaspoon ground ginger**

**¼ teaspoon garlic powder**

**FOR THE LEMON PEPPER MARINADE**

**2 tablespoons vegetable stock**

**2 tablespoons fresh lemon juice**

**1 tablespoon reduced-sodium soy sauce or tamari**

**1 teaspoon freshly ground black pepper**

**½ teaspoon garlic powder**

1. **Make the marinade of your choice:** In a small bowl or jar with a lid, whisk or shake together the ingredients.

2. If you're planning on using the tofu in a bowl or on a salad, cut it into cubes. If you're going to use it on sandwiches or in wraps, cut it into slabs about ¼ inch thick.

3. Place the tofu in a shallow dish and pour the marinade over the top. Set aside to marinate for 30 minutes to 1 hour.

4. Meanwhile, preheat the oven to 400°F. Line a baking sheet with parchment paper.

5. Sprinkle the tofu with the cornstarch and toss to coat it.

FOR THE SRIRACHA
MARINADE

**2 tablespoons
reduced-sodium soy
sauce or tamari**

**2 tablespoons sriracha**

**1 tablespoon
vegetable stock**

**¼ teaspoon garlic powder**

**1 (14-ounce) package
extra-firm tofu, drained
and pressed (see Tip,
page 18)**

**1 tablespoon cornstarch**

6. Arrange the tofu in a single layer on the prepared baking sheet. Bake for 25 to 30 minutes, flipping each piece after 15 minutes.

7. Store the tofu in an airtight container in the refrigerator for up 1 week.

**Time-saving Technique:** If you have an air fryer, you can cut your baking time in half by air-frying the tofu at 400°F for 15 minutes, flipping each piece after about 8 minutes.

PER SERVING (TERIYAKI MARINADE): CALORIES: 121; FAT: 6G; SATURATED FAT: 1G; CHOLESTEROL: 0G; PROTEIN: 11G; FIBER: 1G; SODIUM: 723MG

PER SERVING (LEMON PEPPER MARINADE): CALORIES: 104; FAT: 6G; SATURATED FAT: 1G; CHOLESTEROL: 0G; PROTEIN: 10G; FIBER: 1G; SODIUM: 260MG

PER SERVING (SRIRACHA MARINADE): CALORIES: 105; FAT: 6G; SATURATED FAT: 1G; CHOLESTEROL: 0G; PROTEIN: 11G; FIBER: 1G; SODIUM: 557MG

# REFRIED BEANS

**MAKES ABOUT 1½ CUPS | PREP TIME:** 5 MINUTES | **COOK TIME:** 20 MINUTES

I didn't realize that most brands of canned refried beans weren't actually vegan until I posted a recipe for tacos on Facebook, and a friend warned me that some refried beans contain lard. *Ewww!* Why would someone do that? While there are some lard-free brands available, I prefer the safety of making my own with ingredients I know and trust.

1 teaspoon neutral-flavored vegetable oil

¼ cup minced red onion

2 garlic cloves

1 (15-ounce) can pinto beans, drained and rinsed

¼ cup water or vegetable stock, plus more water as needed

½ teaspoon chili powder

¼ teaspoon ground cumin

¼ teaspoon salt

2 teaspoons fresh lime juice

1. In a large pan, heat the oil over medium-high heat until it shimmers. Add the onion and cook for about 5 minutes, until it begins to brown. Add the garlic and cook for another minute or two, until fragrant.

2. Add the pinto beans, water, chili powder, cumin, and salt to the pan. Bring the mixture to a boil, then reduce the heat to medium-low. Simmer for about 10 minutes, until the beans have softened; if the mixture becomes too dry, add more water 1 tablespoon at a time.

3. Remove the pan from the heat. Using a potato masher or the back of a wooden spoon, mash the beans until they reach the desired consistency. Stir in the lime juice.

4. Store the beans in an airtight container in the refrigerator for up 1 week.

> **Substitution Tip:** You can "refry" just about any type of bean. Black beans and kidney beans work well.

**PER SERVING (½ CUP):** CALORIES: 123; FAT: 2G; SATURATED FAT: 0G; CHOLESTEROL: 0G; PROTEIN: 6G; FIBER: 1G; SODIUM: 388MG

# TEMPEH BAC'UN

**SERVES 4 | PREP TIME:** 10 MINUTES, PLUS MARINATING TIME | **COOK TIME:** 30 MINUTES

It's quite common for strangers on social media to comment "bacon" on vegan posts, thinking they're being original or clever. While I have a strict "don't feed the trolls" policy, I'm occasionally tempted to respond with "tempeh," just to confuse them. Most vegans do like bacon, but we prefer ours to come from plant-based sources like tempeh. Liquid smoke, soy sauce, and maple syrup create the flavor trifecta of smoky, salty, and sweet for which bacon is known.

¼ cup reduced-sodium soy sauce or tamari

1 tablespoon pure maple syrup

2 teaspoons apple cider vinegar

1 teaspoon liquid smoke

½ teaspoon salt

¼ teaspoon freshly ground black pepper

1 (8-ounce) package tempeh, thinly sliced

1. In a small bowl, whisk together the soy sauce, maple syrup, vinegar, liquid smoke, salt, and pepper.

2. Place the tempeh slices in a shallow dish and pour the soy mixture over them. Set aside to marinate for 2 to 4 hours.

3. Meanwhile, preheat the oven to 350°F. Line a baking sheet with parchment paper.

4. Arrange the tempeh in a single layer on the prepared baking sheet. Bake for 25 to 30 minutes, until golden brown and crisp, flipping the tempeh once after 15 minutes.

5. Store the tempeh slices in an airtight container in the refrigerator for up 1 week.

**Time-Saving Tip:** If you'd like your bac'un extra crispy and are too impatient to wait half an hour for it to bake, you can panfry the slices in a little oil over medium-high heat for about 3 minutes on each side. You may need to do so in batches, depending on the size of your pan.

**Substitution Tip:** Thinly sliced extra-firm tofu can be used instead of the tempeh.

**PER SERVING:** CALORIES: 134; FAT: 6G; SATURATED FAT: 1G; CHOLESTEROL: 0G; PROTEIN: 12G; FIBER: 0G; SODIUM: 1,302MG

# CHIC'UN PATTIES

NUT-FREE, SOY-FREE, KID-FRIENDLY

**MAKES 6 PATTIES | PREP TIME:** 20 MINUTES | **COOK TIME:** 1 HOUR

Vegans are often asked why they like to eat foods that mimic meat. Most of us give up meat not because we don't like the taste of it, but rather to reduce the amount of suffering around us. Seitan, made with wheat gluten, has a dense, chewy texture, and it's been used as a meat substitute in Asian cooking for centuries. Serve these patties straight from the oven, chop them up and panfry them, or throw them on the grill.

1 cup cooked chickpeas

4 cups vegetable
   stock, divided

2 tablespoons
   nutritional yeast

1 tablespoon Dijon mustard

1 teaspoon onion powder

1 teaspoon garlic powder

½ teaspoon dried thyme

½ teaspoon dried
   ground sage

½ teaspoon salt

1½ cups vital wheat gluten,
   plus more as needed

**Technique Tip:**
The more you knead the dough, the chewier and denser your chic'un will be. Kneading the dough for 5 minutes will produce a softer texture, whereas 10 minutes of kneading will result in a denser "meat."

1. Preheat the oven to 350°F.

2. In a blender, combine the chickpeas, 1 cup of the stock, the nutritional yeast, mustard, onion powder, garlic powder, thyme, sage, and salt. Blend until smooth.

3. Transfer the chickpea mixture to a large bowl. Add the vital wheat gluten and stir until a dough forms. Knead the dough with your hands for 5 to 10 minutes. If the dough is too wet, add more vital wheat gluten 1 tablespoon at a time. If it's too stiff, add a little more stock.

4. Break the dough apart into 6 equal pieces, and form each one into a flat patty about 6 inches around and ½ inch thick (it's okay if it's an irregular shape).

5. Pour the remaining 3 cups stock into a large baking dish and place the patties in it (it's okay if they overlap slightly). Cover the dish with aluminum foil. Bake for 1 hour.

6. Remove from the oven and let the patties cool in the stock.

7. Take the cooled patties out of the stock and store them in an airtight container in the refrigerator for up to 1 week or in the freezer for up to 3 months. To heat up the patties, bake them, panfry them, or even grill them.

**PER SERVING (1 PATTY):** CALORIES: 181; FAT: 2G; SATURATED FAT: 0G; CHOLESTEROL: 0G; PROTEIN: 25G; FIBER: 3G; SODIUM: 428MG

# SAMMICH SLICES

NUT-FREE, KID-FRIENDLY

**SERVES 6 | PREP TIME:** 20 MINUTES **| COOK TIME:** 1 HOUR 30 MINUTES

I promise you that it is possible to make a midday meal without meat and cheese, but if you find yourself craving something hearty, give these slices a try.

1 cup chopped firm tofu (half a 14-ounce package)

1 cup vegetable stock, plus more as needed (see Tip)

¼ cup nutritional yeast

2 tablespoons reduced-sodium soy sauce or tamari

2 tablespoons tomato paste

1 teaspoon onion powder

½ teaspoon salt

½ teaspoon garlic powder

½ teaspoon ground sage

½ teaspoon ground rosemary

¼ teaspoon freshly ground black pepper

¼ teaspoon liquid smoke

1½ cups vital wheat gluten, plus more as needed

**Ingredient Tip:**
If you can get your hands on vegan chicken stock, use it instead of the vegetable stock. Vegan chicken bouillon can be dissolved in hot water to create stock.

1. Fill a large pot with a few inches of water and place a steamer basket inside. Bring the water to a boil, then reduce the heat to maintain a simmer.

2. In a blender, combine the tofu, stock, nutritional yeast, soy sauce, tomato paste, onion powder, salt, garlic powder, sage, rosemary, pepper, and liquid smoke. Blend until smooth.

3. Transfer the tofu mixture to a large bowl and add the vital wheat gluten. Mix until a dough forms, then knead the dough with your hands for about 5 minutes. If the dough is too wet, add more vital wheat gluten 1 tablespoon at a time; if it's too stiff, add a little more stock.

4. Form the dough into a log. Wrap the log in aluminum foil and twist the ends like a candy wrapper to seal them.

5. Place the log of dough in the steamer basket and cover the pot. Steam the dough for 1 hour.

6. Meanwhile, preheat the oven to 350°F.

7. Transfer the log of dough from the pot to a baking sheet. Bake for 30 minutes.

8. Remove from the oven and let the seitan cool completely. Using a sharp knife, cut the cooled seitan into about 30 thin slices.

9. Store the seitan slices in an airtight container in the refrigerator for up to 1 week or in the freezer for up to 3 months.

**PER SERVING (ABOUT 5 THIN SLICES):** CALORIES: 183; FAT: 3G; SATURATED FAT: 0G; CHOLESTEROL: 0G; PROTEIN: 28G; FIBER: 1G; SODIUM: 912MG

Spicy Green Bean
Stir-Fry, page 124

Cauliflower Piccata,
page 126

White Bean
Shakshuka,
page 158

# CHAPTER TWELVE

# LET'S GET THE PARTY STARTED

## SAMPLE MENUS

# 2-WEEK GETTING STARTED PLAN

If you're just dipping a toe into the world of vegan cooking and aren't sure where to start, I've put together a menu to help. These meals are fairly easy to make, and I've also sprinkled in leftovers, so you won't find yourself in the kitchen morning, noon, and night—life can get hectic, especially on weekdays, and we don't always have time to make an elaborate meal. Weekend meals are a little more involved, since our schedules aren't so busy on Saturdays and Sundays. You may have some extra leftovers, but keep in mind that you can freeze most of these meals. After a couple weeks of vegan meals, you'll be saying, "Come on in—the water's fine!"

## WEEK 1 MENU

|  | BREAKFAST | LUNCH | DINNER |
|---|---|---|---|
| SUNDAY | Carrot Cake Pancakes (page 23) | Vegetable Burrito (page 109) | Lentil Loaf (page 157) with Maple-Mustard Brussels Sprouts (page 56) |
| MONDAY | Peanut Butter Cup Smoothie (page 12) | Leftover Vegetable Burrito | Super Easy Tostadas (page 144) |
| TUESDAY | Baked Apple Cinnamon Oatmeal Square (page 16) | Tempting Tempeh Wrap (page 101) | Leftover Lentil Loaf with Maple-Mustard Brussels Sprouts |
| WEDNESDAY | Sweet Potato Breakfast Bowl (page 15) | Strong to the Finish Spinach Salad (page 74) | Spicy Chickpea Stir-Fry (page 145) |
| THURSDAY | Leftover Baked Apple Cinnamon Oatmeal Square | Leftover Tempting Tempeh Wrap | Pasta Arrabbiata (page 168) |
| FRIDAY | Leftover Sweet Potato Breakfast Bowl | Peanut Mango Tango Salad (page 76) | Buffalo Cauliflower Pizza (page 135) with Kale, Caesar! (page 71) |
| SATURDAY | Broccoli and Sun-Dried Tomato Quiche (page 26) | Leftover Peanut Mango Tango Salad | Stuffed Pasta Shells (page 176) with Balsamic Roasted 'Shrooms (page 54) |

# WEEK 2 MENU

| | BREAKFAST | LUNCH | DINNER |
|---|---|---|---|
| SUNDAY | Leftover Broccoli and Sun-Dried Tomato Quiche | Bring Home the Bacon BLT Salad (page 69) | Cheesy Quinoa Casserole (page 164) with Buffalo Tempeh (page 49) |
| MONDAY | Peanut Butter and Jelly Chia Pudding (page 14) | Chimichurri Bowls (page 116) | Tofu Fried Rice (page 147) |
| TUESDAY | Chocolate-for-Breakfast Overnight Oats (page 13) | Tofu and Kimchi Sandwich (page 106) | Leftover Cheesy Quinoa Casserole with Buffalo Tempeh |
| WEDNESDAY | Leftover Peanut Butter and Jelly Chia Pudding | Leftover Chimichurri Bowls | Red Curry Noodles (page 185) |
| THURSDAY | Leftover Chocolate-for-Breakfast Overnight Oats | Leftover Tofu and Kimchi Sandwich | Leftover Tofu Fried Rice |
| FRIDAY | Breakfast Sandwiches (page 20) | Arugula and Farro Salad (page 75) | Chickpea Mushroom Burgers (page 111) with Polenta Fries (page 38) |
| SATURDAY | Tofu Rancheros (page 18) | Jackfruit White Chili (page 96) | Mushroom Wellington (page 140) with Tahini Greenies (page 52) |

# SHOPPING LIST

## Produce

- Apples (2)
- Arugula (12 ounces)
- Avocados (5)
- Bananas (3)
- Basil (¾ cup)
- Bell peppers, green (2)
- Bell peppers, red (3)
- Blueberries (1 cup)
- Broccoli (5 bunches)
- Brussels sprouts (16 ounces)
- Cabbage, napa (large head)
- Cabbage, purple (large head)
- Carrots (12)
- Cauliflower (2 heads)
- Chives (1 bunch)
- Cilantro (1 bunch)
- Corn (2 cups)
- Cucumber, English (3)
- Dill (1 bunch)
- Garlic (4 heads)
- Ginger (one 4-inch knob)
- Kale, curly (18 ounces)
- Lettuce, butter (1 large head)

- Lemons (6)
- Lettuce, romaine (2 heads)
- Limes (3)
- Mangos (2)
- Mung bean sprouts (1 cup)
- Mushrooms, cremini or white button (3 pounds)
- Mushrooms, portabella (6)
- Onions, red (2)
- Onions, yellow (8)
- Oregano (1 bunch)
- Parsley, flat-leaf (1 large bunch, 2 cups)
- Peas (1 cup)
- Peppers, dried Asian chile (6 to 10)
- Peppers, jalapeño (4)
- Peppers, poblano or Anaheim (4)
- Pepper, red chile (1)
- Potato, russet (1 small)
- Radishes (2)
- Rosemary (1 bunch)
- Scallions (8)
- Shallots (3)
- Spinach, baby (20 ounces)
- Strawberries (2 cups)
- Sweet potatoes (5)
- Thyme (1 bunch)
- Tomatoes (7)

## Beans

- Black beans (15-ounce can)
- Cannellini beans (15-ounce can)
- Chickpeas (six 15-ounce cans)
- Lentils (15-ounce can)
- Navy beans (two 15-ounce cans)
- Pinto beans (two 15-ounce cans)

## Nuts and Seeds

- Almond butter, smooth natural
- Almonds, raw (2½ cups)

- Cashews, raw (3¾ cups)
- Chia seeds
- Flax meal (ground flaxseed)
- Peanut butter, creamy natural
- Peanuts (1 cup)
- Pecans (¾ cup)
- Raisins (¼ cup)
- Sesame seeds, toasted (¼ cup)
- Tahini
- Walnuts (¼ cup)

## Oils and Acids

- Oil, extra-virgin olive
- Oil, toasted sesame
- Oil, vegetable, neutral-flavored
- Vinegar, apple cider
- Vinegar, balsamic
- Vinegar, red wine
- Vinegar, rice

## Herbs and Spices

- Black pepper
- Chili powder
- Cinnamon, ground
- Cumin, ground
- Garlic powder
- Ginger, ground
- Italian seasoning
- Nutmeg, ground
- Onion powder
- Oregano, dried
- Parsley, dried
- Red pepper flakes
- Sage, dried
- Salt
- Thyme, dried
- Turmeric, ground

## Canned and Jarred Goods

- Capers
- Coconut milk, full-fat (14-ounce can)
- Crushed tomatoes (28-ounce can)
- Jackfruit (two 20-ounce cans)
- Red curry paste
- Tomato paste
- Tomatoes, diced (three 14-ounce cans)
- Vegetable stock (three 32-ounce containers)

## Grains and Pasta

- Burger buns (4)
- English muffins (4)
- Farro (½ cup)
- Noodles, rice (8 ounces)
- Pasta, jumbo shells (8 ounces)
- Pasta, penne, rigatoni, or fusilli (8 ounces)
- Polenta, quick-cooking (1½ cups)
- Quinoa (2¼ cups)
- Rice, brown (5 cups)
- Rolled oats, quick-cooking (4½ cups)
- Sandwich rolls (4)
- Tortillas, 6 to 8 inch (16)
- Tortillas, 10 to 12 inch (8)
- Whole-grain bread

## Condiments

- Dijon mustard
- Hot sauce
- Ketchup
- Liquid smoke
- Soy sauce or tamari, reduced-sodium
- Sriracha

## Refrigerated and Frozen

- Frozen kale (12 ounces)
- Mellow white miso paste
- Puff pastry
- Tempeh (four 8-ounces packages)
- Tofu, extra-firm (seven 14-ounce packages)

## Baking

- Agave nectar
- Baking powder
- Baking soda
- Chickpea flour
- Cocoa powder, unsweetened
- Cornstarch
- Flour, whole wheat or all-purpose
- Maple syrup, pure
- Panko bread crumbs
- Vanilla extract, pure

## Other

- Nutritional yeast
- Pizza crust, prepared
- Red wine, dry
- Soy milk
- Sun-dried tomatoes (¼ cup)

# COCKTAIL PARTY

I've earned the title "The Vegan Martha Stewart" from my friends because I like to throw little soirees. I just love putting on a cute dress, mixing up cocktails, and serving fancy canapés and hors d'oeuvres. The recipes on this menu are perfect for such an occasion, since they're mostly finger foods that can be noshed while sipping an aperitif and chatting with chums. I've included both savory and sweet dishes, so that everyone's palates will be pleased. I bet you'll earn yourself a vegan-host-with-the-most moniker in no time, too.

Red Pepper and Spinach Mini Frittatas (page 28)

Potato Angels (page 41)

Crabby Cakes (page 46)

Creamy Queso Dip (page 32)

Polenta Fries (page 38)

French Onion Dip (page 33)

Veggie Chips (page 36)

Stuffed Mushrooms (page 39)

Spinach Artichoke Galette (page 138)

Raspberry Almond Shortbread Bars (page 198)

Lemon Tahini Cookies (page 192)

# SUMMER GATHERING

This menu is for the warm-weather months when you're craving some fun in the sun. These recipes are great for graduation parties, Father's Day gatherings, Fourth of July celebrations, and just-because-it's-summer backyard get-togethers. I've included snacks, salads, sandwiches, and desserts (because you always need dessert). There's a burger thrown in, too, because summer is burger season. With the exception of the burgers and Corsn Fritters, all of these recipes travel well, so they can be packed up and taken with you on picnics or to potlucks.

Summer Rolls (page 59)

Corn Fritters (page 40)

Classic Macaroni Salad (page 63)

Ranch Potato Salad (page 64)

Pesto Is the Besto Pasta Salad (page 62)

Green Goddess Cucumber Salad (page 68)

Lentil Burgers (page 110)

Double-Decker Club Sandwiches (page 102)

Lemon Loaf (page 205)

Raspberry Almond Shortbread Bars (page 198)

# SPECIAL OCCASION

The recipes in this menu are for holiday gatherings and milestone celebrations where friends and family will linger and chat. Chances are, you'll be hosting folks for several hours, so I've included a few appetizers as well as mains, sides, and desserts. These recipes are great for a sit-down dinner or a buffet, and they can easily be scaled up if you have a multitude of guests coming over.

# CHILDREN'S PARTY

Kids have a reputation for being picky eaters, but I'm betting they'll love the dishes on this menu. Heck, I'm pretty sure any kid could happily live on Broccoli Tots, Chic'un Nuggets, and Baked Mac 'n' Cheesy for weeks on end. To make things fun with the Super Easy Tostadas, set out all the components in a "tostada bar" and let the kids put their tostadas together themselves. **Some of these recipes do contain nuts, so be sure to check if anyone has allergies.** The nuts can be omitted from the cheese sauce for the Baked Mac 'n' Cheesy, and they can be left out of the Ooey-Gooey Magic Cookie Bars. When making the salads, I recommend using store-bought dairy-free mayo and ranch dressing rather than my cashew-based sauces.

# MEASUREMENT CONVERSIONS

## VOLUME EQUIVALENTS (LIQUID)

| US STANDARD | US STANDARD (OUNCES) | METRIC |
|---|---|---|
| 2 tablespoons | 1 fl. oz. | 30 mL |
| ¼ cup | 2 fl. oz. | 60 mL |
| ½ cup | 4 fl. oz. | 120 mL |
| 1 cup | 8 fl. oz. | 240 mL |
| 1½ cups | 12 fl. oz. | 355 mL |
| 2 cups or 1 pint | 16 fl. oz. | 475 mL |
| 4 cups or 1 quart | 32 fl. oz. | 1 L |
| 1 gallon | 128 fl. oz. | 4 L |

## VOLUME EQUIVALENTS (DRY)

| US STANDARD | METRIC (APPROX.) |
|---|---|
| ⅛ teaspoon | 0.5 mL |
| ¼ teaspoon | 1 mL |
| ½ teaspoon | 2 mL |
| ¾ teaspoon | 4 mL |
| 1 teaspoon | 5 mL |
| 1 tablespoon | 15 mL |
| ¼ cup | 59 mL |
| ⅓ cup | 79 mL |
| ½ cup | 118 mL |
| ⅔ cup | 156 mL |
| ¾ cup | 177 mL |
| 1 cup | 235 mL |
| 2 cups or 1 pint | 475 mL |
| 3 cups | 700 mL |
| 4 cups or 1 quart | 1 L |

## OVEN TEMPERATURES

| FAHRENHEIT (F) | CELSIUS (C) (APPROX.) |
|---|---|
| 250° | 120° |
| 300° | 150° |
| 325° | 165° |
| 350° | 180° |
| 375° | 190° |
| 400° | 200° |
| 425° | 220° |
| 450° | 230° |

## WEIGHT EQUIVALENTS

| US STANDARD | METRIC (APPROX.) |
|---|---|
| ½ ounce | 15 g |
| 1 ounce | 30 g |
| 2 ounces | 60 g |
| 4 ounces | 115 g |
| 8 ounces | 225 g |
| 12 ounces | 340 g |
| 16 ounces or 1 pound | 455 g |

# RESOURCES

## VEGAN BRANDS I LOVE

In chapter 11, I shared some of my favorite DIY vegan pantry staples, including dressings, sauces, and even "meats" that I frequently make myself. But even cookbook authors need a day off, and I do use store-bought versions from time to time. The lists that follow are by no means comprehensive. We're living in what some might consider a vegan renaissance, where new vegan brands are coming on the market so quickly, it's difficult to keep track of them all.

### NONDAIRY MILK
- Almond Breeze
- Califia Farms
- Good Karma
- Milkadamia
- Oatly
- Ripple
- Silk
- So Delicious

### NONDAIRY CHEESE
- Daiya
- Follow Your Heart
- Kite Hill
- Miyoko's Creamery
- So Delicious
- Treeline
- Violife

### MAYONNAISE
- Follow Your Heart Vegenaise
- Just Mayo
- Plant Perfect

### DAIRY-FREE SAUCES AND DRESSING
- Daiya
- Follow Your Heart
- Organicville

### DAIRY-FREE CHOCOLATE CHIPS
- California Gourmet
- Enjoy Life
- King David White Choco Chips
- Pascha

### PUFF PASTRY
- Pepperidge Farm
- Schär

### SEITAN AND VEGAN MEATS
- Beyond Meat
- Field Roast
- Gardein
- Lightlife
- Sweet Earth
- Tofurky
- Upton's Naturals

# REFERENCES

Barnard, Neal, MD. *The Cheese Trap: How Breaking a Surprising Addiction Will Help You Lose Weight, Gain Energy, and Get Healthy.* New York: Grand Central Life & Style, 2017.

Davis, Brenda, and Vesanto Melina. *Becoming Vegan, Express Edition.* Summertown, TN: Book Publishing Company, 2013.

Food and Agriculture Organization of the United Nations. "Livestock's Long Shadow: Environmental Issues and Options." Accessed July 9, 2020. FAO.org/3/a0701e/a0701e00.htm.

Greger, Michael, MD, with Gene Stone. *How Not to Die: Discover the Foods Scientifically Proven to Prevent and Reverse Disease.* New York: Flatiron Books, 2015.

Marcus, Erik. *Meat Market: Animals, Ethics, and Money.* Boston, MA: Brio Press, 2005.

Moran, Victoria, and Adair Moran. *Main Street Vegan: Everything You Need to Know to Eat Healthfully and Live Compassionately in the Real World.* New York: Tarcher/Penguin, 2012.

Robbins, John. *The Food Revolution: How Your Diet Can Help Save Your Life and Our World.* Newburyport, MA: Conari Press, 2001.

World Wildlife Fund for Nature. "Amazon Deforestation." Accessed July 9, 2020. WWF.panda.org/our_work/forests/deforestation_fronts2/deforestation_in_the_amazon.

# INDEX

# ACKNOWLEDGMENTS

**This book couldn't have been written** without the support of Dennis Mason, who helped test recipes, gracefully put up with some less-than-stellar meals, and washed endless dishes.

I owe a huge debt of gratitude to my recipe testers for all their hard work. Thank you to Brandie Faust, Robin Fetter, Bonnie Goodman and Parke Goodman, Dick Gibbs and Sandy Gibbs, Rhonda Jones, Lisa Kenyon, Donna M. Kaminski, Paulina A. Kaminski, Christine Kaminski Brozyniak, Eileen Mallor and Roger Flahive, Connie Maschan, and Ruth Schlomer and Mike Sojkowski.

Thank you to the amazing authors who have encouraged me to write my own books over the years, including Nava Atlas, Fran Costigan, Kathy Hester, Victoria Moran, Robin Robertson, and Laura Theodore.

I'm so grateful for the support of my family and friends, including Bill Wenz, Cathy Greve, Linda and Ed Halverson, Elizabeth Fischer, Karyn Gost, Sharon Nazarian, Jenna Prochilo, Jessica Caneal, Jen Chaky, Deana Ferreri, Jen Holsman, Venkat Venkatesan, Karla Schultz, Joyce Kent, and Sarah Eastin.

Thank you to all the readers who visit my website and cook my recipes. I'm thankful for the support of my friends in the vegan blogging community, including Cadry Nelson, Becky Striepe, Amy Katz, Jenn Sebestyen, Lisa Viger, and Lisa Dawn Angerame.

This book was written during the COVID-19 lockdown of 2020, while I was ordering all my groceries online. I am beholden to all the grocery store shoppers and delivery drivers who unknowingly helped me write and test these recipes.

And, of course, thank you so much to the team at Callisto Media, especially Rebecca Markley, for entrusting me with this project.

# ABOUT THE AUTHOR

**Dianne Wenz** is a certified holistic health coach, vegan lifestyle coach, and plant-based chef, and she has a certificate in plant-based nutrition. Dianne coaches people from across the globe, supporting them in improving their health and well-being, as well as in making the dietary and lifestyle changes needed to go vegan. She also teaches both private and public cooking classes in the northern New Jersey area. She is the author of *The Truly Healthy Vegan Cookbook* and *Eating Vegan*.

Dianne lives in New Jersey with her partner, Dennis Mason, and their cats, Archie, Clementine, Tallulah Belle, and Rupert.

Visit DiannesVeganKitchen.com for healthy living tips, nutrition information, and recipes.

CPSIA information can be obtained
at www.ICGtesting.com
Printed in the USA
JSHW011431020221
11471JS00007B/15

9 781648 765018